Apocalypse

How Catastrophe Transformed Our World and Can Forge New Futures

Lizzie Wade

WILLIAM
COLLINS

William Collins
An imprint of HarperCollins*Publishers*
1 London Bridge Street
London SE1 9GF

WilliamCollinsBooks.com

HarperCollins*Publishers*
Macken House, 39/40 Mayor Street Upper
Dublin 1, D01 C9W8, Ireland

First published in Great Britain in 2025 by William Collins
First published in the United States by HarperCollins*Publishers* in 2025
This William Collins paperback edition published in 2026

1

A catalogue record for this book is
available from the British Library

ISBN 978-0-00-876145-5

Portions of Chapters 4 and 7, by Lizzie Wade, first appeared in 'From Black Death to Fatal Flu, Past Pandemics Show Why People on the Margins Suffer Most', *Science*, May 14, 2020. Portions of Chapter 9, by Lizzie Wade, first appeared in 'Caribbean Excavation Offers Intimate Look at the Lives of Enslaved Africans', *Science*, November 7, 2019.

Map illustrations by John Wyatt Greenlee, Surprised Eel Mapping

Set in Iowan Old Style
Printed and bound in the UK using 100%
renewable electricity at CPI Group (UK) Ltd

LIZZIE WADE is a science journalist based in Mexico City who has written about archaeology and anthropology for *Science, The Atlantic, Slate, The New York Times, Aeon* and others. *Apocalypse* is her first book.

PRAISE FOR *APOCALYPSE*

'Lizzie Wade is an exceptional journalist and a master storyteller. In *Apocalypse,* she peels back the many myths of the present to reveal the true stories of past apocalypses and, perhaps more important, what happened afterward. She reminds us that survival always has been, and still is, possible' ED YONG, author of *An Immense World*

'This book upended my understanding of the ancient world. Wade renders our deep past in vivid prose, showing us that times of great rupture also bring great possibilities for new ways of living, if we let them. *Apocalypse* is the best kind of history book: vibrant and vital'

ZOË SCHLANGER, author of *The Light Eaters*

'A timely examination of catastrophes that humanity has faced through history. There are lessons, warnings and solace to be drawn from this deep time perspective on the existential challenges facing us today'

ALICE ROBERTS, author of *Ancestors: The Prehistory of Britain in Seven Burials*

'A fascinating dive into the tragedies – and comebacks – of those that came before us. Lizzie Wade combines detailed research with clear writing to bring these historical events to life – they're stories that will stick with me for a long time'

HANNAH RITCHIE, author of *Not the End of the World*

'Lizzie Wade's vivid descriptions bring the latest archaeological research to life in this fascinating and timely book. Despite its sobering subject matter, *Apocalypse* is ultimately an inspiring read, revealing how lessons from past crises can help us survive the looming apocalypse, which is likely to be the greatest challenge our species has ever encountered'

JONATHAN KENNEDY, author of *Pathogenesis*

'This book tells the grim story of how our species has bounced from one apocalypse to the next catastrophe. The good news is that, through human ingenuity, we survived – and there is much we can learn from how our ancestors managed these natural catastrophes'

ROBIN DUNBAR, Professor of Evolutionary Psychology, University of Oxford

'*Apocalypse* is an inspiring book for challenging times and [...] a rewarding read for everyone intrigued by archaeological discovery and the deep history of human social change'

Science

'In addition to her exhaustive research, Wade also manages to include personal anecdotes and immersive narratives. In fact, it is through the depth of her scholarship that Wade is able to craft these vignettes that, oddly enough, *humanize* the apocalypses of the past'

Chicago Review of Books

'The world has ended many times and usually, amazingly, humans keep going. Rooted in solid science that never loses sight of the human and the possible, this book shows us why good stories and an understanding of history matter more than ever'

AGUSTÍN FUENTES, author of *The Creative Spark*

'With her knack for bringing the ancient world to life, Lizzie Wade turns the idea of apocalypse on its head, showing us how endings offer new opportunities for freedom, community building, and cultural change. *Apocalypse* is a fascinating chronicle of our deep past, written with extraordinary wisdom and clarity'

ANNALEE NEWITZ, author of *Four Lost Cities*

'An extraordinary book. Wade invites us to turn away from despair and apathy and embrace the creativity and compassion that has made humans so resilient. I found myself up late at night thinking of the lessons of the book long after I finished it'

JENNIFER RAFF, author of *Origin*

'A richly imagined new view on the great human tradition of apocalypse that defies conventional wisdom and long-held stories about our deep past to reveal how cataclysmic events are not irrevocable endings, but transformations' *The Next Big Idea Club*, 'May 2025 Must-Read Books'

'In this surprisingly hopeful book, Wade reports on what archaeologists see when they look at sites of upheaval and invites us to look at the past – and our own troubled time – in a new way' *MIT Review*

For Luckez

CONTENTS

PART 3: NEW WORLDS

AUTHOR'S NOTE

This book is built on the foundation of scientific evidence and journalistic rigor. I've read countless research papers and interviewed scores of scientists, both remotely and in the field. I've done my best to both capture the latest archaeological evidence about the societies and events I write about and reflect the generosity, compassion, and empathy with which today's archaeologists approach the past and the people who lived in it. They've taught me to see our history as a place of surprises and possibilities, where any story I thought I knew could be reinvented if only I could manage to see it from a different perspective. And so this book is also an act of imagination. Throughout, you'll find narrative scenes set in the past. Some of them trace the full arc of a past apocalypse, and others attempt to see one moment in time through the eyes of a particular person. Some of those people are known historical figures, indicated by the fact that they have names. The others I've created through doing deep research into daily life in particular places and times and imagining what it might have felt like to occupy them in the same way we experience our own lives: day by day, year by year, never knowing what will happen next. For a detailed list of sources and explanations of how I used them—as well as some exciting alternative viewpoints—please see the Selected Bibliography and Further Reading at the end of the book.

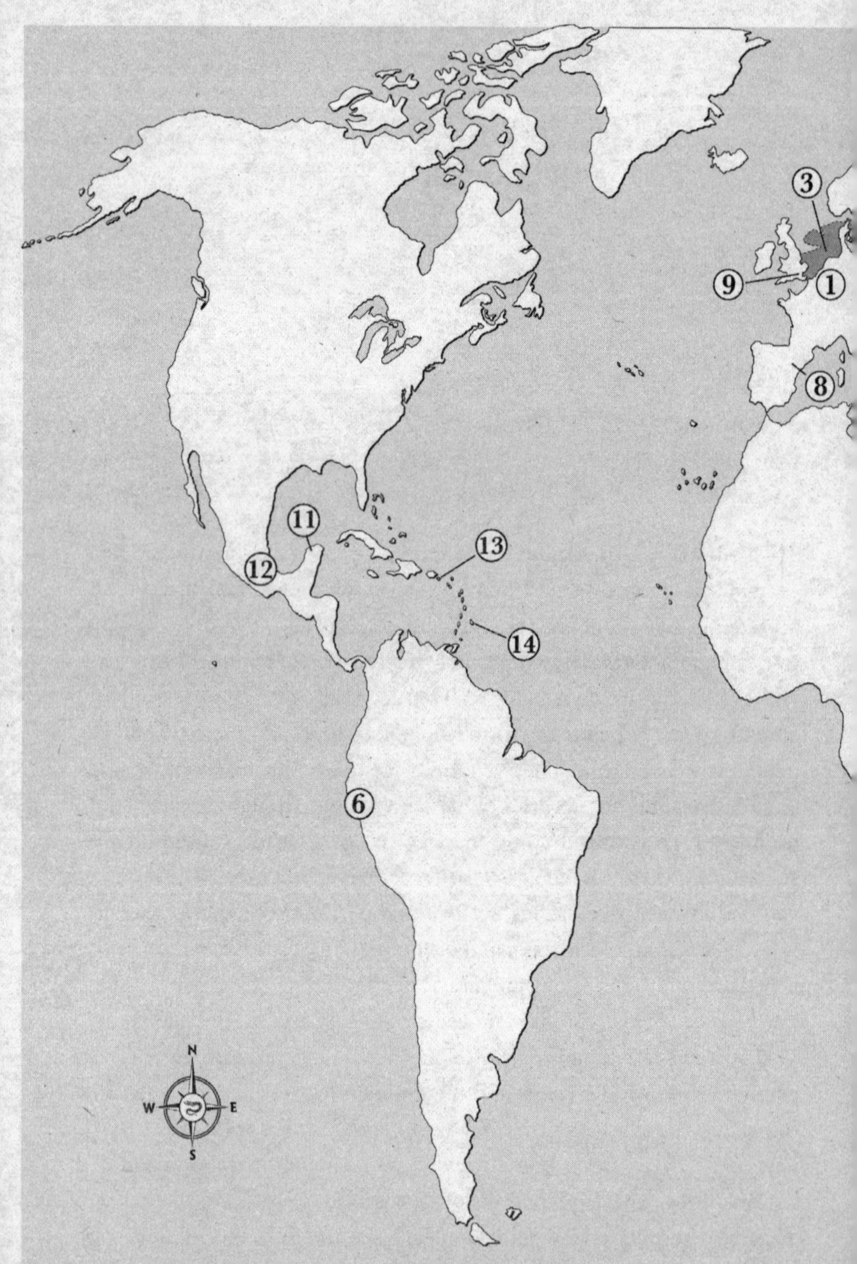

Map of Key Sites

1. Neander Valley
2. Denisova Cave
3. Doggerland
4. Tel Hreiz
5. Kangaroo Island
6. North coast of Peru
7. Harappa
8. Tàrrega
9. London
10. Giza
11. Aké
12. Mexico City
13. St. Croix
14. Barbados
2
7
5

INTRODUCTION

The End

Seven thousand years ago, the world ended. The sea ate the land, creeping up shorelines with the steadiness of a predator closing in on its prey. First it devoured beaches. Then it filled river mouths and estuaries where fresh water flowed to the ocean, sending poisonous torrents of salt water upstream. It strangled the life out of the plants people collected and the animals they hunted and fished. At first, those people could learn to gather new plants and hunt different animals, but that only worked for a time. Eventually, the sea covered their homelands, and they had to find new ones. But as soon as they settled into the rhythms of a new place, learned which animals lived there and how best to hunt them, which plants would nourish and which would kill, the sea came again.

The water followed them everywhere, relentless in its pursuit, all over the world. People who once lived on vast continents now found themselves on islands, cut off. Children paddled boats over the villages their grandparents had grown up in. Eventually the sea gave up, but the damage had been done. People were left living in a mere remnant of the world their ancestors once inhabited.

◉

Four thousand years ago, the world ended. The city was a marvel, almost a miracle. People came from far and wide to trade there, and many of them stayed to build their fortunes and their futures. Ideas, cultures, religions, and goods mixed and mingled, as did the people who brought them to the city. Life was exciting, so exciting, but also comfortable, with a government that busied itself building homes and roads to serve its booming population. And then the rains that filled the city's reservoirs each year stopped falling. People lost faith in their leaders, and when those leaders were toppled there was no one to replace them. Pristine streets became trash dumps, and sturdy houses that had stood for generations were scavenged to build makeshift shacks. As their city disintegrated, so did people's sense of citizenship, of belonging. They retreated into family and kin groups and turned on anyone deemed an outsider. People grew accustomed to going to sleep hungry and startling awake many times in the night, ever vigilant to possible attack. The lucky ones had somewhere else to go, and the smart ones left even if they didn't. Eventually, the bustling city became an empty ruin, its orderly streets serving only its ghosts.

◉

Seven hundred years ago, the world ended. The people heard rumors of a plague sweeping across entire continents, and they knew it was only a matter of time before it reached their shores. But when it came, it was worse than anyone could have imagined. Half a city could die within a single year. The plague snuffed out entire family lines, with no one to remember or mourn them. Bodies piled up in the streets, and the gravediggers worked night and day until they, too, fell ill. Those who could afford it fled to the countryside, but nowhere was truly safe. The country was dotted with villages of the dead, their few survivors having staggered away from the homes they couldn't maintain or bear to live in anymore. Life before the plague seemed like a distant memory, and no one could imagine an after.

◉

Five hundred years ago, the world ended. The conquering army marched into the defeated capital, determined to remake it in their own image.

The invaders installed themselves in the most opulent palaces and razed the rest to the ground. They tore down the temples of the old religion and used their stones to build churches of the new. Men who had been little more than beggars and outlaws in the old world killed the leaders of the former city and married their widows, claiming the right to noble lineages. Those residents of the capital who hadn't died in the war were forced to work, erasing the place they had known while building its replacement. New diseases tore through their already ravaged communities, and those seeking comfort had no choice but to turn to the new religion. Meanwhile, the conquerors trumpeted their heroic victory against the barbarians to all corners of the world. People flocked to the center of this new empire, eager for a piece of its stolen wealth, and soon enough the horrors started to seem like fate.

◉

Today, the world is ending. The climate is changing, and it's too late to stop it. Crops are failing as vast areas of the world's farmland dry up into desert, driving famine and war. Storms and wildfires are growing more powerful, consuming towns and threatening cities. Coastal communities, as well as entire island countries, are sinking under the rising seas. Fresh water is becoming ever scarcer, destabilizing the cities that remain. Millions of people are being driven from their homes and being met with violence when they try to move elsewhere. New pathogens are jumping from animals to the humans invading their territory, and terrifying novel diseases are spreading around an interconnected yet destabilized world with lightning speed. The wealthy and powerful are beginning to close themselves off, and governments are taking a turn for the authoritarian, controlling everyone but protecting no one. Some borders, and the countries they defined, are disappearing; others are growing violent and militarized. The changes are sometimes too slow to see, but they quickly become too fast to stop.

◉

Life in the 2020s is not for the faint of heart. Less than a decade ago, the apocalypses we knew were coming—climate change, a novel pandemic, state collapse, unexpected invasions, and brutal wars—seemed, for many of us, like they could still be far away. We dreaded them, we may have even been expecting them, but we didn't yet live inside them. Now, undeniably, we do. It feels like history suddenly sped up, leaving us scrambling for a foothold in a future we didn't believe we'd be the ones to experience.

Against that backdrop, I have what I hope will be good news: We've been here before. Not every generation, or even every century. But history is long, and people in the past have confronted just about every apocalypse we're facing today, from megadroughts to plagues, the end of empires to the extinctions of entire human species. What unites those past apocalypses isn't suffering and death, though those things certainly happened. It isn't the complete collapse of social order. It isn't mass violence. It isn't the hardening of hearts against outsiders. It isn't the total loss of hope. What unites them is survival.

Not only have people already confronted almost every possible apocalypse, they have lived through them. All of them. Every time. Survival wasn't always easy, and it definitely wasn't pretty. Some of those apocalypses made life unquestionably worse, at least for a while. Many times, they meant that certain people suffered more than others—though who the unluckiest happened to be in any given apocalypse is surprisingly variable. But lots of people made it through.

That's not to say life continued just as it had before apocalypse struck. It didn't, and that's a good thing. Apocalypses transformed the people and societies that experienced them. They were turning points, moments in which everybody, individually and together, had to make a decision. Are we going to keep going as we always have? Or are we going to change?

And so they changed. They had to. The beginnings of the new worlds our ancestors found themselves creating were chaotic and haphazard, and what would happen in their tomorrows was never certain.

No change was guaranteed to improve anything in the moment, much less in the future. We're still suffering from some of the changes born from past apocalypses. But sometimes, apocalypses made societies more equal. Sometimes they made people more creative. Sometimes apocalypses made communities stronger.

To understand who we are and where we came from, we need to understand those past apocalypses and how they shaped everything that came after, for better and for worse. We need to understand what survival, resilience, and transformation mean—and what they cost—under conditions we'd prefer not to imagine. Our own apocalypses are coming, or maybe they are already here. The more we know about the apocalypses that came before, the more prepared we will be to walk forward into our own uncertain tomorrows. We need to change how we think about human history—not as an inevitable march of progress but as a story of crises, cataclysms, and endings. Only when we do that will we be able to see our current world as just one, imperfect, already postapocalyptic option among many ways of being, and to understand each coming ending as a chance for a new beginning.

◉

What, exactly, do I mean by *apocalypse*? The word has held many different meanings over millennia, from a religious judgment day to a city-destroying natural disaster to the imagined decimation of modern society by zombie hordes. But its layered meaning is also its strength. We need a way to conceive of, and talk about, existential threats to our societies and our species that transcend specific disasters and catastrophes, their relatively localized and temporary effects, and their iconic but particular symbols, from the bodies cast in ash in Pompeii to news footage of people stranded on roofs after Hurricane Katrina. Disasters can be part of apocalypse, but apocalypse has tentacles that reach farther and deeper into a society than any single crisis or calamity could.

In this book, I define apocalypse as a rapid, collective loss that fundamentally changes a society's way of life and sense of identity.

First, an apocalypse is a loss experienced by an entire society. It's not an individual tragedy but a collective experience. What is lost can be environmental, like a coastline dotted with settlements that drowns under a rising sea or a stable climate that suddenly becomes unpredictable. It can be political, like a government that collapses or a country that fragments. It can be human, like the almost inconceivable number of people who died in epidemics such as the Black Death and the diseases introduced to the Americas by European colonists. Often an apocalypse fits in more than one of these categories, when, for example, an environmental loss spurs a political one in a feedback loop of destruction. An apocalypse can be provoked by outsiders, as in a conquest, or brought upon a society by its own actions. It can also be completely random—undeserved, unpredictable, and unpreventable.

Next, for a loss to be experienced collectively, it must happen relatively quickly. All societies experience gradual, non-apocalyptic change, which they are able to absorb and adjust to over time. Part of what distinguishes an apocalypse is its sheer speed. The loss must be noticeable and disruptive within the span of a community's collective memory, which can mean anything from a few years to a few generations. Sometimes an apocalypse plays out within a person's lifetime. Sometimes an apocalypse causes grandparents and grandchildren to grow up in fundamentally different worlds. But for a change to be experienced as an apocalypse, the Before must be remembered during the After. The faster the changes happen, the likelier that will be.

Finally, an apocalypse must transform a society. An isolated drought might make for a few bad harvests and some rough years, but it won't force a society to give up on farming entirely. A drought that lasts for decades, however, might do just that. It could also lead to the overthrow or disintegration of the government that didn't adequately prepare for such a crisis. An apocalypse can break up empires and empty out cities. It can force people to learn new ways of keeping themselves alive. It can plant the seeds for entirely new religions or forms of government, which will then shape the lives of generations to come. An apocalypse sets a society on a new path, often one that was unimaginable during the Before.

It may seem that my definition of apocalypse is missing an essential element: that it has to be a tragedy. Apocalypses can include mass death, unfathomably cruel violence, and the sudden disappearance of cooperation or even empathy. But they don't have to, and not all of them have. What is lost in an apocalypse may be mourned for centuries, or its end may be welcomed. Sometimes different kinds of people in the same society react to an apocalypse in entirely opposite ways. To qualify as an apocalypse, a loss must be felt by the entire community or society—but each individual doesn't have to respond to it in the same way. In fact, they almost certainly won't.

In short, apocalypses are not endings. They are transformations.

◉

It can be surprisingly hard to understand, or even recognize, an apocalypse while you're living through it. There is, however, a whole group of people who study the ones that have already happened: archaeologists, the scientists who use the objects, buildings, and bones past people left behind to reconstruct their cultures and understand their lives.

I'm not an archaeologist, but I do spend a lot of time with them, trying to see the past through their eyes and understand how their knowledge might help the rest of us better navigate the present and the future. As a science journalist, I've crawled through tunnels, dug into pyramids, bushwhacked through undisturbed jungle hunting for lost ruins, searched for signs of the first ancient humans to reach a desert island, and visited laboratories where ancient genomes from all over the world are revealing their stories. It's fun, and it's fascinating. There are so many ways to be human and so many ways to build a society. Seeing even a handful up close opens a dizzying window into the complexity of the past, of how we came to be who we are, and who we could be if history had taken a slightly different path.

Much, though not all, of archaeology is about reconstructing and understanding the cultures that have come and gone before us. Inherent in that study is the question: What happened to them? Why don't

Egyptian pharaohs still build pyramids? Why aren't Maya cities like Tikal and Chichén Itzá still thriving capitals? Why, for that matter, aren't we all still hunter-gatherers, as our ancestors were for the vast majority of human history? Why, after centuries or millennia of living one way, do people and their cultures radically change?

Apocalypse is one answer. But archaeologists see apocalypse differently from the rest of us. We tend to think of such events as entirely out of our control. A natural disaster hits, a drought lasts for decades or centuries, a disease rips through a city. Archaeologists, on the other hand, can see the whole story, reflected in the objects, architecture, and sometimes bones past people left behind. They see what happened before a world-shattering event, and they see what happened after. They can see the trends that made a society vulnerable, and they can see how survivors regrouped and transformed. For archaeologists, the most important piece of the story is not the apocalypse itself but how people reacted to it—where they moved their settlements to escape, how they changed their rituals to cope, what connections they made with other communities to survive. That's where they find countless stories of resilience, creativity, and even hope.

Much to these scientists' frustration, these moments of survival and even revival are the parts of apocalyptic stories that often don't get told. If a city, empire, or culture came to an end sometime in the past, it's assumed to have failed, and it's all too easy to turn it into a fable. We look for what they did wrong, both to assuage our fears and confirm our expectations. Look, we say, they cut down trees and ruined their soil. Look, we say, they couldn't survive a drought. Look, we say, they didn't know how to protect themselves against outsiders. It's easy to turn them into a lesson, or perhaps a wake-up call.

But past civilizations were not parables, and their citizens were neither heedless fools nor passive victims. They were people, just as complicated, emotional, capable, strange, and imaginative as you and I are. Even Neanderthals, once considered the ur-brute of our family tree, are finally getting their due as sensitive, artistic, and human. And that means there are no easy answers about how any of these past people and their cultures lived, and even fewer about why they died. If we want to understand how and why apocalypse forever changed their worlds, it's up to us to ask better questions.

Once an apocalypse comes to pass, there is no going back. But no apocalypse is inevitable. They only appear that way in retrospect, from vantage points firmly situated in the new world, on the other side. The routes leading up to and through any apocalypse are full of choices, decisions, successes, and failures made by people who didn't know how their stories would end. People who made the best decisions they could in the world they knew, only to find that world utterly changed around them within a matter of months or years. People who were, like any of us, more concerned with surviving the immediate future than with how their choices would be remembered, understood, and misunderstood centuries later.

This book will tell the real stories of past apocalypses, using the latest archaeological evidence to illuminate them in all their complexity. Don't get me wrong: Many of them were absolutely horrible to live through. We will see what it was like to lose your homeland under rising seas, to have everyone you know die of an incurable disease, to live in a once-great city as it collapsed under the weight of war. But we'll also see that even in the worst of times, people had choices. They moved, they adapted, they changed. They survived.

◉

Archaeology has never been as powerful or exciting as it is today. After a century or so of being defined by swashbuckling foreign explorers raiding other countries' ancient tombs, palaces, and temples for breathtaking artifacts to bring home, archaeology is now a fully scientific enterprise. Its practitioners no longer seek to procure stand-alone artifacts destined for static existences in museum vitrines. Instead, they want to understand the full context of the cultures that produced those artifacts, including exactly when their people lived, what they ate, which diseases they suffered from, what jobs they did, and how they thought about big questions like religion, government, and leadership. Archaeologists are still explorers, but they are no longer plundering ancient ruins for the treasure of long-dead monarchs. They are flying planes equipped with lasers over impenetrable jungles to spot the ruins hidden underneath. They are sequencing the DNA of ancient people to see how our ancestors' migrations and cultural mixing formed our identities today—and occasionally discovering a whole new human species in the process. They are scuba diving into shipwrecks and caves filled with mysterious ancient offerings. They are analyzing the isotopes preserved in long-dead people's teeth and bones to reconstruct their diets and rediscover their homelands. Knowledge about the human past is simply exploding, often in completely unexpected ways.

Archaeologists' trove of new data from every corner of the world allows them—even requires them—to ask previously unimaginable questions about the past, from rediscovering otherwise invisible, and long-since forgotten, migrations through dietary isotopes and ancient DNA to reconstructing, sometimes with year-by-year detail, how local and global climate patterns changed and affected the people who lived within them. In the process of asking new questions, archaeologists often find their new answers rewriting the stodgy historical narratives too many of us still grow up learning. Archaeologists can see the experiments, the dead ends, the alternate worlds that past people built and lived in, sometimes for centuries, that don't fit with the story of progress our societies like to tell us. They can see that human history is not a straight line of economic growth, technological improvements, and cultural advancements, inevitably leading to where we are today. They can see that the past was much messier, less certain, and more contingent than we are taught to believe—and they can also see the contemporary prejudices and hierarchies working to obscure that truth and limit the possibilities we can imagine for ourselves and our societies, in the past, present, and future.

More than anything, many of today's archaeologists are seeking to tell the whole stories of past communities, not just the official narratives that tend to be preserved and codified in written history compiled and popularized by its "victors." Archaeologists are hunting for information about the lives not only of the kings or the overlords but of the workers, the commoners, the women, the children, and the outsiders. Many kinds of voices are excluded from historical documents, and that can make us feel like a society's outsiders didn't matter or didn't even exist. But no type of person is invisible to archaeology.

That expansive view makes archaeology a particularly extraordinary tool for studying apocalypses, which by definition affect every rung of a society—but rarely in the same way. Archaeologists can examine mass graves that preserve evidence of massacres and widespread death, and they can rediscover when cities were abandoned, left to decay into the ruins we visit today. But in artifacts moving along trade routes, new architectural styles being invented, chemical residues left behind on ceramics, and DNA preserved in ancient bones, archaeologists can also see people migrating to new places, trying out new foods, and forming entirely new religions and governments. They can see not just the destruction of an apocalypse but also the regeneration that comes after.

◉

We'll begin by traveling deep into the past, to when *Homo sapiens* went from being one of many human species on the planet to being the only human species on the planet, after a wave of extinctions—the apocalypse that in some ways started it all. We'll watch global sea level rise with devastating speed, drowning countless homelands around the world in just a few generations, but also creating new ones. In some places, natural disasters became regular occurrences, and preparing for them shaped the kinds of societies we still live in today.

You've heard of some of the apocalypses that came next: the fall of Old Kingdom Egypt, the collapse of the Classic Maya, the Black Death. Others might be less familiar, like the fall of Harappa in what is now Pakistan. We'll examine how societies sometimes organized themselves in ways that invited these apocalypses in and multiplied the suffering they caused, and also how people learned, or didn't, from their ancestors' mistakes. We'll see how people reacted to apocalypses with violence and cruelty, but also with creativity, solidarity, and a sense of liberation. We'll also learn to see the modern world not as a triumph of technological and cultural progress but as the child of apocalypse, built from the rubble that hides in plain sight all around us.

I've almost certainly left out many of our shared history's familiar apocalypses, but I hope I've included others you didn't know to expect. I've tried to choose examples from many different places in the world, from what you could (perhaps) call the beginning of human history until the present day. Just as no two cultures or societies have ever been exactly alike, no apocalypses were, either. No single story can or should overwrite all others, but it is in each one's specificity that we can see the outlines of broader truths.

As the forces of the next apocalypse gather on the horizon, it's time for a new understanding of the endings that have led us here, not as sites of suffering and destruction—or at least not only that—but as times of change, uncertainty, resilience, survival, renewal, and opportunity. This book is that history, reckoning with what apocalypses are, how people have survived them, and the legacies they've imprinted on us and our cultures. The more I've learned about past apocalypses, the more hopeful I've become that we can and will survive our own. It won't be pleasant. It won't be fair. The world will be different on the other side, and our cultures and communities—perhaps even our species—will be different, too. We are cursed, and we are lucky, to be here to see the beginning.

PART 1: FOUNDATIONS

Chapter 1

HOW WE MISUNDERSTOOD THE APOCALYPSE OF HUMAN EXTINCTION

The Düssel River snakes through a valley in west Germany, flowing westward toward the Rhine and the metropolis of Düsseldorf. The trails along the Düssel offer a respite in the middle of the Rhine-Ruhr region, a conglomeration of cities that forms Germany's largest urban area. But something is missing from today's version of the landscape, something that generations upon generations of people saw and experienced, beginning long before the river was named the Düssel or the faintest notion of Germany—or any country—existed. For millennia, in what would come to be called the Neander Valley, towering walls of limestone stood sentry over the banks of the Düssel. In those cliffs were countless caves.

During the long, late summer days of August 1856, a team of workmen scrambled down one of those cliff faces onto a ledge about sixty feet above the river, which jutted out in front of one of the caves. The men were the advance guard of industrialization, tasked with chipping the limestone walls into pieces that could be carted off and used in the construction boom that was busy transforming Düsseldorf and the rest of the Rhine-Ruhr. Although the limestone surrounding the cave was newly valuable, the five feet of mud blanketing its floor was not. In preparation for quarrying away the cliffs, the workmen hauled out load after load of mud, heaving it off the ledge and onto the valley floor below.

It was in this tossed-out muck that someone first noticed the skull. Well, part of a skull—it was missing its face below the forehead. The owner of the quarry was a member of the local natural history association and told the workers to keep an eye out for more bones. They might belong to an extinct animal like a cave bear, whose bones turned up all over northern Europe. Their fossils, as well as those of other extinct creatures such as mammoths and dinosaurs, were of increasing interest to scientists, who had recently realized the Earth was much older than the Bible taught, and its deep past much stranger. Eventually the workers found fifteen other bones in the cave, including long, sturdy limb bones and curved ribs.

Johann Carl Fuhlrott, a teacher and the founder of the local natural history association, was called out to take a look. Based on their general anatomy, he immediately recognized the bones didn't belong to a cave bear. He suspected they belonged to a human, albeit a very unusual one, and likely a very old one. Fuhlrott needed some help understanding what he was looking at, and so he sent a letter, along with a cast of the partial skull, to Hermann Schaaffhausen, a respected anatomist at the University of Bonn. Soon, Fuhlrott would make the trip himself carrying the originals so that Schaaffhausen could examine them.

Schaaffhausen agreed with Fuhlrott that the bones belonged to a human. But what kind? Schaaffhausen got to work measuring the bones in order to compare them to the skeletons of modern and ancient people from all over the world. He immediately noticed the bones from the Neander Valley—or, in the German of the time, the *Neander Thal*—were very different from those of any known human. The limb bones and ribs were unusually thick, and the skull had a distinctive shape. Instead of the round dome of known human skulls, the Neanderthal skull was flatter and longer. It also had strikingly prominent brow ridges, which jutted out dramatically above the eye sockets. Schaaffhausen could find nothing quite like it in the museums of Europe. Its "extraordinary form" was "hitherto not known to exist," Schaaffhausen wrote.

In addition to the question of its humanity, the Neanderthal skeleton presented another mystery: its age. Both Fuhlrott and Schaaffhausen suspected the skull was ancient because it had been buried under four or five feet of mud and dirt, a fact Fuhlrott made sure to confirm with the quarry workers as soon as he realized the bones might be special. But unlike some human bones found in different parts of Europe and the world, the Neanderthal skeleton was found alone, unaccompanied by the bones of mammoths, cave bears, or other extinct animals that were, in the nineteenth century, the only unequivocal proof of antiquity.

Unable to place the bones in an ancient context, Schaaffhausen decided to test whether they were fossilized. If not, the bones would be assumed to date to the historical period and therefore have little to say about humanity's deep past. But if they were, it would imply they had been in the cave for a very long time, perhaps before any known European people or culture had existed. So Schaaffhausen employed the nineteenth century's gold-standard dating technique: He licked them. Fossil bones would stick to his tongue, whereas more recent bones would slip off. The Neanderthal bone stuck. It was ancient, belonging to, Schaaffhausen believed, the world of the last ice age or perhaps an even older, and still largely unknown, geological era. He and Fuhlrott presented their findings at a scientific conference in Bonn in 1857, and Schaaffhausen published his study of the fossil bones in 1858.

Schaaffhausen's paper sparked a flurry of interest and heated debates among the European scientific establishment, especially after it was translated into English in 1861. Some agreed with Schaaffhausen's theory that the skeleton belonged to a "barbarous" member of *Homo sapiens*. Others weren't so sure. The English geologist William King was the first to take the leap and suggest the Neanderthal represented a new species. He found its skull to be "eminently simial," closer to those of chimpanzees and gorillas than those of *Homo sapiens*. King named the new species *Homo neanderthalensis*.

◉

And so it was that science realized *Homo sapiens* had not always been alone. We had once shared the world with other humans. The discovery of Neanderthals in the mud from that cave revealed the staggering unfamiliarity of the deep past, and it hinted at a previously unsuspected apocalypse lurking within it: human extinction. Whatever had happened, however the Neanderthals—and perhaps as yet unknown others—had succumbed and why, we were now the only survivors.

With few real clues to solve the mystery, assumptions and biases seeped in to fill the yawning gaps in scientific knowledge. Making assumptions based solely on one set of Neanderthal bones, Schaaffhausen, King, and other early paleoanthropologists felt confident in characterizing them as primitive, barbarous, and savage. In the absence of any information about the Neanderthals' culture or era, the ways their skulls differed from those of *Homo sapiens*—namely their longer, flatter shapes and pronounced brow ridges—were immediately taken to be not only marks of their inferiority but also the causes of it.

These same scientists had already spent decades studying *Homo sapiens* skulls from around the world, largely in service of classifying and ranking them by race. For Schaaffhausen, Neanderthals slotted perfectly into the bottom position of this hierarchy of humanity, as he thought their cranial features existed on a continuum with those of "living savages." King, on the other hand, believed the Neanderthal skull had more in common with ape crania than the skulls of even the "most degraded race" of *Homo sapiens*, whom he considered to be the people of the Andaman Islands, an archipelago in the Indian Ocean. Andaman Islanders were "very little above animals," King thought, so Neanderthals must fall out of the category of human altogether. "I feel myself constrained to believe that the thoughts and desires which once dwelt within [its skull] never soared beyond those of the brute," he wrote in 1864.

Gradually, more and more Neanderthal bones were identified in other parts of Europe, from Gibraltar and Belgium (where the bones had been discovered before the skull in Germany but had languished unidentified) to France and Croatia. The more these early paleoanthropologists looked at Neanderthals, the more distant from us these ancient people seemed. In the early twentieth century, paleontologist Marcellin Boule analyzed the first nearly complete Neanderthal skeleton, discovered in France's La Chapelle-aux-Saints cave. He looked at its warped vertebrae and damaged joints and concluded Neanderthals had a hunched, slouching posture, which reflected their clumsiness and stupidity. "Even the primitives at the peripheries of the earth are considerably more advanced," Boule wrote in 1908. It wasn't until the 1950s that other scientists reexamined the bones and discovered the La Chapelle-aux-Saints skeleton belonged to an elderly Neanderthal man with arthritis.

As anthropologists solidified their impression of Neanderthals as primitive brutes, they also began to consider the question of their extinction. Based on the stratigraphic sequences at many European sites, their bones and the types of artifacts associated with them seemed to endure for many centuries, if not millennia, only to abruptly vanish around when the first *Homo sapiens* appeared in the region. The possibility of directly dating archaeological material was still decades away, so no one knew exactly when this replacement of Neanderthals with us had occurred. Most anthropologists, however, were quite sure of what it meant. "Those who observe the fate of the aboriginal races of America and of Australia will have no difficulty in accounting for the disappearance of *Homo neanderthalensis*. A more virile form extinguished him," wrote anthropologist Arthur Keith in 1915.

When these early anthropologists gazed back into the deep past of human evolution, they saw violence, domination, and replacement. To them, *Homo sapiens* was not merely the survivor of an apocalypse that wiped out our close cousins. We were its perpetrators, and, importantly, its victors. We *were* the apocalypse, clearing the stage of our inferior, less evolved relatives so that we could step into our rightful role as the planet's most advanced and widespread species. Early paleoanthropologists saw no reason to lament Neanderthal extinction as a loss, nor to doubt its rapidity and totality. As a lower form of human, extinction was simply their evolutionary destiny.

◉

On many days when Johannes Krause reported for work at the Max Planck Institute for Evolutionary Anthropology in Leipzig, Germany, he had to make sure to avoid absolutely everyone. Using a special entrance that led directly to a series of rooms in the basement, Krause was forbidden from chatting with, or even being in the presence of, his colleagues working upstairs in different labs. He couldn't risk being contaminated—or at least any more contaminated than he already was.

To that end, Krause would go straight to the basement and change his clothes. He would put on a face mask, affix paper booties over his shoes, and pull a puffy shower cap–like cover over his mop of blond curls. He snapped on not just one but several pairs of surgical gloves. He knew that once he was inside the lab, shedding a single hair, or smudging just one surface with a fingerprint, could set his whole team back years.

Krause, then working on paleogeneticist Svante Pääbo's team, was after a prize that still might have been a fantasy: Neanderthal DNA, preserved for tens of thousands of years in the bones they left behind. The *Homo sapiens* genome had been sequenced less than a decade before, from blood samples collected from living people under immaculate conditions. But Pääbo, Krause's adviser, had already been making progress on extracting and studying DNA from the bones of extinct animals, including the mammoths and giant ground sloths that had roamed the Earth during the last ice age. It seemed possible that DNA in Neanderthal bones that had been preserved in similar environments and kept in the same museums might have also stood the test of time.

If Neanderthal DNA had survived—and that was a big if—the team would have to make sure that what they were sequencing was the real thing, and not more recent human DNA from anyone who had handled the bones, contamination that would discredit any results. So, the team had to do everything they could to keep their own DNA away from the Neanderthal remains. Hence the isolated basement lab, the sterile clothes, the shower cap, and the several pairs of gloves Krause—who happened to be from the same village where Johann Carl Fuhlrott was born—carefully put on before each and every time he touched a Neanderthal bone. In the lab, he breathed air filtered of 99.99 percent of the dust, skin, pollen, bacteria, and other particles that typically float around in any indoor space, and he worked under the blue glare of UV lights that would break down any offending double helixes the filters missed. Only under such meticulously clean conditions would Krause dare to touch the Neanderthal bones that had been sent to the laboratory from sites all over Europe. Then he pulled out a dentist's drill, set it whirring, and carefully touched its delicate tip to the bone.

Many of these bones had been discovered decades before and had been sitting in museums ever since, exposed to veritable avalanches of modern DNA. Countless scientists had touched them—or worse, licked them—during that time, leaving minuscule pieces of their modern selves behind. Krause employed the drill to meticulously grind away a tiny amount of each bone's surface, along with—he hoped—any modern DNA clinging to it. Then he drilled a small hole into the bone, as delicately as any dentist grinding away a cavity. Perhaps even more carefully, as he had to pause every few seconds to avoid heating up the bone with the friction from the drill, which could destroy already fragile ancient DNA.

The drilling created a fraction of a gram of pulverized bone powder, which Krause painstakingly collected, hoping it would contain what they needed. He added it to a solution that released any surviving DNA molecules from the rest of the bone's minerals, and then used an enzyme to add short, artificial DNA sequences to either end of the extracted molecules. Those artificial sequences made it possible for newly developed DNA sequencing machines to read and amplify the ancient genetic material in between, which could then be compared to the genomes of modern humans and other primates to reveal what made it unique.

Krause's careful work paid off—the Neanderthal bones contained DNA that couldn't possibly have come from the researchers or museum handlers. Pääbo's team published the first Neanderthal genome in 2010. This genome and others that followed would reveal much about the genetic characteristics of different Neanderthal groups over time, including their likely group size (small) and potential linguistic abilities (strong). But it was in comparing the Neanderthal genome to the *Homo sapiens* genome where Pääbo, Krause, and the rest of the scientific world would find the biggest surprise. They found pieces of the Neanderthal genome within the genomes of every living person tested outside of Africa. It turned out the genomes of Europeans, East Asians, Native Americans, and everyone else with ancestry outside Africa are about 2 percent Neanderthal. Anthropologists now had definitive, scientific proof that modern humans had mated with Neanderthals, and their offspring had survived to go on to have their own children.

Some twentieth-century anthropologists had always thought Neanderthals could be our direct ancestors, but among those who subscribed to that theory, Neanderthals were mostly envisioned as an evolutionary "phase" of archaic humans passed through and left behind on the way toward the appearance of anatomically modern and behaviorally advanced *Homo sapiens*. Neanderthals weren't driven extinct by us, those scientists thought, but rather had evolved into us through the forces of natural selection and, perhaps, mating with other archaic species. But by the time Pääbo's team sequenced the Neanderthal genome, the majority view of Neanderthal evolution and extinction was not so different from the vision of replacement that prevailed a century earlier. In 2010, most paleoanthropologists thought *Homo sapiens* and Neanderthals were distinct species and that *Homo sapiens* had evolved in Africa and Neanderthals in Europe and western Asia, geographically separated from each other's lineages. Once modern humans expanded into Neanderthal territory, the theory was that we quickly replaced them without any of the kinds of interactions that would have left a genetic or cultural trace, and perhaps with a fair amount of violence.

Whether they thought we replaced them through evolution or competition, most anthropologists had considered Neanderthals a stepping stone on the way to a better, smarter, fitter version of humanity, the *Homo sapiens* destined to inherit the Earth. The revelation that almost all living people carry a small amount of Neanderthal DNA turned that assumption on its head. The genetic evidence showed that while Neanderthals hadn't transformed into modern humans, they had met and mixed with us once we spread out of Africa. That meant Neanderthals were not a less evolved version of *Homo sapiens*, nor did we immediately drive them to extinction. Our family trees didn't stand apart from each other, one long since withered and one still thriving. They were intertwined, reaching into the future together. Maybe, the genetic evidence suggested, Neanderthals didn't go extinct at all. Instead, they became us—but we also became them.

◉

With the discovery of widespread Neanderthal ancestry in modern humans and intensive archaeology looking at how our ancient relatives lived in the hundreds of thousands of years before our species met, scientists' image of Neanderthals, and their place in human history, is now very different than it was fifteen years ago, much less one hundred and fifty years ago. The oldest known Neanderthal bones, found in Spain, date to four hundred thousand years ago, making them one hundred thousand years older than the most ancient *Homo sapiens* fossil discovered so far, in Morocco. Neanderthal bones—sometimes, it seems, intentionally buried or interred in caves—have been found from Portugal to Wales, Croatia to Iraq, Uzbekistan to Siberia. Remains of their ancient meals suggest they hunted giant camels in the Middle East, gathered shellfish along the shores of the Atlantic, and brought down scores of prehistoric horses by ambushing migrating herds. Direct dating techniques have shown that cave paintings of geometric patterns and the ghostly outlines of hands predate the arrival of *Homo sapiens* in Europe by twenty thousand years, making Neanderthals the only possible artists. Fragments of their bones, identified by Neanderthal-specific proteins, have also been found in the same archaeological layers as jewelry carved from animal teeth, shells, and ivory. All told, Neanderthals roamed Europe and western Asia for more than three hundred and fifty thousand years, finally disappearing around forty thousand years ago. Our genetic mixing happened in many places and time periods, with the most influential burst possibly occurring for several millennia around forty-seven thousand years ago.

Debates continue to rage over the extent of Neanderthals' cultural and cognitive capabilities, and how similar or different they were to those of *Homo sapiens*. But given the fact that the two populations had viable, fertile children together, as evidenced by our widespread Neanderthal ancestry today, some scientists have even started to question whether they were really separate species at all. The categories set in place by the first scientists to identify and study Neanderthals—us and them, superior and inferior, winners and losers, extinct and alive—have definitively blurred, even if the full picture of their abilities and our relationship is still coming into focus.

Along with ancient DNA, direct dating techniques have played a crucial role in rewriting Neanderthal history. A technology like radiocarbon dating would have been unimaginable to early paleoanthropologists like Schaaffhausen and Fuhlrott, who depended on fossils being found alongside the bones of extinct animals to determine their antiquity—or, at least, sticking to their tongues. Early archaeologists, meanwhile, relied on the handful of ancient cultures that had left behind written dates they could decipher, primarily ancient Egypt. Using ancient calendars, they could define the precise span of years during which a certain style of pottery, jewelry, or tool was made and used. Ancient Egypt traded with other cultures all over the eastern Mediterranean, so if a specific kind of Egyptian pot, weapon, or piece of jewelry turned up in an excavation in Athens, Rome, Damascus, or Tunis, archaeologists could work backward and link it to the date range they knew from Egypt. Chains of dates, all tracing back to Egypt and other cultures with known dates, "spread out rather like ripples upon a pool," says Tom Higham, a radiocarbon dating expert. But the farther archaeologists got away those cultures, both geographically and temporally, the weaker the ripples became. Dating an ancient site in Britain, Siberia, China, or the Americas using this method was all but impossible. And reaching back as far as the prehistoric world Neanderthals inhabited was even more out of reach.

That all changed with the invention of radiocarbon dating in the 1940s. The physical chemist Willard Libby discovered that all living organisms absorb a small amount of the radioactive isotope carbon-14 from the atmosphere. As long as the organism is alive and absorbing carbon-14, the ratio of carbon-14 to the other carbon isotope in its body, carbon-12, stays fixed. When an organism dies, the carbon-14 it contains starts to decay at a steady rate. Within about 5,700 years, half of it will have disappeared. The amount of carbon-12, however, will remain the same. By measuring the ratio of carbon isotopes in a bone, the wooden shaft of a spear, a seed, or a piece of burned food or charcoal from an ancient hearth, archaeologists can figure out how long ago the organism died.

Libby won a Nobel Prize in Chemistry in 1960 for radiocarbon dating, and his work transformed the study of the past. For the first time, archaeologists could figure out the precise age of ancient artifacts and bones, using only information contained within the object itself. The field began to be able to present testable hypotheses, to be confirmed or refuted by data that any researcher in the world could replicate or question. Archaeology, in other words, became scientific.

Radiocarbon dating has an upper limit. In bones or seeds or charcoal older than about fifty thousand years, there is no radiocarbon left to measure. But Higham was developing sampling techniques that could isolate even tiny amounts of carbon, allowing him to date organic material closer and closer to that natural limit. He wanted to use his techniques to precisely identify when Neanderthals disappeared and when *Homo sapiens* arrived in Europe, which happened just about as far back as radiocarbon dating can go. When Higham embarked on the project, he said, "I was wedded to the idea of modern humans being superior—culturally, technologically, and so on. And I was of the view modern humans swept into Europe and Neanderthals went extinct very quickly."

To date Neanderthal bones, Higham and his team also had to destroy them, or at least small pieces of them, drilling out a few hundred grams of bone powder from their interiors and subjecting the powder to acid washes and other chemical solutions to isolate and purify its collagen, which would offer the most reliable date. Those collagen molecules then went into a particle accelerator to measure their carbon-14 and, thus, their age. Just a few years after the first Neanderthal genome was published, in 2014, Higham's radiocarbon dating of late Neanderthal and early *Homo sapiens* bones from all over Europe showed that the two species overlapped for up to 5,400 years, and the likely upper limit has only been pushed even earlier since. Neanderthals survived for many millennia after the arrival of *Homo sapiens* in their territory, complicating previous assumptions about their quick, and perhaps violent, replacement. The two species may have even occupied the same caves in different years, as evidenced by a baby tooth that likely belonged to a young *Homo sapiens* found in between layers of Neanderthal bones and tools in a cave in France.

With such a long time to get to know each other, and both archaeological and genetic evidence of close, even intimate, contact, Higham now sees this period as one of likely exchange and experimentation. "You can imagine—a group of new people arrive, and they're doing things slightly differently than you. Maybe they have some ideas, some materials you've never seen before. And what do you do? Well, as a human, you copy. You imitate." And the more Higham learns about what Neanderthals were capable of, the more it seems possible that knowledge and ideas flowed in the other direction as well. These meetings were "fertile ground," potentially changing both species, he says. Our relationship began to look less like an immediate, inevitable replacement and more like a more fluid dance around, and occasionally with, each other.

And yet, an apocalypse still lurks at the heart of this story. Neanderthals no longer walk the earth beside us. They are our ancestors but not our contemporaries. Their genetic contribution to modern humans, while significant and widespread, is still only a small portion of our genomes. After millions of years during which different species of humans shared our planet, *Homo sapiens* are the only ones left.

Compared with their nineteenth- and early twentieth-century predecessors, today's anthropologists are far more willing to admit they don't know why we are our genus's sole survivors. Some do still believe we outcompeted Neanderthals, that something about *Homo sapiens* really did make us more capable, more adaptable, more resilient. Others are eager to give Neanderthals their due as hunters, craftspeople, artists, and humans after more than a century of casting them as a "lower form" or "degraded race" warped both scientific and public opinion about them. When it comes to Neanderthals and their extinction, anthropologists have moved away from thinking they have a single, all-encompassing answer, or that the hypothesis that convinces them today won't be overturned by new evidence tomorrow. That shift from confidence in a coherent story to uncertainty as the narrative we trusted falls apart can leave us feeling unsatisfied, or even betrayed. It is also, almost always, a sign of scientific progress toward something closer to the messy, unpredictable truth.

Bolstered by these new facts and possibilities about Neanderthals, we might give ourselves and our ancestors the gift of imagining a different kind of story about the apocalypse of their extinction. Stories that center the best of our natures, instead of the worst, and that allow people of the past—of all species—to have desires, fears, and imaginations of their own. Stories like those recognize the contingency of history rather than insisting on the inevitability of the narratives we think we know. These new stories might be wrong, but just as possible, they may not be as wrong as the ones that came before.

◉

A more complete story of Neanderthal history, including its ending, starts with recognizing just how capable and adaptable they were. Over the course of their more than four hundred thousand years of existence, Neanderthals successfully inhabited many different ecosystems and climates, from mountains to forests to coasts. Some Neanderthals lived in cool mountain caves and others on the balmy shores of the

Mediterranean. They survived as those climates slowly shifted, as the Earth naturally entered and emerged from periodic ice ages. These climates could be challenging, especially the coldest ones, but once they had settled over the Neanderthals' homelands, they were generally steady and predictable. Bands of Neanderthals could adapt to the new conditions, focusing their hunting on cold-loving animals like reindeer and probably smoking and storing meat for the long winters.

But in Neanderthals' final millennia on the planet, the climate grew jumpy and unstable, especially in northern Europe. Conditions swung between cold and warm and back again relatively quickly. The paleoanthropologist Chris Stringer, who has studied Neanderthals and other ancient humans for over fifty years, envisions Neanderthals of this period regularly retreating to a handful of relatively warm places during the cold snaps, hunkering down in small and shrinking populations, and then expanding again as their ancestral territories thawed. "Things improved for a couple of thousand years, and they bounced back in numbers," he says. But then the cold returned, quickly and unpredictably, and "most of those migrants got wiped out," leaving only those who had remained in warm areas to repeat the whole process again. "They were continually pruned back," Stringer says. "They could never build up diversity, they could never build up numbers consistently." By the last ten thousand years or so of their existence, Neanderthals, he says, "were already in trouble"—and then in walks another human species, looking to hunt the same animals, gather the same plants, and live in the same caves. In walks us.

Those modern humans may not have had any intellectual or behavioral advantage whatsoever over Neanderthals. But from the genetic data, we know that most Neanderthal bands at the time were small and getting smaller. Newly arrived *Homo sapiens*, however, had more diverse gene pools and traded stone and other materials across longer distances, meaning they may have lived in slightly larger groups or had stronger social connections with other bands of modern humans living both nearby and far away. "Being welcome at the fires of friends many valleys away might make the difference between infants getting by on milky dregs, or tiny hollow bodies being laid down in cold crevices," writes archaeologist Rebecca Wragg Sykes. Perhaps the new arrivals also had sewing needles for stitching up animal skins into warmer baby clothes, or another seemingly trivial technology that would turn out to make all the difference to surviving climate fluctuations, Stringer says.

Faced with shrinking communities, an unpredictable climate, and another kind of human who may have been noticeably more successful at weathering social and environmental challenges, Neanderthals didn't stagnate or apathetically wait out their remaining time on Earth. Perhaps, as small Neanderthal bands suffered, some of their members took a chance on joining a group of those other humans, choosing community and life over isolation and death. As an apocalypse bore down on them, they took the ultimate risk and allowed themselves—and, perhaps more importantly, their children—to cross cultures, languages, and traditions, and to become something entirely new in the mosaic of humanity. A process that now looks like extinction could have looked, to the people who enacted it, like the surest path toward survival.

◉

Neanderthals were the first "extinct" humans to be discovered, but they wouldn't be the last. Scientists now know of several other species of human that shared the planet with *Homo sapiens*, including *Homo erectus*, which evolved in Africa and may have been the first human to travel beyond its borders; *Homo floresiensis*, a diminutive human that might have evolved its tiny body size over millennia of isolation on the island of Flores in Indonesia; *Homo naledi*, of whom the only known remains were found deep in a cave in South Africa, raising evocative questions about how they thought about death, burial, and the afterlife; and *Homo luzonensis*, another small, island-dwelling human, found in the Philippines, whose curved finger and toe bones suggest they could have swung through trees.

Many of these species' bones have been recovered from environments that don't favor the preservation of ancient DNA, such as the hot and humid tropics, and without being able to look at their genomes, scientists aren't sure if they actually met contemporaneous *Homo sapiens*. But the fifth kind of human who coexisted with us was discovered from ancient DNA alone, both in their bones and our genomes. They are the Denisovans, and their story goes the farthest in revealing just how much we don't know about the human past and the apocalypses it contains.

It was Johannes Krause, working in his surgical getup in the basement lab in Leipzig, who stumbled upon the first sign of the Denisovans. He was deep in his years of "play[ing] dentist," as he described it, drilling tiny holes into ancient bones and developing cutting-edge chemical and computational methods to isolate and sequence any DNA they contained. He and Svante Pääbo had been given a tiny fragment of a pinky finger bone; "the size of two grains of rice put together," as Pääbo would later describe it. It had come from Denisova Cave in Siberia's Altai Mountains, near where Russia, Kazakhstan, and Mongolia meet. The bone was too small and nondescript to tell what species it came from, but it seemed possible it was Neanderthal—and at the time, while they were building the first Neanderthal genome, Krause and company were eager for any Neanderthal DNA they could find.

When Krause extracted and sequenced the bone's DNA, he quickly realized its genome didn't match up with those of Neanderthals. But it didn't match the *Homo sapiens* genome either. It was something else, a lost human species no one had even dreamed existed, much less thought to look for. The team announced their discovery in 2010, the same year they published the first Neanderthal genome. They named the new group the Denisovans, after the cave where the bone was found. Krause and colleagues couldn't tell what the Denisovans looked like, where they lived, or how their bodies and cultures differed from those of Neanderthals and *Homo sapiens*. They could only determine that the Denisovans were about as genetically different from *Homo sapiens* as Neanderthals were.

More than a decade later, very few other Denisovan bones have been found. At the time of this writing, scientists have yet to confirm discovery of a complete Denisovan skeleton, or even a skull. Neanderthals, from nearly the moment of their discovery, have been the subjects of countless reconstructions from the "brutish" and apelike to the friendly and human. Denisovans, on the other hand, are still ghosts, their physical form invisible and unimaginable. This will almost certainly change one day, and possibly soon. Their bones may, in fact, already be in museums, unrecognized and misclassified by past generations of scientists who didn't know how to look for them—or that there was anyone else there to look for at all.

In the meantime, however, scientists interested in the Denisovans have started digging not in caves (or at least not only in caves) but also into the genomes of living, breathing *Homo sapiens*, where a surprising amount of Denisovan DNA still survives. Denisovans apparently had babies with modern humans from Siberia to China to Southeast Asia, and they also mated with Neanderthals; in a stunning bit of luck, scientists found, also in Denisova cave, a fragment of a bone belonging to the daughter of a Denisovan father and a Neanderthal mother. Based on where their bones and genes are found today, Denisovan communities likely lived in tropical rainforests, frigid tundras, and even some of the world's highest habitable altitudes in Tibet—successfully adapting to a huge range of ecosystems in a way some anthropologists thought only *Homo sapiens* could do. But Denisovans are still known only through their DNA. Without Denisovan sites, tools, or skeletons, archaeologists can't yet study their lives or cultures the way they can with Neanderthals.

If Neanderthal extinction presents a mystery to which we may never be sure we have the full answer, Denisovan disappearance is even more puzzling. Unlike Neanderthals, whose genomes point to dwindling numbers toward the end of their existence, Denisovans seem to have been a thriving, impressively adaptable species. Until they weren't. "It doesn't look like they were in trouble the way the Neanderthals were," Stringer says. "And yet they also disappeared." As for our other extinct cousins—*erectus, naledi, luzonensis, floresiensis*—we know even less. Their disappearances could have had everything to do with us and our arrival in their homelands, or nothing to do with us at all.

Despite, or perhaps because of, this wide-open mystery with so few clues, we have the chance to imagine better for the Denisovans and others than early paleoanthropologists did for the Neanderthals. Faced with these very old, but also new, human ancestors, we can use the evolution of scientific thinking about Neanderthals to reject outdated assumptions about inferiority and replacement from the start—or at least begin from the premise that other more interesting and generous ideas are equally likely to be true. What could we learn if we looked at the apocalypse of human extinction through the lens not of violence, competition, and disappearance but of community, creativity, and survival? What if we could see our ancestors—all of them—as partners and collaborators, not victors and victims? What if we could believe not only that Neanderthals, Denisovans, and perhaps more were capable of joining our communities but that we were capable of welcoming them?

◉

The people were always on the move. They walked through valleys and along rivers. They walked up and over hills. Mostly they walked between places they had already been, places where they could still see the ashy smudges of fires they and their ancestors had kindled. The chain of knowledge and experience stretching far back into the past told them where the best caves were to pass a night, a month, a season. It told them when the horses would begin to move to warmer places, and where to best meet them for the hunt that would sustain their group through the winter. It told them how to take apart the animals they killed, cure their hides, and smoke their meat so it would last. It told them where the best stone could be found and how to turn it into the tools they needed to do the work that made up their lives.

One day, around forty-seven thousand years ago, the people arrived at one of their caves and immediately saw that someone else had been there. The ashes in the fire circle were fresh. Discarded animal bones lay on the floor, cooked and eaten so recently the hyenas hadn't yet found them to pick off the final scraps of meat and marrow. They didn't know who else would come here. This cave was right in the heart of their territory. They only ever met with other bands on the edge of their lands, and even that happened rarely. Some generations could go their whole lives without seeing a stranger. The people knew bears used their caves sometimes, but bears didn't light fires.

The people were unsettled, of course, but night was falling, and this was the cave they knew. They stayed the few days they had planned and then continued their journey, which was carefully timed to intercept a herd of horses during its seasonal migration. They didn't have time to waste looking for the Others, although the band's best trackers remained on high alert for signs of where they had gone and who they might be. The trackers could see the broken twigs and churned-up earth that marked the path the Others took away from the cave, just as they could see where the aurochs, deer, bears, and wolves had been. The people went in another direction, as they knew to do with animals they wanted to avoid, and soon all traces of anyone else vanished. They didn't think about the Others again for a long time.

One day, when the children who remembered encountering signs of the Others had grown to be adults, the trackers among them picked up an unusual trail. It looked like the trail they themselves left behind, the one the trackers could always find. But they hadn't walked over this land in a long while. This trail was fresh, and it was heading in the same direction they were going.

When they came within sight of their destination, a limestone cave in a river valley, the Others were already there. The group kept a safe distance, the hunters standing guard with their spears. While the people were discussing what to do, the Others noticed they weren't alone and gathered outside the cave to look at them. The Others were taller and slimmer than the people were, and their eyebrows and noses seemed so small in relation to the rest of their face. *Can they even smell?* the people whispered to each other. *How can they hunt if they can't smell?* It was like seeing their own reflection distorted by a rippling, churning river after a storm. You, but different. You, but changed.

One of the Others' young ones was wearing the teeth of an animal around his neck. Their own young ones were pointing and talking about it excitedly. The other boy, with the necklace, could tell they were talking about him. A woman—his mother, presumably—tried to hold him back but he walked a few steps away from his group and toward the visitors. They drew back a bit, but what could a boy do to them with their best hunters standing right there with their spears raised? The boy took off the string of teeth and put it on the ground in between the groups and then scampered back to his mother.

Before anyone could stop her, one of their girls darted away from the group of children, grabbed the teeth, and dashed back to her friends. She put the string around her neck like the other boy had been wearing it. The children were wild for it. It was the most special thing they'd ever seen. Inspired and more than a little jealous that she hadn't been the one to retrieve the necklace, another girl removed one of the feathers she was wearing in her hair, walked toward the Others—not quite as far as the boy had come toward them, but far enough—and placed it on the ground. Tomorrow, the boy with the necklace would be wearing it in his hair.

It was too late in the season to move on, and the people had grown familiar enough with the dangers of unpredictable weather to take the risk. But it seems the Others had, too. Both groups knew that this valley was the best spot to pass the winter, and they were both determined to stay. With the Others occupying the first-choice cave, the people had to seek out another, which they had used before, in years when a bear had beaten them to their normal over-winter spot. It would do.

Sometimes the hunters from the two groups would meet each other in the woods; other times an adult would look around for their child, only to find them playing with one of the Others' children and have to drag them back to camp. Once, when they had had a good hunt and the Others hadn't, the people cautiously placed a reindeer haunch within sight of the Others' cave. They whistled to get the Others' attention before the hyenas smelled it but left before they reached the gift. It wasn't the best meat by far, but they knew what it was like to be hungry enough to eat almost anything. They didn't want the Others to starve while they feasted. Who knows what that kind of hunger could drive them to do?

Just after the snow began to melt and the rivers began to thaw, one of the trackers took the route that would take him closest to the Others' cave, to see how they were getting by. They were gone, having moved on in the dawn light. When he went back to the group, the people were abuzz with news of their own—a young woman was nowhere to be seen. She had been spending an unusual amount of time away from the group, and once a tracker had seen her in the woods with a young man belonging to the Others. They couldn't talk to each other—the Others' language was indecipherable to them—but they were still smiling and laughing together, their bodies drawing close against the cold. As winter wore on, the elder women had started to suspect the woman was carrying a child, her first, though the woman herself didn't say anything about it, and none of their young men had been with her. Once the tracker told them the Others had gone, too, it seemed obvious what had happened.

There were legends of people who joined other groups, adventurous souls who, sometime deep in the undefined past, had left their communities for lives with other bands. Some of those stories spoke of newcomers whose helpful knowledge and novel ideas saved their new companions in a time of need. Other stories warned against such a choice, telling of the misery and homesickness that crept into the newcomers' hearts once the first blush of excitement and attraction had worn off, and sometimes of the violence with which they were greeted. The young woman's life had now forked away from them, her family, and would take one of those directions. They would never know which. They would never see her, or the Others, again.

Chapter 2

HOW SEA LEVEL RISE SPURRED INGENUITY

Doggerland was doomed, but no one knew it yet. To the thousands of people who lived there, it still seemed like paradise. This was a land of water, and they were water people. Many of them lived on the shores of a lake so large it might as well have been the sea. It stretched far beyond the horizon, and almost every river flowed into it. The people had lived around the lake and along the rivers for generations, and they knew their environment in exquisite detail. They fished with nets and pronged spears, trapped birds, and collected eggs. They waded into the shallows and pried shellfish off the rocks. They cut the reeds that grew along the shore and wove them into baskets, mats, and roofs for their huts. In the nearby forests, they hunted deer and aurochs, plucked sweet berries off bushes, and picked bitter herbs to use as medicine. They paddled boats around and across the lake, meeting and trading food and crafts with their neighbors. When the season was right, they followed spawning salmon; at other times, migrating birds. The whole landscape was their home, and they moved with these times of plenty, periodically coming together in large groups for celebrations that could last for days. But the waterways of Doggerland teemed with so much life all year round that its people rarely went hungry. Doggerland gave them everything they needed, and they loved it in return.

That love expressed itself in profound attention to the landscape and its every detail, no matter how subtle. So of course the people noticed the change right away: The sea was getting closer. It sounded impossible, and yet it was unmistakable. Generations of elders said that when they had climbed the hills on the north side of the lake in their youth, they had seen forest and rivers stretching between them and the distant glimmer of the sea on the horizon. Now, the young people who climbed those same hills saw the coast just on the other side.

As they grew old and became elders themselves, salt water snaked around the hills and up the rivers the people knew so well. Finally, it reached their lake. The water turned brackish and began to flow in and out with the tide. Those tides carried sand with them, gradually building up banks that sliced the lake into smaller and smaller pieces. The lake became a marsh, a liminal space that connected land and sea but belonged to neither.

The people of the lake were now people of the coast. Doggerland was no longer the place their ancestors remembered, but they could still make do. They had always been water people, and the sea was still water—just a different kind. It wasn't as gentle as the lake had been. Floods and storms were more dangerous, and the new currents could easily pull a boat off course. Hemmed in by rough waters and sand banks that shifted unpredictably, people lost touch with the neighbors they had once visited by paddling across the lake's tranquil waters. But the fishing was still good, the marsh was still full of reeds, and there were still plenty of birds to catch and eat. Instead of hunting aurochs, they hunted seal. They came to know the marsh plants and seaweeds as well as they had ever known the herbs and berries of the forest.

Sometimes the people would visit the old lands, paddling their boats over the drowned valleys, gorges, and rivers their ancestors had known. They still knew the names of some of these places, even though nobody had seen them for generations. At low tide, they could walk among ghostly forests of petrified tree stumps, their long-dead roots still snaking across and into the sand. Their ancestors had known these woods when they had been brimming with life, and the people continued to care for the trees that had crossed over to the afterlife. When one of their own died, the people would sometimes bury them on the shore, covered in shells, or row their bodies to small islands they used as cemeteries. It was a way of returning the dead to the home of the ancestors.

Eventually the hills that had once risen beside the lake became an island. The people crowded onto its shrinking footprint, fighting each other for space. Those who managed to eke out a life there became travelers and traders who navigated the new sea, bringing people and goods from one community to the next, just as their ancestors had done around the lake. They braved floods, one of which sent thirty-foot waves crashing over what little land remained. And then one day, even the island was gone. Doggerland became a memory, and soon enough it wasn't even that.

◉

About twelve thousand years before it disappeared, the place that would become Doggerland, along with much of the rest of Earth, would have been unrecognizable to its future inhabitants. Deep in the last ice age, about twenty thousand years ago, vast sheets of ice reached down from our planet's poles, covering much of the land we know today. Glaciers obscured much of Canada, Norway, Scotland, and a good part of northern England; others extended up from the Antarctic and across half of Chile. These glaciers had sucked so much water out of the oceans that they transformed our planet's geography. The continents we know today were all quite a bit wider, with coastlines that extended miles and miles beyond where our beaches end. Many of today's islands were connected to the mainland or to each other. Land stretched across the Bering Strait, linking Asia and North America. Several of Southeast Asia's archipelagos were joined into a continent almost as big as India. Doggerland filled the southern part of what is now the North Sea, the cul-de-sac of the Atlantic Ocean that sits among England, the Netherlands, Germany, and Denmark.

With glaciers looming on its northern edge, Doggerland was, at this point in its history, an inhospitable tundra. Mammoths and woolly rhinoceros roamed its frigid plains, grazing on hearty Arctic grasses and shrubs. It's possible small groups of human hunters followed them, but if they did, there weren't many of them. Most people had probably retreated to the warmer and more welcoming climates of southern Europe after the glaciers began their advance.

And then, so slowly at first as to be imperceptible, apocalypse struck. Earth's orbit shifted out of the elongated oval shape it had traveled during the ice age and into something closer to a circle, which brought the planet slightly nearer to the sun for more of the year. The planet's tilt changed, too, increasing the intensity of sunlight hitting the surface. Doggerland, like so many places around the world, began to thaw. Retreating glaciers left behind huge lakes, and rivers crisscrossed its expansive plains. Mammoths disappeared, and deer and aurochs arrived. Trees sprouted into temperate forests. Between about fifteen thousand and ten thousand years ago, a warming climate and sea level rise transformed Doggerland into one of the best places to live on the European continent.

But the sea didn't stop there. As the ice sheets melted and freed Doggerland and other places from their frigid grip, water rushed back into the sea. The ocean itself grew warmer, slowly dissolving ice sheets from underneath, a steady decay that led to sudden collapses. The sea sloshed into low-lying areas, including Doggerland. By nine thousand years ago, breached lakes and river valleys had transformed into salt marshes that flooded with every high tide. Patches of higher ground became islands as the land around them was submerged more and more quickly. By seven thousand years ago, the last vestiges of Doggerland disappeared beneath the waves. Worldwide, sea levels had risen over four hundred feet. We can call this apocalypse the Great Drowning.

Doggerland may have been erased from the maps scientists and cartographers drew of the world and from the narratives the people of northern Europe told about their history. But every so often, over the centuries and millennia that followed, pieces of the lost land would reappear, as if they were trying to show us how much we were missing, how much we had forgotten, how much we didn't understand about the past.

Most obviously, there were the drowned forests. Just as residents of Doggerland might have walked among the remains of trees that had been drowned by the rising sea, low tides along the east coast of England often expose eerie landscapes of petrified tree stumps and undulating roots that now sit well below the waterline. Long before scientists would be able to explain them, locals called them Noah's Woods. They were right about these drowned forests belonging to an antediluvian world, though Doggerland disappeared thousands of years before even the earliest versions of the biblical flood myth were written down. The people of England may not have remembered Doggerland, but some of them still walked among its ghosts.

Scientists had also been collecting evidence of Doggerland before they knew what their finds meant. In the middle of the nineteenth century, trawlers plying the waters around a shallow area of the North Sea—named the Dogger Bank after a type of medieval Dutch fishing boat, and the source of the name Doggerland—started to heave up bones, sometimes very big ones, as well as blocks of peat. Some of their unusual finds made it back to port and into the collections of researchers and eventually museums. Many of the bones belonged to species that had disappeared from Britain long ago, including wolves, wild horses, mammoths, and woolly rhinoceroses. The peat contained seeds from wildflowers that grew in freshwater ponds, bits of wood from birch trees, spores from ferns, and pollen from hearty flowering weeds. These ecological time capsules revealed that the Dogger Bank had once been dry land.

A particularly staggering discovery came in 1931, about seven thousand years after Doggerland drowned, when the trawler *Colinda* dropped its net into the murky water about twenty-five miles off the English coast. As the ship glided across the water's surface, the net churned up the ocean floor about one hundred feet below and trapped scores of fish between its mesh walls. It also shook loose a block of peat, which drifted into the net and was hauled onto the deck along with the rest of the catch. Sealed inside the peat was a point that had once been one prong of a fish spear, about eight and a half inches long and carved from the antler of a red deer. One end was particularly sharp, and delicate teeth were notched along one of its long edges. It was clearly a tool made by human hands; in fact, it was the first direct evidence that people had once roamed Doggerland's lakes, marshes, and river valleys. Archaeologists suspect the point had once been lashed to a wooden shaft and used for harpoon fishing. Five decades after it was first studied by scientists, radiocarbon dating of the antler would suggest it was carved over thirteen thousand years ago.

For nearly one hundred years after the *Colinda*'s discovery, these pieces of evidence "just stood there, effectively in the middle of the North Sea, screaming at people," says archaeologist Vince Gaffney. There was a lost land under the waves, and remnants of it were out there, waiting to be found. But archaeologically speaking, "there wasn't anything you could do," Gaffney says. Scientists could study only the pieces of Doggerland that happened to come to them, mostly by way of fishing nets. The faintest beginnings of underwater archaeology were still decades away, and most archaeologists, trained in a firmly terrestrial vision of history, believed that even if submerged landscapes could be found, they would reveal little more than ancient land bridges that had once connected currently habitable regions and allowed people to move between them.

Doggerland's time period was also treated as something of a bridge between more interesting eras, rather than an epoch that had been foundational to human history. The time during which it had been most welcoming to humans—and then, in relatively short order, disappeared—is known as the Mesolithic, or the "Middle Stone Age." This era came after the Paleolithic and its breathtaking cave paintings of animals in motion, and before the Neolithic, when people adopted farming and the texture of human life changed forever. Europe's climate and geography changed radically over the course of the Mesolithic, and life and land were inherently unstable. That instability led most archaeologists to treat it as a transitional time in human history, a stepping stone rather than a stopping place. "One occasionally gets the feeling when reading archaeological text books that the Mesolithic was merely something that had to be passed through, possibly until the world became one that the authors felt more familiar and comfortable with," Gaffney and two colleagues wrote.

By the late twentieth century, however, archaeologists increasingly suspected Doggerland was not a peripheral bridge for migrating hunter-gatherers but the cultural and geographic heartland of those nomadic people's world. Excavations of submerged sites under Denmark's shallow coastal waters had revealed huge numbers of Mesolithic artifacts, from flint axes and blades to wooden stakes arranged into fish traps to ancient dugout canoes and paddles, some decorated with geometric patterns. Ancient objects crafted from organic materials such as wood, bone, and antler would have long since decayed in terrestrial sites, but their swift inundation by the rising sea and the sediments it carried created ideal conditions for their preservation. The people of these submerged sites had hunted deer and gathered hazelnuts, but the large quantities of fish bones, fishing tools (including one hook carved from antler with a piece of line still attached), and of course boats spoke to their profound relationship with water, including the nearby rising sea.

Following these finds and their suggestion that what was submerged under the North Sea hadn't been a mere land bridge, the archaeologist Bryony Coles advocated for calling this new, still speculative country Doggerland. She, Gaffney, and others were increasingly sure not only that this lost country might harbor information about the last time people lived through a period of prolonged and extreme climate change, but that at least some evidence of their lives and environments still existed to be found.

Gaffney was no longer content to wait for evidence of Doggerland to come to him. He was determined to go after it himself. But how?

◉

When I first started going into the field with archaeologists, I was pretty sure the only thing they did was excavate. Ancient people's houses, belongings, hearths, and graves would be preserved and waiting underground, but, I thought, any trace of their presence would have clearly long since disappeared from the surface. But while excavation is the most famous part of an archaeologist's job, it's really an intermediate step in a long process of exploration, and nowhere close to the first. Archaeologists can do years of survey work on an ancient place before a shovel ever meets the earth. During that time, they roam all over the landscape, paying meticulous attention to everything from their GPS coordinates to their position relative to rivers and mountains to the ancient artifacts literally lying at their feet.

Survey can and does help archaeologists figure out where to excavate, eventually. But it's also an expansive study of an entire landscape in its own right, aimed at teasing out where, exactly, its previous inhabitants lived. During survey, archaeologists home in on, for example, natural features that would have attracted people for centuries or millennia, such as the bottom of a fertile river valley or a freshwater spring. They also pay particular attention to large-scale landscape alterations humans likely had something to do with, like an unusually large pile of mollusk shells, earthen mounds covering the remains of monumental buildings, or the remnants of long-unused irrigation canals. And then, in survey's most basic form, archaeologists walk, hunched over, staring at the ground with incredible concentration. They look for anything clearly made by humans, which for sites the age of Doggerland tend to be stone tools. Some of these tools have shapes too refined and deliberate to occur in nature, like the points of ancient spears. Others are more subtle, identifiable by surfaces covered in the telltale scars made when ancient artisans chipped off pieces. To an untrained eye, they look like any other stone, but archaeologists can see human ingenuity and craft in the patterns of their sharp angles and deliberate breaks.

It takes practice to learn to see like an archaeologist, but that concentrated gaze and the patterns it begins to pick out can reveal extraordinary amounts about ancient settlements and landscapes long before excavation begins. A cluster of tools in an otherwise barren landscape may point to the long-ago location of a campsite or even a village. Their styles can tell archaeologists something about the culture of the people who made them; a preponderance of spear or arrow points, for example, suggest a culture that prioritized hunting, while crescent moon–shaped scrapers or stone spindle whorls show how ancient people processed plant fibers and animal skins into textiles. In many places around the world, stone tools are eventually joined by ceramics, whose shapes and decorations tend to change over time and can thus provide a preliminary clue to when the people who made them lived. Survey allows archaeologists to begin to map an ancient landscape and make some educated guesses about the people who inhabited it, and when. Like any first draft, the result is meant to be revised and built upon by the years of excavation, dating, and laboratory work that are still to come. But without the starting point survey provides, none of that future work would be possible.

Doggerland wasn't entirely closed off to excavation—the finds in Denmark had confirmed that. But the vast majority of this lost land didn't lie near modern coastlines, and whatever was left of it was now covered not only by the North Sea but also by sediment. Layers of sand had settled atop the drowned country, and seven thousand years of ocean tides, currents, and storms had shaped those sediments into their own unique topography that didn't necessarily reflect the more ancient geography below.

With a literally invisible landscape, survey seemed impossible. But it was also particularly vital, as it presented the best chance to see Doggerland's environments through the eyes of the people who lived in them. Ancient Doggerlanders were hunter-fisher-gatherers, and as such they would have been drawn to places of natural abundance, whatever that meant to them. It could have been hills where they quarried stone for tools, or tidal zones where they collected shellfish, or forests where they could hunt deer and source trees to build bows, boats, and huts. It's possible that some or all of Doggerland's people would have moved seasonally or even more frequently, living a nomadic life in their world of plenty. It's also possible that some stayed rooted to their chosen places, building more permanent settlements and negotiating territorial boundaries with other groups. To have any chance of finding traces of either kind of community in the middle of the North Sea, archaeologists would have to understand Doggerland's landscape and its attractions in great detail, including how the environment had changed as the sea encroached. If they wanted to find the people of Doggerland—and Gaffney, for one, very much did—they would have to figure out not only how to survey their landscape but how to reconstruct it.

While mulling over this problem, Gaffney and his colleagues realized that archaeologists weren't the only ones interested in peering under the floor of the North Sea. Beneath whatever might remain of Doggerland lay extensive reservoirs of oil and natural gas, which the energy industry had been exploiting for decades. To know where to drill, energy companies needed maps not of the seabed but of the geology deep underneath it. Making these maps was expensive, but it wasn't impossible. In order to map the seabed, the energy companies would send out ships towing a device that emitted sound waves targeted at the seafloor, as well as receivers that measured how long it took those waves to bounce off sediments and echo back. High-frequency sound waves would bounce off the surface of the seabed or just underneath it, but low-frequency sound waves could travel deep into buried geology before reflecting back to the sensors. Using this data, scientists could create maps of the geological formations that lay beneath the seafloor.

It wasn't a sure thing that this technology would help Gaffney and his colleagues map Doggerland. Any oil and gas reservoirs would be deep underneath whatever might remain of a land that started to drown ten thousand years ago—a blink of an eye in geological time. It was possible that the energy industry's typical mapping technology, aimed at those deeper sediments, wouldn't pick up anything of Doggerland at all. But Gaffney and his colleagues decided it was worth a try. A geologist on his team approached a researcher at the company Petroleum Geo-Services to see if they would share some of the information they'd already collected from the area. The researcher had never heard of Doggerland and was somewhat baffled by the request—a drowned country? In *my* data?—but he agreed to give the archaeologists access to data that covered about twenty-three hundred square miles of the

North Sea, near the Dogger Bank, close to what once had been the northern edge of Doggerland.

Gaffney and his colleagues began the painstaking work of piecing together the seismic data and translating its chaotic collection of sound waves into comprehensible images and maps. They focused particularly on places where the buried landscape dipped, which was a relatively easy geological change to pick out. As they traced those dips, the researchers realized they fit together like puzzle pieces into an ancient river channel that meandered across their computer screens. This was no minor stream—the width and depth of the channel suggested that the river had been almost as large as the Rhine. The researchers could follow its course for twenty-five miles and pick out wisps of the tributaries that had once fed into it.

There it was: Doggerland, a real-life drowned country, in previously unimaginable detail. Gaffney and his colleagues were the first people to "see" this river in roughly ten thousand years. They couldn't know what it had been called by the people who had walked along its banks or fished in its waters. So they gave the river a new name: the Shotton, after a storied British geologist.

Petroleum Geo-Services would go on to donate thousands of square miles of data from the North Sea, an area larger than Wales. Not all of it yielded the kind of clear picture Gaffney's team was able to make of the Shotton, but overall the researchers were able to map nearly one thousand miles of rivers and identify twenty-four lakes and marshes, firming up the picture of Doggerland as a place where water was just as important as land, if not more important. Among the most significant features of Doggerland they identified was an enormous lake that sat just south of the Dogger Bank—or rather, the Dogger Hills, as what was now a shallow section of the seabed would have been the rare piece of high ground in flat and watery Doggerland. The lake extended over 650 square miles; today it exists as an undersea basin, well known to modern fishermen, where the seafloor suddenly drops to 260 feet below the surface of the water. As with the Shotton River, its old name has been lost to time, but today the lake is called the Outer Silver Pit. When

Doggerland existed, the lake's abundant and diverse natural resources would have made it a magnet for people, possibly even the center of their world.

The team could also begin to see how this piece of Doggerland changed as the sea drew higher and closer. Long before the land was fully inundated, the lake was invaded by sand banks, which form as ocean tides push sediments to and fro and whose rippling shapes were still preserved under the seafloor. Over time, salt water pushed out fresh water and the lake became a marsh, crisscrossed by streams whose channels now appeared as wispy dark lines on the computer screens of Gaffney and his colleagues. Their survey of under-sea Doggerland had not just documented a landscape, as archaeologists usually did. It had essentially re-created it.

Their maps of lake giving way to marsh, and then to sea, showed that a drowning Doggerland would have been a very different place to live, but not necessarily a worse one, especially for people who already organized their lives and livelihoods around water. Their homelands' gradual transformation from lake to marsh, from river lands to coast, from hills to islands, may not have seemed like a loss at all, or at least not only a loss. As it destroyed existing places, sea level rise created new ones.

As their homelands changed, Doggerland's people changed with it. Almost ten years after Gaffney's survey, Dutch scientists collected over fifty pieces of human bone retrieved from Doggerland sediments, dated them using radiocarbon, and measured their ratios of nitrogen and carbon isotopes, which would tell them about the chemistry of ancient people's diets. The results, published in 2016, showed that over time, Doggerlanders switched away from terrestrial sources of food and toward freshwater ones, reflected by an increase in their nitrogen values. As their environment transformed from forest to wetland, people figured out ways to reap its new bounty.

Like any survey, the work done by Gaffney and his colleagues to reconstruct Doggerland's landscapes was just the first step. In the decade and a half since, dozens of archaeologists have walked through the door it opened. They've set out for expeditions to the North Sea with their own seismic mapping equipment, more finely tuned to the uppermost layers of sediment they want to study. They've plunged vibrating tubes deep into the seafloor and pulled up long cores full of wood, flint, and other tiny traces of Doggerland's lost environments, to better understand the ecosystems where people lived. The expansion of offshore wind farms in the United Kingdom has led to extensive offshore mapping, generating data on submerged landscapes similar to that once donated by Petroleum Geo-Services, as well as archaeological salvage work that can identify and protect possible sites before they are destroyed. In 2019, archaeologists even dredged up a piece of worked flint, the first human artifact from offshore areas of Doggerland to be discovered on purpose. Closer to the coasts, researchers have identified and started to excavate a handful of submerged sites once occupied by humans. In the Netherlands, archaeologists are working with volunteer beachcombers to find artifacts in Doggerland sediments that have been dredged up and used to extend the coastline, now shrinking once again.

◉

After every winter storm in northern Israel, the archaeologist Ehud Galili races from his home to the Mediterranean beaches south of Haifa. He used to ride along the shore in a Jeep, until driving across the sand was prohibited. Now he walks, his eyes trained on the shallow water just beyond where the waves break. He's often the only person there, as the off-season chill and lack of car access keep less committed visitors away. That's fine with Galili. He doesn't need anyone disturbing what the storm may have churned up.

Under the water lie the remains of ancient villages, most abandoned during the Great Drowning between about nine thousand and seven thousand years ago. Usually, in addition to being underwater, they are covered by a layer of sand. This sand has protected the ruins over many millennia by preventing the displacement and erosion of their artifacts, houses, hearths, and graves, but it also makes them all but impossible to find. The region's ferocious winter storms, however, can kick up and clear away that sand—for a few days at a time. As soon as the wind, rain, and waves die down, Galili needs to be ready to look.

Unlike the archaeologists searching for Doggerland beneath the North Sea, Galili isn't trying to reconstruct an entire drowned country. He's trying to find individual villages that are relatively close to the present-day shoreline. So close, in fact, that sometimes when Galili walks along the shore he finds broken bits of ancient clay pots lying at his feet. Other times the sea delivers to him a piece of animal or human bone, battered by the sea and sand into a barely recognizable shape. If low tide and the effects of a storm line up just right, Galili will occasionally find himself walking among the remnants of stone structures like hearths and houses, waves lapping at his feet as he explores a long-lost place. If he can find these kinds of artifacts or even structures on the shore, he knows there must be more underwater.

Other times, however, no obvious evidence of the underwater world washes up. Then Galili must stand on the beach and gaze into the shallows, alert to any anomaly. The light Mediterranean sand throws the darker color of ancient soils and exposed stones into relief, making them stand out even underwater. The ruins of houses, wells, walls, and stone circles, when briefly relieved of their sand covering, also disrupt the waves' typical smooth, unperturbed path toward the beach. So, when Galili sees a dark smudge underwater or an odd pattern in the waves, he wades, snorkels, scuba dives, or takes a boat out to see what it might be. Sometimes it's a bushel of algae or kelp, agitated and brought to the sea's surface by the storm's waves. But sometimes, it's a village no one has seen for at least seven millennia. "It's like magic," Galili says.

This is how, in 2012, Galili found himself scuba diving among the remains of a drowned village now called Tel Hreiz. Unlike in Doggerland, where people likely made dwellings out of wood from the trees that surrounded them, these Mediterranean villagers had built most of their houses and other structures from stone, and their sturdy rectangular foundations still stand in their original locations. Employing underwater survey methods he'd been perfecting since the

1980s, Galili quickly drew, photographed, and mapped these easily identifiable structures. He also looked for features he'd seen in other submerged villages, such as ancient hearths, smatterings of stone tools or animal bones, fragments of mats or baskets woven out of reeds, and mounds of stones perhaps marking a grave or outlining the mouth of a well. In addition to undertaking a speedy survey, Galili's team sampled bits of wood and bone to send off for identification and radiocarbon dating. The dates showed that people lived in Tel Hreiz sometime between seventy-five hundred and seven thousand years ago, toward the end of the Great Drowning. Within that span, the village probably existed for two hundred or three hundred years.

In many ways, Tel Hreiz was a typical coastal village from its place and time period. Its people survived through a combination of fishing, farming, herding, and hunting. They built permanent houses where they could live year-round, rather than moving with the seasons as so many people around the world still did at the time. They planted crops such as wheat, barley, and lentils, tended to goats and cattle (perhaps with the help of dogs), fished by dropping nets into the sea, and hunted the occasional deer. They were among the first people in the world to press olive oil, as shown by hundreds of waterlogged olive pits preserved from decay by the sand and sea.

But Galili saw something in Tel Hreiz he hadn't seen in any other drowned village. Out past the village's houses and most of the rest of its remains, he spotted a straight line of boulders stretching more than three hundred feet. Each one weighed hundreds of pounds, much bigger than the stones used to build houses. They'd been arranged by people into a wall.

Using waterproof notebooks and underwater cameras, Galili and his team drew and photographed the stones in the partially exposed wall in just two days, doing the meticulous work of archaeological survey while in a race against the returning sand. It would be three years before the archaeologists saw the wall again, after a storm in 2015. Once again, they rushed into the sea to document it, confirming and expanding on their initial data. Using the information gathered during those two brief survey windows, Galili and his team mapped the wall in relation to the rest of Tel Hreiz. It had once stood on the ancient beach, between the village and the sea. Although the archaeologists couldn't tell exactly how tall it had been now that the boulders lay scattered on the seabed, the size of the stones hinted at its sturdiness and strength. The closest place one might find boulders of that size were riverbeds at least a mile away from the village. Everyone who lived there probably worked together to haul the boulders to the beach and stack them into position, one by one.

At the time the villagers of Tel Hreiz built the wall, the Mediterranean was creeping up the beach. Its approach wasn't always steady. Sometimes it would be a slow crawl; other times it would pause for long enough that the people might have wondered if it had stopped for good—until a violent winter storm sent huge waves crashing toward the beach and water surging toward Tel Hreiz once again. There, as in Doggerland, the apocalypse didn't take the form of one single catastrophe but rather an accumulation of smaller ones. Floods happened often, and perhaps the salt spray from the waves fell on fields and poisoned crops. All the while, the beach eroded under the constant pounding of the waves, bringing the sea ever closer and making the next storm even more dangerous.

In Tel Hreiz during the Great Drowning, the sea rose between four and seven millimeters each year. Over the course of a century—perhaps three or four generations—the water rose more than two feet, a rate on par with what's expected by 2100. The wall, like seawalls around the world today, would have impeded the flow of floods and high tides, shielding the village from the rising sea for as long as possible. The people of Tel Hreiz responded to apocalypse with ingenuity and cooperation, taking time away from their typical work to build a massive barrier to protect their collective home. Perhaps they were inspired by knowing they were the inheritors of a long line of communities that had faced the same apocalypse. As fishers, the villagers of Tel Hreiz and beyond would have been intimately familiar with the waters close to their shores. In those waters, after storms or at low tide, they also would have been able to see the shadowy outlines of stone houses, pick up the battered remnants of ancient tools and bones, and swim among the ruins of settlements long since drowned. They would have known their ancestors had lost their homes to the sea, too.

By venturing further into northern Israel's coastal waters, Galili could find the even older drowned villages the people of Tel Hreiz would have already known as ghosts—and see an even earlier chapter in the story of their adaptation to sea level rise. About three miles south of Tel Hreiz, people lived in the settlement now called Atlit-Yam between about ninety-three hundred and eighty-four hundred years ago, an earlier phase of the Great Drowning. Today it's more than six hundred and fifty feet from the coast and under more than twenty-five feet of water, but seven thousand years ago, its ruins were as close to the beach as Tel Hreiz's are now. Much changed in the time between the two villages' existences. In Atlit-Yam, pottery had not yet been invented, and people fished far more than they farmed. Tel Hreiz and others were their descendants, preserving some of the old fishing traditions while expanding their use of terrestrial plants and animals. They may have also inherited, directly or indirectly, the knowledge that they could protect their communities from sea level rise, at least for a time, through technological creativity and invention. While excavating Atlit-Yam's well, Galili found a layer of large stones about six and a half feet from the bottom of its shaft, evidence the villagers had tried to partially fill it in. At the time, salt water from the rising sea would have been seeping into the area's fresh groundwater. Raising the level of the well with stones would have helped the villagers draw from a higher, still uncontaminated part of the aquifer, thereby extending the life of the well and perhaps Atlit-Yam itself.

Perhaps people told stories of this innovation, in tones admiring or disbelieving or both. Over time, those stories may have been transmuted into fable or myth, an example of resourcefulness and survival that staved off apocalypse, or gave a community just a little more time when they needed it most. Maybe when it happened again, people remembered that story, or rumor, or myth, and knew they could do it again. They would have known their inventions couldn't save their homes forever. Every village, like every person, would one day pass into the afterlife. But that was no reason to give up on their home while they could still protect it, no reason not to help it exist as long as possible. The well, and the wall, carried into the future the memory of one possible response to apocalypse, ancient whispers of imagination, perseverance, and rescued time.

◉

Ngurunderi's wives had run away. He could hear and see them in the distance, so he chased after them. But every time he arrived at the place where he had spotted them, they were already gone. Ngurunderi followed his wives down the river and all along the coast, to the point where a thin strip of land stretched across a strait to another shore in the distance. Ngurunderi was right behind, however, and determined to punish them. He reached the edge of the strait when his wives were halfway across.

Ngurunderi roared in a voice of thunder, *"Prenkulun prakuldun!"—water rise, water fall.* A mighty swell rushed into the strait. It swept his wives off their feet and out to sea, where they drowned and turned to stone. There they became small islands, trapped forever in the middle of their journey. The terrible flood never receded, and the shallow strait grew deep. Ngurunderi swam to the land where his wives were once headed, now an island cut off from the mainland by the water he had summoned. He listened to the wind blowing through a large tree. It sounded like crying, and it reminded him of his wives.

Ngurunderi knew it was time for him to leave this world. He traveled to the western end of the island, threw his spears in the sea, and dove in after them. From the ocean, he ascended to the sky and became the brightest star in the Milky Way. For the people of the nearby mainland, the island became known as the land of the dead. The souls of the departed followed Ngurunderi's journey, traveling to the island on their way to the sky.

In addition to being a myth about the afterlife, this legend of Ngurunderi and the creation of Kangaroo Island, told by the Ngarrindjeri Nation and other Aboriginal peoples of southern Australia, may also be an oral history of the Great Drowning. Called Karta Pintingga by Aboriginal groups, Kangaroo Island lies about eleven miles off the coast of southern Australia, across a narrow ocean strait formed when the sea level rose. Dozens of similar tales—of floods, of death, of places old and new—were and are told by Indigenous communities all around the Australian coast.

Many cultures around the world have myths about floods and drowned places, and it's tempting to connect them to an ancestral memory of the Great Drowning. But in most places, the link between specific stories and sea level rise nine thousand to seven thousand years ago is symbolic, if that. The flood myth most familiar to Westerners stretches back to only around 2,000 BC—about three thousand years after Tel Hreiz drowned and the last remnants of Doggerland disappeared—when the story of a man tasked by a deity with building a boat to save Earth's living beings from a supernatural flood first appeared in poems that would go on to form the Epic of Gilgamesh. That tale would influence many more, among them the story of Noah and his ark. If we could hear all of the even more ancient tales, told around fires or performed during rituals, that eventually gave rise to the written versions we know today, we might indeed discover that they are echoes of the destruction and renewal of the Great Drowning. But with the information we have, all we can say is that the flood stories in Gilgamesh and the Bible aren't connected to the formation of a specific landscape, like the myth about Kangaroo Island clearly is. What's more, the Western stories end with the water retreating. After the Great Drowning, it never did.

In Aboriginal Australian stories, the flood doesn't end. The sea rushes in and never recedes. The landscapes people knew don't return. Nothing goes back to the way it was. The land and the people who belong to it are forever changed, reshaped and remade by an apocalypse. If these stories do indeed document the Great Drowning, it means the memory of these past landscapes and the apocalypse that destroyed them has been passed down for at least seven thousand years, when the sea level around Australia stopped rising. That would make them some of the oldest cultural memories in the world.

Some of these Aboriginal stories may preserve just how difficult and uncertain survival may have been during the Great Drowning. In the stories of the Narungga people, the drowning of the marshy land that would become the gulf just north of Kangaroo Island is foreseen in the nightmares of an emu and a willie wagtail, a common species of songbird. The willie wagtail dreams of being trapped on an island while waves crash all around him; the emu dreams of familiar lagoons becoming "a dry, dusty, and parched country. Desolation was everywhere. Animals, birds, and reptiles were lying dead all round." That same day, their kangaroo companion unwittingly opens the land and invites in the sea by dragging the bone of a magic being across the ground.

Other stories speak more directly of a relentless sea and the people who feared its approach would never stop. The Yidinjdji people of northeastern Australia remember when land stretched twenty-five miles or so beyond today's coast and what is now the Great Barrier Reef—one of the richest marine ecosystems in the world—was dry scrubland. Their stories tell of a man who led some of his people up a mountain to escape a flood. There they built a fire and heated boulders, which they rolled into the sea to stop the water's rise. They managed to halt its advance, but the sea never retreated back to where it had been. Meanwhile, in southern Australia, the Andingari, Wirangu, and Wati Nyiinyii peoples all tell of how their ancestors feared the sea would spread over everything they knew. In response, they built barriers—of tree roots in some stories, of spears in others—that stopped the flood from coming any closer. Like the wall builders of Tel Hreiz, it seems the ancestors of these Aboriginal communities went to great lengths to stay in the places they knew and loved.

And stay they did, even when their land and lives changed. On the islands of Murujuga, or the Dampier Archipelago, off the coast of arid western Australia, archaeologists have documented thousands of pieces of ancient rock art. Before about eighteen thousand years ago, all the engraved figures represented humans and terrestrial animals such as kangaroos. Then the sea began to rise, slowly turning the landscape into a series of islands. Murujuga's artists began engraving figures of turtles, fish, sea birds, and sea mammals. When the sea came to them, these formerly desert people adapted to island life. There was still plenty of land for everybody, if they just changed the way they were living on it.

Memories of ancestral homelands were passed down through countless generations in myths, legends, ecological knowledge, and even languages. The Yidinjdji people, who tell of how their ancestors stopped the sea with hot stones, preserve a kind of map of their drowned country in their language. In the Yidin language, "daruway" means both "small hill" and "island," capturing how the landscape transformed as the sea crept in. Fitzroy Island, now about three miles offshore of Australia's northeast coast, is named "gabar," or lower arm—"a reference to the time when it was a mainland promontory enclosing a river valley." The Yidinjdji people even still know the name of a long-drowned island off their coast: Mudaga, named for the type of tree that once grew there. Around the North Sea, scientists must rediscover submerged and forgotten landforms like the Dogger Hills (turned Dogger Island, turned Dogger Bank) and the Shotton River. In Australia, similar places are vividly remembered by Aboriginal groups who have relied on and cared for what they call Sea Country since time immemorial.

Even though myths and memories directly linked to the Great Drowning don't survive to the present in Israel or the countries around Doggerland, they could have been just as central to ancient people's lives, identities, and spiritual practices as Sea Country is for Aboriginal groups today. At Mesolithic sites in the Netherlands, Denmark, and Norway, archaeologists have found offerings of stone tools and sometimes animal bone buried along the ancient shorelines, now underwater. People in Europe and beyond also buried at least some of their dead along the coast, their graves intentionally placed in what may seem to be precarious proximity to the rising sea.

For example, at one of the first submerged sites excavated in Denmark in the 1990s, archaeologists discovered a nearly seven-thousand-year-old boat burial. The body of a man, about twenty-five years old, had been placed in a partially burned dugout canoe and wrapped in sheets of bark. A paddle, a bow, and pieces of antler were placed around him. The boat had been staked into mud close to the coast, holding it in place but also ensuring it eventually would be inundated and buried underneath the new seafloor. Large boulders seem to have been positioned in a line connecting the shoreline to the burial, perhaps creating a path so people could visit the site even after it was submerged. Two thousand miles to the southeast off the coast of Israel, in a village that was a neighbor of Tel Hreiz, now called Neve-Yam, Galili and his colleagues found the region's first separate cemetery, right next to the contemporary village along the shore. They also discovered the bones of a one- or two-year-old child interred on what is now a small island and was then a hill that stood in between the village and the sea, in a similar position to Tel Hreiz's wall.

Perhaps the shallow waters offshore, dotted with visible ruins in Israel or ghostly drowned forests in Doggerland, represented the land of the dead, foreboding and taboo. Burying offerings and interring loved ones—or perhaps making sacrifices—along the inundating shore may have been a desperate spiritual response to sea level rise, "a cry to the gods to make it stop," writes the archaeologist Jim Leary. Or perhaps people saw these vanished and vanishing places as their ancestral homelands, dearly missed but still remembered. The offerings could have been made, instead, to the ancestors who had lived there, and coastal or island burials could have been ways of returning home to join them.

These memories and traditions may have endured for thousands of years. Among the many artifacts that have been dredged from the North Sea are several stone axes of a style not invented until a few millennia after Doggerland had drowned. Farming had arrived in Britain by then, and Doggerland's hunter-fisher-gatherer lifestyle had long since disappeared from the region, as had the land where it had been practiced so successfully. The usual explanation is that the axes were cargo on boats that sank during a trading voyage six thousand years ago or so. But some archaeologists, including Leary and Gaffney, think they might have been offerings made in the same tradition as the Mesolithic tools buried along the shore.

The axes were dredged from highland places, including the Dogger Bank, that could have survived as islands as the rest of Doggerland disappeared around them, gaining new meaning as landmarks and refuges. They would have been the last pieces of Doggerland to vanish, and so possibly the last to be forgotten. Perhaps the descendants of Doggerland's water people rowed their boats out to these remembered places and made the same kind of offerings their ancestors had, dropping some of their most precious objects down to the watery world they could no longer access but had not yet lost.

Chapter 3

HOW APOCALYPSE BROUGHT PEOPLE TOGETHER

The north coast of Peru, stretching six hundred miles from the capital of Lima up to the border with Ecuador, is one of the driest deserts on the planet. Fewer than twenty miles wide in some areas, it's wedged between the chilly waters of the Pacific Ocean to the west and the craggy peaks of the Andes Mountains to the east, which block humid air rising from the Amazon rainforest from drifting over the coast. The cool sea that hems in the desert on one side is teeming with life, especially small fish like anchovy and sardine. But fresh water is scarce. Life on land revolves around its only reliable source: the rivers flowing down from the Andes, fed by mountaintop glaciers and highland rains. Often, they are little more than trickling streams. Still, the ecosystem is primed to take advantage of them, and their valleys are shocking explosions of green against the tan, dusty desert that surrounds them.

For thousands of years, the north coast's economy has been centered on two main activities: farming and fishing. Both are astoundingly productive, especially in an environment that seems, at first glance, to be marginal and unforgiving. Irrigation canals, a technology in use there for thousands of years, draw water from the rivers to the fields. Today, they nourish large farms of sugarcane, rice, and other tremendously thirsty crops, thriving incongruously amid the desert. At sea, enormous fishing operations pull anchovy, sardine, squid, and mahi mahi from the Pacific by the ton. The

Key river valleys on the north coast of Peru

steady upwelling of cold, nutrient-rich seawater supports mind-bogglingly huge schools of fish, easy to catch and ship around the world.

Most of the time, this delicately balanced system works. But every three to seven years, the north coast's environment—and all the lives that depend on it—literally turn upside down. It usually starts just after Christmas, when a current of warm water suddenly appears in the normally chilly Pacific. Local fishermen on Peru's north coast, beginning by the late nineteenth century, called this current El Niño, after the Christ child whose birth they celebrated at the same time. With the arrival of the warm current, fish adapted to the Peruvian coast's cold water must migrate or die. Masses of dead fish rot on the beaches, and the normally plentiful catch plummets. The warmer sea sends more water evaporating into the atmosphere, and clouds bulge with moisture over land that typically receives barely more than an inch of rain per year. The downpours are torrential. Rivers overflow their banks, destroying the canals and fields they usually nourish. Normally dry ravines funnel flash floods directly into the valleys where most people live. The floods sweep away farms, canals, crops, houses, livestock, and people, sometimes in a matter of hours. The streets of cities become raging rivers. The floodwaters carry tremendous loads of earth along with them, blanketing homes and fields under thick layers of mud and silt that remain even after the rains stop and the floods recede. Pools of standing water where there is normally none become breeding grounds for mosquitoes, leading to outbreaks of diseases such as malaria and dengue fever.

Scientists now know an El Niño event, which lasts between twelve and eighteen months, affects weather around the world, from unusually strong winter rains in California to drought in southern Africa. Nowhere, however, is hit harder than the north coast of Peru. In 2017, even a short, unusually localized El Niño killed 158 people in Peru, displaced more than a million others, and resulted in over three billion dollars' worth of damage. More than 1 percent of the country's GDP was lost in only two months.

Scientists now understand that El Niño happens because of complex interactions between the atmosphere and the ocean's surface. But they still aren't sure why it happens in some years and not others, or exactly how strong it will be once it arrives. All anyone can be sure of is that someday, not too far in the future, it will happen again.

For ancient societies, such a regular, destabilizing catastrophe, in which an arid landscape suddenly receives enough rain to transform it into a malevolent mirror image of itself for over a year at a time, would almost certainly have been an apocalypse. People could recover from any single El Niño, eventually. But knowing that its destruction would inevitably return, literally and figuratively washing away years of restoration and progress, with no pattern and almost no warning—that would have thrown life and society's precariousness into sharp, unavoidable relief.

Many of us instinctually believe that communities fracture after such catastrophes. And so we might expect that the level of climate instability and periodic but inevitable destruction suffered by the ancient people of the north coast would have discouraged them from building anything that could be destroyed, up to and including civilization itself. But archaeology has revealed that living in the shadow of recurring apocalypse didn't drive the people of the north coast apart. Instead, it may have been the force that brought them together.

◉

In 1980, a young American graduate student named Dan Sandweiss found himself in the Santa Valley of Peru, poking around some six-thousand-year-old garbage. The people who left it behind had lived without pottery, political leadership, or intensive agriculture. They didn't need any of those things to live comfortably, because they had the sea. Like the people of Doggerland, they were hunter-fisher-gatherers, but the bulk of all of those activities was the ocean and its bounty. When they hunted, they hunted sea lions and other aquatic mammals. When they gathered, they gathered shellfish. The only plants they cultivated with any serious commitment were cotton and bottle gourds, which they used to weave nets and create floats. Mostly, these people fished.

By the time Sandweiss arrived in the Santa Valley, one of those thin strips of green in the midst of an unforgiving desert, he already had an encyclopedic knowledge of the shellfish these ancient people ate. Shellfish come in their own virtually indestructible containers, which the ancient residents of the north coast threw out in huge piles. Unlike delicate fish bones or organic cotton nets, shells don't easily decay, disintegrate, or otherwise disappear back into the landscape from which their raw materials once came. They stay where they are put, which makes them "treasure troves of information" for archaeologists.

Sandweiss had come to the Santa Valley to check out a collection of sites containing ancient shell middens, the repository of the remains of generations of meals and, as such, a tremendous source of information about ancient people's diets, the location of their settlements, and the ecosystems they relied on. Even though he was just beginning his scientific career, Sandweiss had already examined countless shells from sites like these, both on the ground and in collections held in laboratories and museums. In the Santa Valley, he adopted the hunched posture familiar to any archaeologist doing survey, his eyes trained on the evidence of past lives still scattered across the ground. He expected to see the same species he'd been examining for two years already. But instead, he saw the oblong shells of oysters.

"I had never seen oysters in Peru," Sandweiss says. His eyes snagged on other anomalies as well, species of clams and scallops he'd never seen before. "I thought I knew all the shells," but ones he was familiar with were nowhere to be seen at this site. Intrigued and more than a little confused, he picked up some of the strange shells lying on the surface and tucked them into his backpack. The next time he was in Lima, he took his impromptu collection to a shell expert at Peru's Institute of the Sea. Maybe a more experienced researcher would be able to explain what he was looking at. The shell expert asked him to give her two weeks to take a look at what he'd found.

When Sandweiss returned for the results, the shell expert had compiled a list of species in Sandweiss's collection and compared it to collections of species that lived in various nearby ecosystems. "So, what were you doing in Ecuador?" she asked Sandweiss as she handed him the results. Ecuador, just north of Peru but out of the range of the current that keeps Peru's coastal waters cold, was the closest place with the warm, tropical waters that could have produced Sandweiss's collection of shellfish.

"I wasn't in Ecuador," Sandweiss said. The Santa Valley was about three hundred miles south of the Ecuadorian border.

"You had to be in Ecuador!" the shell expert said. "These don't live in Peru." It was like finding massive amounts of shellfish from tropical Puerto Rico on the beaches of New Jersey.

"*What?*" Sandweiss remembers thinking to himself. Looking back, he says, "That was the beginning. The clue that something was really different."

◉

The field of archaeology is predicated on the truth that societies and cultures are always changing. Sometimes the changes are small, like when a new style of tool or decoration is invented, and sometimes they are monumental, like the development of a new religion or the creation of an empire. Archaeologists are trained to spot how these changes are reflected in the objects people used, the food they ate, and the way they organized their homes, towns, and cities. A new religion, for example, could lead not just to new temples reshaping a cityscape, decorated with pictures of new gods, but also to the adoption of new dietary laws—and the sudden disappearance of the remains of that newly forbidden food in the middens of the most humble commoner houses. But archaeologists also need to be attuned to the possibility of another kind of change, one over which ancient people had little control. Archaeologists need to be on the lookout for environmental change. Anywhere they work, archaeologists must not assume that the local ecosystem and climate were the same in the past as they are today.

Over the past five decades or so, as contemporary climate change has made understanding previous climate regimes more urgent, scientists have identified a wide range of natural materials that preserve records of past environments from which we can glean insight for our own future. They drill ice from mountain glaciers and polar ice sheets and pull tubes of sediment from the floors of the world's oceans and lakes. They chip stalagmites and stalactites out of caves and slice them into pieces. They even bore tiny samples from the inside of corals to reconstruct how the temperature and chemistry of the water around them has changed over time. All these materials formed in layers, like tree rings, and each layer preserves organic or chemical signatures that reflect the environment in which they formed. By counting back through the layers, scientists can reconstruct snapshots of past environments and trace how they changed, sometimes stretching back hundreds of thousands of years.

These natural climate archives have been a tremendous boon to archaeologists who previously might have struggled to understand how past environments differed from those of today, but they have limitations for studying human societies and cultures. The climate information these archives capture tends to cover a very broad region, up to an entire hemisphere, over time spans of decades or centuries. Those averages, while vital for reconstructing global climate trends over eons, don't necessarily reflect the kinds of shorter-term, more localized climate and weather patterns that actually affect human lives and society-level changes in the time frame in which they occur.

Sandweiss's shellfish from the Santa Valley, on the other hand, were both a climate and a cultural record. By showing us that people who lived there six thousand years ago ate oysters—now nowhere to be found in Peru—the shells offered a tantalizing, if confusing, clue about the marine ecosystems from which they were plucked. By combining local information like shellfish species with regional data like oxygen isotopes from ice cores, archaeologists can both build a more complete picture of ancient environments and understand how particular people and societies experienced them.

Today lots of archaeologists mine their data for similar information about ancient climates and their fluctuations—including the environmental challenges that contributed to the apocalypses we'll explore in Part 2. But it wasn't as common back when Sandweiss found his unusual shellfish. Still, his discovery was so intriguing that a small crew of more experienced archaeologists and geologists asked to see the sites in the Santa Valley. There the crew collected more shells from the surface, and they also dug a small test pit, a first foray into what further trash-turned-treasure lay buried underground. Digging allowed them to find bits of ancient charcoal amid the shells they could radiocarbon date, with the goal of eventually creating a firmer timeline of what species were found where and when. For the moment, however, all the scientists could be sure of was that the warm-water shells were there, only a few miles from a cool sea teeming with an entirely different set of species.

Like many days of archaeological fieldwork, this one ended over beers. To process what they'd seen, the team gathered at a hotel bar in Chimbote, the closest city and, in those days, a major producer of fish meal. It's a particularly stinky product to make, and the noxious smell of burnt rotten fish permeated everything. But the bar was welcoming, the ocean view was spectacular, the drinks were cold, and, most important for buoying the scientists' good moods, they had a mystery on their hands.

They spent the evening debating possibilities. The only time in contemporary memory or circumstances when such shellfish species had even an outside shot at survival in the Peruvian sea would have been during an El Niño, when the sea in front of them could grow over fifteen degrees Fahrenheit warmer than normal. But El Niños were, by definition, occasional events. They might leave a few stray tropical shells behind among the typical collection of cold-water species. But at the Santa Valley sites, there were nothing but warm-water species, in places where people had presumably collected shellfish for centuries. El Niño could have transformed the environment for a short time, but not the entire life of this settlement.

Cautiously, the scientists began circling around the only explanation that made sense. Maybe, they posed, the Pacific Ocean and its currents were once "radically different." Maybe Peru's coastal waters had once always been warm. And maybe, without a cold current to drive away, El Niño hadn't existed at the time.

Those six-thousand-year-old oyster shells were the first evidence that El Niño hadn't always loomed over the people of the north coast. The people of the Santa Valley lived their lives and developed their culture free of its threat. Their descendants, however, wouldn't have simply lived with apocalypse—they would have seen its birth. Transforming from a warm sea to a cool one, a world of oysters to a world of anchovies, was an environmental change extreme enough to remake people's diets and perhaps their technologies, if they changed how they fished to take advantage of the new cold-water species. But going from trusting in a stable environment to fearing an unpredictable, dangerous one would have been an even more profound transformation, and it could have rippled through and reshaped north coast societies in ways Sandweiss could only begin to imagine that day in Chimbote.

And so, after his chance discovery as a graduate student, Sandweiss would go on to devote his career to unraveling the mystery of El Niño's past, in hopes of better understanding its effects on the ancient cultures of the north coast. By weaving together local archives like fish and shellfish remains from sites up and down the north coast with regional climatic records like ice cores, he's built a picture of when El Niño came and went. Between eleven thousand and nine thousand years ago, he's found, El Niño probably happened, but exactly how often is still fuzzy. Then, around nine thousand years ago, El Niño disappeared, granting the oyster gatherers of the Santa Valley, as well as many generations of their ancestors, three millennia of environmental tranquility. That peace was shattered fifty-eight hundred years ago, when the cold current reappeared and El Niño was reborn. Apocalypse loomed over the north coast. And not long after, civilization as we know it began.

◉

What would it have been like for these coastal fishers and shellfish gatherers to experience the return of El Niño after three thousand years? It's possible they had legends about times when the environment their ancestors knew so well betrayed them, and it's possible those legends contained hints of what to do when the ocean temperature flipped and rain started to fall: Leave the river valley, get to high ground, stay away longer than you think you need to, don't tempt the floodwaters that can gather again in seconds. It's also possible, so long after a perennially returning El Niño had faded away, that its threat had been forgotten. The people might have struggled to believe the sea and their valleys could ever turn on them, even after it had already started happening.

During this initial phase of El Niño's rebirth, it seems to have happened once or twice per century, rather than once or twice a decade as it does now. Perhaps not every generation saw one, but it happened regularly enough, was certainly shocking enough, for the experience to be remembered and passed on, vivid in the culture's collective memory. Apocalypse wouldn't have been something in the distant past, processed through myths, if at all. It would have become something the people of the north coast knew they had to be ready for, that could and would come again with little warning. That dread, worry, and foreboding expectation of loss may have felt like its own kind of apocalypse, especially when the experience of El Niño was still new.

We might expect communities and cultures to disintegrate under the pressures of catastrophe. And perhaps they did, in a way. Survivors who staggered away from a river valley churned up by floods and blanketed by mudslides might have lost family and friends, homes and belongings, a sense of safety and security. Maybe they moved on by never looking back, or perhaps they pined for what they once had. They wouldn't have had our names for post-traumatic stress, climate anxiety, and ecological grief, but they may have had their own words, and their own ways of understanding and managing similar feelings.

It's easy to imagine displacement after disaster as a lonely, isolating experience, and it's easier still to imagine the emotional and societal damage inflicted by the same disaster unpredictably but inevitably striking generation after generation. But our instincts about such experiences, while deeply rooted, rarely reflect how people and communities actually respond to disaster. Our modern-day disaster myths flatten a complex event into only its worst moments, feelings, and reactions and insist that's all we can expect.

In reality, "disasters are extraordinarily generative," writes Rebecca Solnit in *A Paradise Built in Hell,* which documents the communities of care and solidarity that consistently arise in the wake of such events, from improvised street kitchens after the 1906 San Francisco earthquake to community bomb shelters in the London underground during the Blitz to self-organizing volunteer rescue operations in Lower Manhattan after 9/11. Again and again, ordinary people spring into action during and after disaster, dissolving old boundaries between individuals and creating new communities based on our unwavering, but often suppressed, need to give and receive help, and to come together to heal. "Suffering and loss are transformed when they are shared experiences," writes Solnit. Disasters give us "a glimpse of who else we ourselves may be and what else our society could become."

Although Solnit is writing about modern-day disasters and their power to loosen "the shackles of conventional belief and role" in societies that are much larger and less adaptable than those of foragers in the distant past, ethnographic and archaeological evidence suggests ancient hunter-gatherers would have reacted to disaster with just as much compassion, generosity, and flexibility, if not more. Research on more recent hunting and gathering societies, from pre-Columbian Cuba to the Kuril Islands strung between northern Japan and Russia's Kamchatka Peninsula, show that their principal strategy for surviving disasters such as hurricanes or volcanic eruptions was to depend on their neighbors and friends. Sometimes that took the form of moving in with a less affected group for decades or up to a century. Other times, people could stay in their homes thanks to long-standing trade networks and relationships providing a more-than-usual amount food and other resources during recovery. Long-distance social connections and a willingness to absorb new members may have even saved *Homo sapiens* during the period of climate instability that tipped Neanderthals over the edge into extinction, as we saw in Chapter 1. As far back as we can see, humans have survived apocalypse through cooperation and generosity.

On the north coast, El Niño's environmental impact extends well beyond its initial phase of sudden destruction. As the rains stop and the floods recede, the sudden influx of moisture into a desert incapable of absorbing it leaves behind temporary wetlands in the river valleys and along the coast. These are the places the north coast's foragers would have gathered after the threat had passed. They would have been looking to take advantage of the sudden abundance of fresh water, but also, assuredly, to share their experiences of the floods that had transformed their valleys and their lives. After a disaster, "every stranger can be spoken to and all share the experience," Solnit writes, which explains in part why "crises and stresses often strengthen social bonds rather than breed competition and isolation."

After an El Niño on the ancient north coast, everyone in the affected valleys would have lost something, and possibly many someones. Talking through that experience, or processing it through communal rituals, likely would have helped them heal and reorganize. Drawn together in unfamiliar, suddenly fertile landscapes created by the disaster itself, everyone would have been rethinking the traditions and taboos they previously thought immutable, like animosities or territorial boundaries between groups. Perhaps some bands had been hit harder than others, and other, more fortunate ones shared their resources or even took the less fortunate in as they recovered. Maybe when the next El Niño struck, the groups' fortunes would be reversed, and any debt, if they saw it as such, could be repaid.

◉

It had happened again. Ever since the sea had mysteriously turned cold, the people of the north coast of Peru had been enjoying a surprising abundance of fish and mollusks, different from the ones they ate before but even more plentiful. But once every few generations, the cold water disappeared, as if the sea had changed its mind. The following months would be catastrophic as everything in the environment also reversed its normal course. Rather than the gentle fog they usually enjoyed, menacing clouds swelled with rain. Just as one storm ended, another would start, overwhelming the dry earth of the desert. The tranquil streams where the people collected fresh water transformed into terrifying, fast-moving rivers barreling over anything that stood in their way, including their camps, tools, and stores of food and supplies. The massive schools of fish that would have nourished them for months, years, instead washed up on the beaches en masse, dead and rotting. Afterward, the landscapes they knew so well were blanketed in mud, the places they once knew erased so completely it was as if they had never existed.

During the first cataclysm, the people had no idea if it would ever end, if their home would return to being a place they recognized. Now, they knew each cataclysm would eventually subside, but they were also learning their havoc could last for a year and sometimes even longer. They were learning that another cataclysm would always come. Sometimes the next one arrived sooner than they expected, striking the same generations twice. Sometimes the time between them extended for so long that the people wondered if whatever caused the cataclysms had finally decided to leave their land in peace. Eventually, however, their anxious hope was betrayed again.

The people were also learning what to do during the cataclysms, as well as after. They had started to gather supplies and leave their homes immediately after their fishers noticed the return of warm water. It might be weeks, even months, before a flood came for their particular valley, but they were learning it was better not to wait and see. The people had always moved around the land and sea, following food and taking care never to exhaust the resources of a particular place. Now they were learning how different it felt to run from something.

They would stay on high ground for as long as they could. Sometimes they would meet other groups there, people who had escaped from a different valley. Sometimes their personalities and practices clashed, and they couldn't figure out how to work together. Most times, however, they were grateful to be able to combine their resources and knowledge to brave the hard months ahead. When a cataclysm ended, sometimes these new communities decided to stay together rather than returning to their separate homes, especially if each had lost people or formed new bonds across groups. They were like two damaged schools of fish weaving themselves together into a larger, stronger one after an attack by a predator.

When it was finally safe to go home and the people saw what was left, they wept for the places they had known. The environments left behind after a cataclysm were nothing like what they were used to. They were muddy and buggy and wet. They had scars where floods had burst free of riverbanks, where earth and rocks from the mountains had been stranded by the rushing water. But suddenly, for months after a cataclysm, the people didn't have to work so hard to haul fresh water from the rivers back to camp. Suddenly, there was fresh water everywhere. They could camp in new places, and gather new plants, and savor, just for a bit, the warm-water oysters and scallops that had sustained their ancestors but they only rarely got to taste.

In the blessedly tranquil years after a cataclysm receded, some valleys eventually went back to the way they were. Others, the people noticed, were changing. For as long as they could remember, there was one place on a valley floor where no one had been able to live. Even though the ocean curved inland into a bay, the river itself was a long walk away, too far to bring back enough fresh water to support more than the occasional overnight camp, if that. Like everywhere, the cataclysm sent floods hurtling through this place and left unfathomable amounts of mud in their wake. As the cataclysm happened again and again and again, water and mud built up along the flat shore of the bay; no one cared about this place enough to try to clean it up. After many generations and not quite as many cataclysms, the place became home to wetlands and lagoons that teemed with birds and fish, and that seemed to slow down and absorb the force of the cataclysms in a way the desert couldn't.

And so, when a cataclysm calmed down enough for them to come down from high ground but not enough to be safe at home, the people gathered in these new wetlands. There they met those they had sheltered with in the past and others they didn't yet know. Each group had traditions and protocols for greeting strangers, but after a cataclysm, those rules dissolved along with so much else. After a cataclysm, no one was a stranger. Those who had escaped with more shared with those who were forced to run without warning. Groups who ventured home to find their valleys miraculously untouched brought back supplies for the rest, and they eventually welcomed those who would realize they no longer had homes to return to.

Between cataclysms, when their increasingly large and intermingled groups needed to come together for ceremonies or negotiations or feasts, the people began coming together in the new wetlands, the place where the world was born anew. Its bay and lagoons and heaps of mud and clay became landmarks as important as the mountains that rose in the east and the mounds of unfamiliar shells their ancestors had left along the shore. And so, the people decided to build a special space befitting this place, using what the cataclysm had provided: slick, slippery clay. They cut blocks of it directly from the thick banks left behind by one cataclysm after another and laid them out to dry in the sea air. When they had enough, they turned to a woman who had lost her whole family in the last cataclysm—from her grandparents to her young children—and they asked her where they should place the first brick.

Every July, Ana Cecilia Mauricio Llonto leaves her comfortable life as a professor in Lima and sets off to spend a month in a particularly inhospitable part of the north coast. The place is tucked into the Chao Valley, only thirty miles north of the green strip of the Santa Valley, but its landscape is practically lunar in comparison. It's a desert within a desert, more than four miles from the nearest river and two and a half miles from the sea. The pale sand of salt flats stretches out in every direction. No one lives here, and aside from Mauricio Llonto and her team, hardly anyone visits. There are no farms, no houses, no towns. "It's like it was frozen in time," she says.

Interrupting this desert plain is a fifty-foot-high mound of sand and rocks known as Los Morteros. For centuries, perhaps millennia, people thought it was a natural hill, possibly an ancient sand dune that ossified when wind patterns shifted. That changed in 2006, when a team led by Sandweiss used radar to peer inside the mound. The beams bounced back in patterns that revealed ancient walls and floors, outlining long-buried rooms and staircases. On its surface archaeologists found stone tools (including mortars, *morteros* in Spanish, giving the site its name), animal bones, and shell middens. Radiocarbon dating put these objects, buried close to the mound's surface, at about five thousand years old. The structure underneath had to be even older, making it one of the most ancient monuments in Peru.

Mauricio Llonto was particularly keen to study this formative period in her country's past, when hunter-fisher-gatherers first began to work together to build such structures. In order to build a place like Los Morteros, especially for the first time, a society had to develop ways to organize massive amounts of labor, promote cooperation among smaller social groups with differing interests, and distribute food and other resources to people working on the project. Many of the world's most famous ancient monuments were built within the strictures of large, complex, settled societies whose agricultural economies and social hierarchies made organizing the logistics of such projects, if not easy, then at least relatively straightforward, politically and ideologically. The pyramids of Giza, nearly one thousand years younger than Los Morteros, served as tombs for divine kings who sat at the head of sprawling royal bureaucracies. Those in the heart of Maya capitals like Tikal, almost four thousand years younger than Los Morteros, were royal palaces and temples anchoring green cities dotted with commoners' small-scale farms. The people who built Los Morteros, on the other hand, still lived in small, egalitarian groups spread out across the landscape. The mound wasn't the center of a city or a town, concepts that were still thousands of years away. There was no king to glorify and no ruling class to command and organize labor. There were no stores of grain to feed the people busy constructing it. So why did they do it? And why here?

The return of El Niño may hold some clues. Before the rebirth of this apocalypse around fifty-eight hundred years ago, the landscape of Los Morteros would have been nearly as uninviting as it is today.

Its only possible attraction would have been that the ocean was once much closer; in a curve of sloped earth that now cuts across the desert, scientists can see the outline of an ancient bay. But the Chao River, the only nearby source of fresh water, was still nearly five miles away. No amount of excellent fishing could make up for that distance, especially in a world where mobile people lived lightly and had their choice of where to camp or settle for a season.

Once El Niño returned, however, the landscape in this particular part of the Chao Valley quickly changed. As flash floods and mudslides inundated the desert plain and hit the edge of the bay, the fresh water, and the sediments it carried, slowed down. Gradually, perhaps after several El Niños, enough earth and fresh water accumulated to transform this strip of coast into rich wetlands that persisted long after the rains and floods stopped. Elsewhere, El Niño floods engulfed and destroyed everything in their path. Here, they created, and then expanded, a coastal oasis, lush with vegetation, fish, and birds. People weren't far behind.

These people lived less than a millennium after the warm-water oyster gatherers of the Santa Valley, but the return of El Niño had already transformed their world. They faced the threat of regular but unpredictable apocalypses, occurring about every three or four generations. But they must have also realized these new coastal marshes and lagoons that provided so much sustenance were themselves sustained and renewed by the unusual years of rain and floods that took so much else away. Perhaps they also saw how the disasters were expanding and nourishing their own communities by bringing disparate, damaged groups together to give and receive help in their wake.

It was in this precarious and symbolically potent context that people began to work together in a new way. The connections and skills learned during recoveries from repeat apocalypses may have taught people how to organize themselves, their resources, and their labor for the benefit of all—skills they could now use on a new kind of collective project. El Niño had also given them the raw material for such a project: massive deposits of mud and clay left behind by the floods.

Starting sometime well before fifty-one hundred years ago, after the people of the north coast had likely experienced somewhere between five and ten El Niño events, they began cutting rectangular bricks of damp clay straight from the debris, itself a sort of natural memorial to this apocalypse. They stacked the sun-dried bricks into the Los Morteros monument. It is the oldest adobe monument in the Americas, predating the local use of pottery by millennia, and one of the oldest monumental structures of any kind in Peru. Although Los Morteros's architecture and artifacts have not yet revealed what kinds of rituals people practiced there, or exactly what they believed about the natural and supernatural forces that governed their lives, it seems possible that the mound, constructed from the very material that destroyed homes and created new ecosystems, could have been a kind of monument to the power of El Niño itself.

The rituals performed at Los Morteros might have been a spiritual plea to deities or natural forces to stop El Niño's devastation, or grateful tributes to the newly fertile environment this recurring apocalypse left behind. Building and maintaining Los Morteros could have also helped the people of the Chao Valley and beyond solidify what otherwise could have been a temporary "disaster utopia," as Solnit calls the communities of care and recovery that spring up after catastrophe. The monument could have been a place where people formed and strengthened social bonds they knew would get them through this apocalypse, and the next. Maybe it was all of that, and more.

At and because of Los Morteros, people may have started thinking of themselves as a small part of an increasingly large and complicated whole. Each existing band or social group could have taken on a specific task—one became the brick makers, another the bricklayers, another the fishers who made sure no one went hungry while working on the monument. Perhaps it made sense for one person from each group to carry word of their activities to the others, and then for this committee to coordinate what each would work on next. Maybe a class of architects emerged, made up of the people who delighted in figuring out how to make their houses and now the monument as sturdy and long-lasting as possible. Still others would have naturally understood how to hold the attention of larger and larger groups of people, possibly gathered to commemorate the anniversary of an El Niño–related loss or celebrate the completion of a new phase in the monument's construction. Perhaps those gifted speakers became the priests.

To us, the idea that a society would have a leader, or a group of leaders, seems obvious and maybe even natural. But at some point or other, everywhere in the world, it was a new idea. To the people who started gathering in the Chao Valley near what would become Los Morteros, living in a hierarchical society wouldn't have seemed natural at all. Throughout history and into the present day, most hunter-gatherers live in small, egalitarian bands. No one person has more power than another, and decisions are made by the group as a whole. Their lives also tend to be the opposite of the "nasty, brutish, and short" stereotype so many of us imagine. Studies of their remains show that ancient hunter-gatherers had more varied diets, fewer cavities and diseases, and much more free time than early farmers. One of the perennial mysteries of archaeology is why, all over the world, so many people gave up the comfort and inherent equality of the hunter-gatherer lifestyle and built complex, unequal societies instead.

For archaeologists, complexity and inequality are an inseparable pair. Complex societies structure themselves around social divisions and hierarchies. They contain leaders and followers, farmers and kings, artisans and bureaucrats. By dividing roles and responsibilities, and investing a small number of people with the power to make decisions for the whole community, complex societies can grow to be extremely large, as large as any nation in the world today.

Los Morteros captures one culture's first steps toward this mysterious transition. It shows that complexity isn't a prerequisite for cooperation; instead, it may suggest that cooperation on a collective project can lay the foundations for complexity, and perhaps its attendant hierarchy, to arise in the first place. For after Los Morteros, the societies on the north coast would never slide back to the atomized constellation of egalitarian foraging bands they had been before. They would only ever grow more and more complex, with all the benefits and drawbacks that entailed.

The people who built Los Morteros didn't yet live in a society with political divisions or differences in wealth. Perhaps any kind of hierarchy was only apparent when the community imbued a priest with the responsibility to perform a ritual at the top of the mound. These emerging leaders didn't yet command an elite status that allowed them to live a different kind of life, nor did they wield any kind of decision-making power over the lives of others. "But they were heading down that path," Mauricio Llonto says.

◉

By thirty-six hundred years ago, the people of Peru's north coast had entered a veritable monument-building craze. In the fifteen hundred years since Los Morteros had been constructed by hunter-fisher-gatherers, agriculture had caught on in the river valleys. People had adopted irrigation canals, which brought fresh water directly to their fields. Rather than moving across the landscape, they settled into more permanent farming settlements, some that exploded to staggering sizes within a few centuries after Los Morteros was built.

Then, as farming settlements spread, a pattern emerged: Every village built its own temple pyramid. Unlike Los Morteros, which was built close to the shore of a bay, the temple pyramids were further inland, tucked into river valleys amid farms and villages. They all had a central pyramid flanked by two long, low platforms, forming the shape of a U and creating a semi-enclosed plaza where the community could gather. The temple pyramids weren't smooth-sided, like those of ancient Egypt, but terraced, like a staircase for a giant. The walls and floors of those terraces were smoothed over with white plaster and likely decorated with the colorful images of gods and other mythological figures. Inside, the temple pyramids were full of rooms and stairways, which grew increasingly narrow as one climbed toward the top. During festivals and ceremonies, their interiors would have buzzed with backstage activity, as priests prepared to step out onto the terraces and communicate with the gods on behalf of the people gathered in the plaza below. Each river valley could be home to several temple pyramids, perhaps as communities grew, splintered, and reorganized into independent groups in need of their own monuments.

If Los Morteros hints at the possibility of emerging leadership, the temple pyramids coincide with evidence of priests, warriors, and perhaps something approaching rulers. Some of it is indirect: The restricted access to the upper levels of the pyramids, combined with the plazas demarcated below, speak to a difference between the individuals or small groups who would have performed ceremonies on top of the temple and the masses of people who would have gathered to watch. Some of it is more direct: At the site of Cardal, near Lima, archaeologists found an elderly man buried in the community's temple pyramid. Unlike the fifteen other men, women, and children buried alongside him, his body was adorned with a necklace of sea lion teeth and earrings of whale bone—"the largest and strongest animals occupying" the Pacific Ocean. The unusual and symbolic jewelry suggests his community saw this man as particularly powerful, and the site of his grave links his exceptional status to the pyramid where he was buried. Other sites show evidence of social stratification. At the site of Sechín Alto in the Casma Valley, sixty miles south of Los Morteros, archaeologists have found iconographic evidence of two separate, powerful groups: priests in charge of the religious sphere, shown wearing scalloped tunics in art on the site's temple; and warriors, depicted with weapons on more secular buildings.

Although archaeologists will likely never know the particulars of the religion—or religions—practiced in these temple pyramids, there are hints it had to do with water and agricultural cycles. Some of the preserved murals and friezes depict waves, fish, and sea lions. And many of the pyramids sat near the places where irrigation canals drew water from the rivers flowing down from the mountains in the distance. These were the places where human ingenuity met natural abundance and made this farming culture possible.

It was also a "horrible hazard zone," says the archaeologist Jason Nesbitt, who spent several years excavating one of these temple pyramids, called Huaca Cortada, or "the cut mound." (The name comes from the fact that in the colonial era, Spanish treasure hunters dug a trench through it.) It sits in the Moche Valley, thirty-five miles north of Los Morteros, one temple pyramid among seven in the part of the valley that abuts the foothills of the Andes. Like many of the temple pyramids, Huaca Cortada sat at the intersection of a canal and a river, and it also faced several dry streambeds carved into nearby mountains. During an El Niño, the river and the streambeds would flood, and the fast-moving waters would surge into the canal and slam directly into the temple pyramid.

Given the location of the temple pyramids right in the path of El Niño floods, some archaeologists wonder if part of these priests' ritual responsibility could have been to stand up to—and perhaps even control—this recurring apocalypse. These were people who had already learned to manipulate the inhospitable desert of the north coast to their benefit. They had domesticated crops and employed an incredible new technology—irrigation canals—to keep themselves fed. They might have been confident in their ability to control other parts of nature, too.

"Overall, if you're on the north coast, [El Niño] is really bad. But it's not without opportunity. One of them is the political opportunity to take advantage of a crisis," Sandweiss says. Charismatic and ambitious people might have risen to the top of a religious system that promised, in part, to keep El Niño at bay, or at least ensure that its potent balance of creation and destruction would work in their favor. "So long as the events were infrequent, the system would appear to be working." And at the time the temple pyramids were built, they *were* infrequent—still only once or twice a century. Trading a bit of social equality for decades of safety might have made perfect sense.

Sooner or later, however, an El Niño flood was bound to hit each temple pyramid, leaving behind unmistakable physical evidence and marking a Before and After for the communities that built them. During his excavations at Huaca Cortada, Nesbitt found a thick layer of mud blanketing some of the pyramid's earliest terraces. It seems that in addition to the sediment carried by the flood, El Niño rains also essentially dissolved the pyramid's earthen outer layer, the remains of which flowed down its sides and settled on the terraces below. Nesbitt was able to date the El Niño that nearly destroyed Huaca Cortada by radiocarbon dating a twig stuck in that mud to between 3,600 and 3,450 years ago, near the beginning of the temple pyramid's life.

Nesbitt also found the remains of a small house near the base of the pyramid. It lies under a thick layer of gravel, showing it was likely leveled by a river flood. No one rebuilt the house on top of the stones, suggesting the house's inhabitants fled to another part of the valley after the flood. Or perhaps they didn't survive at all.

The larger community at Huaca Cortada carried on, however. Instead of trying to clear away the mud covering the pyramid, they used it as construction material, echoing the Los Morteros adobes so many centuries before. They leveled out the mud that covered the early terraces and turned it into the foundation for a new plaza floor. The twig Nesbitt radiocarbon dated was likely placed in the mud by a person, to be used as a marker during this remodel. After they were done, Huaca Cortada was even bigger than it had been before.

As the people came together to repair and expand the pyramid, they may have once again created one of Solnit's "disaster utopias." Gathered in one place again after being displaced by the flood, they would have learned who had survived and who was missing, and they would have been able to mourn and celebrate together. Perhaps the priests who had failed to prevent this apocalypse performed ceremonies of penance, seeking forgiveness from their people and from the gods who had punished them. Working together on the damaged pyramid, the people and their leaders would have absorbed, processed, and transformed the material that threatened to destroy the symbol of their village into the foundation of its future greatness. Maybe people from temple pyramids that had been spared this time came to help, and some of them might have stayed at Huaca Cortada once it was rebuilt. By the time the work was done, the people would have woven themselves back into a community.

◉

Six hundred years or so after the rebirth and expansion of Huaca Cortada, El Niño changed again. Around twenty-nine hundred years ago, according to Sandweiss's natural climate archives, El Niño suddenly went from happening once or twice a century to once or twice a decade, the pattern we know today. For a brief window right around the shift, El Niño occurred even more often than that. Climatically speaking, scientists still aren't sure why this happened, just as they aren't sure why El Niño returned in the first place. All they know is that within a single generation, El Niño went from being a rare apocalypse to a frequent one. Recovery times plummeted from several decades to a few years, or maybe, in some cases, just months.

How would the people of the temple pyramids have experienced this shift? It probably would have taken them several years, maybe up to a decade or two, to realize the full extent of what had happened and to be sure nature wasn't about to swing back to its old pattern. They would have been very familiar with the fear that accompanied a flood or an evacuation, but now they would have also felt the same ecological betrayal their ancestors experienced nearly three millennia before, when El Niño first returned out of nowhere. In response, the priests might have intensified the frequency or duration of their ceremonies, throwing all their charisma and metaphysical resources at the problem of a newly fickle and untrustworthy environment. Repairing and maintaining the temple pyramids went from the occasional necessity that brought people back together after a disaster to a near-constant obligation, its increasingly obvious futility grinding away at people's hope for their community's future.

At Huaca Cortada, Nesbitt found evidence of this final, desperate phase in the life of the temple pyramids. The El Niño mud returned, once again engulfing the pyramid's terraces. Once again, people used that mud to build a new floor and expand the pyramid. And then it happened again. And again. Three floods in very quick succession, three floors that attempted to contain and transform the destruction. But shortly after they built the third one, the people walked away from Huaca Cortada, and they never looked back.

They did the same at every temple pyramid in every river valley up and down the north coast, definitively abandoning them all within a century. At Sechín Alto, the site decorated with images of warriors and priests, people went so far as to tear down the pyramid and destroy the art within it. The society the pyramids represented—and had once held together—could not adapt to the new El Niño regime. Perhaps the people felt their religion had failed them, that they had been betrayed not only by nature but by the leaders who promised everything was under control. Those leaders may have been the ones to insist on rebuilding the pyramids even after the third, fifth, tenth flood in a row, and being coerced into useless labor to prop up the foundations of the priests' increasingly irrelevant power could have undermined the people's trust even further. The north coast had entered the era of a new kind of apocalypse, and its people couldn't rely on the old systems to protect them. They needed new leaders, new temples, and new homes, and they would go on to create them all.

The society of the temple pyramids was an early experiment with leaders and hierarchies, nowhere near as complex as the north coast states and empires that would follow in the centuries and millennia to come. But its disintegration in the face of sudden environmental instability and uncertainty carries a warning that echoes throughout history, all over the world. Complexity cannot prevent apocalypse, nor does it protect anyone, or any society, from it. In many ways, complexity invites and magnifies an apocalypse's worst effects, creating the conditions for inequality, climate change, disease, and floundering governments to intertwine into a monster that can tear society apart.

PART 2: TRANSFORMATIONS

Chapter 4

HOW APOCALYPSES TURN INEQUALITY INTO VIOLENCE

Around four thousand years ago, a young man packed up his belongings, said farewell to the people he'd known his entire life, and moved from his tiny farming village in the Indus Valley to what, in his mind, had to be the greatest city in the world. Tens of thousands of people lived in Harappa, and more were arriving every day. Like the young man, most had family in the villages, but the climate was getting drier and farming was getting harder, and so they'd come to try their luck as artisans, traders, merchants, builders, or any number of the other jobs the city had to offer.

The streets of Harappa were bustling but orderly, laid out in a grid established by the city government many centuries before. Everything was precisely planned and coordinated, from the drains that whisked rainwater and sewage off the streets to the size of the clay bricks used to construct buildings. Walls separated each neighborhood from the next, but everyone mingled in the markets, plazas, and baths, and they all cooperated to keep the city's infrastructure running smoothly. Traders from as far away as Mesopotamia came to Harappa to acquire the city's expert, intricate crafts, from jewelry carved from seashells to clay seals imprinted with images of water buffalo and unicorns. Some of these traders, along with the many migrants from the villages and beyond, stayed in Harappa and became an integral part of the city.

Even though the young man had never been to Harappa before, he knew exactly where to go when he arrived. He had an uncle who worked in the city making shell bangles, a type of jewelry popular in the city and the surrounding villages alike. Harappa wasn't particularly near the coast, but flourishing trade networks ensured that the city's workshops always remained stocked with shell. The young man's uncle had learned the craft back when he had arrived in the city seeking his own fortune. Thanks to his deft touch with shell and people alike, his uncle had become a trusted figure among his neighbors and fellow artisans. He was often called upon to sort out conflicts and had been sent several times to represent the neighborhood's interests in the city-wide meetings. He didn't always get the results his community was after, but they all understood that their life in Harappa depended on compromise and cooperation.

When the young man had become an old man, he would think back on his early days in Harappa and recognize that the signs of the apocalypse were already all around him, if only he had known how to see them. The city was stuffed to the gills and growing more crowded by the day as new arrivals fled the droughts in the countryside. Farmers in the villages like the one he had left had enough different crops on hand that usually one could grow even in a bad year. But as the summer monsoons and winter rains both became more unpredictable, so did the size of their harvests. The surpluses that had once been bound for Harappa's markets shrank, and sometimes there was nothing to send at all. Harappa's government, which once precisely managed everything from new construction to waste disposal, struggled to keep up with the increasing demand for its services. People without houses took to living in formerly public spaces, and trash piled up in the streets—signs of disorder that never would have been permitted just a few decades before, according to his uncle.

Other, even more unfortunate people eked out difficult lives just outside the city walls, subject to levels of violence and disease that would have provoked outrage and shame if they had been afflicted upon the citizens of the city. Harappa may not have had a king or much of a ruling class, but it did have outsiders. How foolish he had been, the man would think after everything had happened, to believe their suffering meant nothing for the city. To believe the pain, disease, and squalor those outside the walls were forced to endure wouldn't eventually become the fate of all Harappa.

Back then, however, the young man was simply grateful to have been granted a place in a city that may not have been as great as it once was but still offered a life that was unimaginable in his village. Tucked under his uncle's wing, he learned the art of carving and polishing shells into bangles. He also tried to learn the craft of politics and the kind of relationship-building at which his uncle excelled. But as the city grew more crowded and resources became scarcer, the kinds of negotiation and compromise that had built and sustained Harappa for seven hundred years became all but impossible. Desperate people found it harder and harder to trust each other. Shared urban citizenship had once outweighed all else, but as the bad years gave way to worse ones, neighborhoods and communities became more insular. If people could be convinced to cooperate with anyone, it would be others from their villages or regions over fellow city dwellers. The man's uncle, frustrated by these new dynamics, saw his charisma and connections quickly decay into obsolescence.

Just as the new scarcity eroded city politics, it also undermined the trade networks and economic activity that had been Harappa's foundation. Food shortages worsened as farmers found themselves with nothing left over to sell. Trade decreased as communities turned inward and dedicated themselves to conserving what they had instead of exchanging it in hopes of bringing in more. The man and his uncle had an increasingly hard time finding shell, and what items they could fashion didn't sell nearly as well as they used to. Who wanted bangles when they didn't have food?

The man stayed in Harappa until his uncle died. After that, he couldn't bear it any longer. The city that once seemed so full of opportunity was a husk of itself. The once cooperative government now existed in name only and would soon crumble altogether. Without the government's attention and maintenance, Harappa's infrastructure decayed, and people took to scavenging its carefully constructed buildings for bricks and other materials to throw together into slipshod huts. Those who had flowed into the city seeking refuge in its final years were now flowing back out. Their home villages, which had once seemed doomed by the weakening monsoon rains, now appeared to be their only hope. At least there they could grow their own food, however small the harvests might be. At least there they could be with their families instead of surrounded by strangers. So once again, the now not-so-young man decided it was time to say goodbye to the life he knew. His parents had died years ago—he had traveled back to the village for their funerals—but his sister and her husband had taken over their fields, and their children would soon do the same. The man had been a farmer once. He could learn to be one again.

Sometimes, in the years after his return to the village, the man would find himself thinking of all that Harappa had been. He was the only person he still knew who could read the text inscribed on the city's clay seals; when he died, that knowledge would disappear with him. There was no need to write down trade records or even shared myths in a village, where everyone knew each other and local knowledge could be stored in memory alone. He had once yearned for the excitement of city life, but now the younger generations recoiled at the thought of so many strangers, so much uncertainty, so much risk. The man had heard that some people still lived in Harappa, but their lives were hard and violent, and they only stayed because they had nowhere else to go.

Once, when the man was very old, a trader came to the village with some shells. They weren't as beautiful as the ones he had worked with in Harappa, and the trader only had a few. The man exchanged some grain for one, which he carved and polished into a bangle for his great-grandniece. She was delighted, if confused by the stories he told her about where he'd learned to make it. Harappa, swallowed by apocalypse, might as well have been a dream.

◉

Around five hundred years after communities on the north coast of Peru banded together in the face of apocalypse to build Los Morteros, people on the other side of the world were experimenting with an entirely new way of living. In places such as Egypt, Mesopotamia, and the Indus Valley of Pakistan and India, people—and their ambitious leaders—took social complexity to a level never attempted before. They lived in cities of tens of thousands, united large territories under shared cultural and political identities, developed economies that supported and required specialized jobs ranging from farmers to artisans to bureaucrats, established far-flung trade networks, and formed and followed the rule of powerful governments. These were the world's first states and, in the case of Mesopotamia, the first empires.

One of these early states is known as the Indus Civilization, which extended over nearly four hundred thousand square miles in what is now Pakistan and northwestern India. At its heart were five cities, including the place now known as Harappa, in the province of Punjab, Pakistan. As in ancient Egypt at the same time, the Indus cities brimmed with monumental architecture, bustling neighborhoods, art, markets, and workshops. Unlike in Egypt, however, archaeologists excavating in Indus cities have never found a palace, a royal tomb, a portrait of a political leader, or any other material evidence of a monarch.

Instead, Harappa and the others were anchored by grand public spaces, such as baths and plazas. Streets were laid out in grids, just as they are in many of today's big cities, which made them easy to navigate for locals and visitors alike. Sewers and drains kept the streets clean and dry and prevented floods from the heavy rains that fell during the annual summer monsoon, the region's primary source of water. In Egypt and Mesopotamia, wrote Indus archaeologist John Marshall in 1931, "much money and thought were lavished on the building of magnificent temples for the gods and on palaces and tombs of kings, but the rest of the people seemingly had to content themselves with insignificant dwellings of mud. In the Indus Valley, the picture is reversed, and the finest structures are those erected for the convenience of the citizens."

Some archaeologists have posited that such successful urban planning and standardization imply a level of control, centralization, and order that could only have been executed and maintained by an authoritarian ruling class, even in the absence of any art or monuments depicting them. But most others, starting with the first excavations of Indus cities in the early twentieth century, have interpreted their unique gridded layouts and lack of royal residences or tombs as signs that these cities weren't ruled by kings. It's impossible to reconstruct exactly how Harappa and the other Indus cities governed themselves, especially since archaeologists haven't yet been able to decipher—or even identify the language of—their writing. But it seems likely that political and economic power were somehow shared rather than being concentrated in one family, neighborhood, or social group. Perhaps in Harappa, the city's many plazas were home to neighborhood councils or craft guilds, and these groups fed into a larger, collaborative city government that negotiated conflicts, provided services, and maintained the urban infrastructure for the benefit of all.

Harappa's social equality and investment in making itself a livable, welcoming city made it wildly successful as an economic center. There, merchants could sell their wares and acquire others, traders could access an economic network that extended from India to Mesopotamia, and craftspeople could learn, refine, and sell their art. Grains and other foods flowed in from the farming villages, and art, culture, and riches flowed back out. The streets, drains, and public spaces made it possible for anyone, from migrants from nearby villages looking for opportunity to foreign traders hailing from the other side of the known world, to quickly learn the city's layout and enjoy its comforts. Despite the many different kinds of people who mixed and mingled in Harappa, archaeologists haven't found vast differences in wealth, either in the form of larger homes or an unequal distribution of precious goods. Although it would be naive to think that Harappa and the other Indus cities were blissfully free of political tension or interpersonal strife—no human society is, or ever will be—there's no evidence they engaged in war.

Then, around forty-two hundred years ago, apocalypse struck. Stalagmites and stalactites from caves in Israel, India, and even South America, as well as cores taken from oceans and lakes around the world, show that many places became much drier right around that time, in what's become known as the 4.2-kiloyear event. Drought struck Eurasia particularly hard. In the Indus Valley, the summer monsoon grew weaker and less predictable. The already meager winter rains ceased. Rivers slowed to a trickle, and entire lakes dried up.

Weather and especially rainfall in the Indus region had never been entirely predictable, and farmers there were already accustomed to cultivating many different crops, each able to thrive under different conditions. But the new drought would have been unlike anything they'd seen or known how to prepare for. As the archaeologist Cameron Petrie writes, the Indus Valley's climate went from being "predictably unpredictable," with frequent variations that stayed within familiar parameters, to "unpredictably unpredictable," where no one had any idea how the weather would behave from one year to the next.

At the beginning of the drought, farmers were on the front lines of the water shortages, and life in Harappa seemingly became more attractive. People poured into the city, and it grew larger than it had ever been. Perhaps the new arrivals expected that the drought would last only a few years, and they were seeking a safer place to ride it out; in the city, their fortunes didn't directly depend on the vagaries of each harvest the way they did in the villages. Perhaps their plan was to go home one day, as soon as home became a more viable place to be. Harappa had always been a gathering place for those in search of economic opportunity. Now it might have been the best hope for survival.

The trouble with counting on Harappa in a time of apocalypse was that Harappa had always counted on everyone else, as cities usually do. Its food was grown and processed in the very villages where crops were withering, the raw materials needed for its craft economy could come from hundreds of miles away, and the value of its products depended on trade routes that carried them far and wide. Harappa was a node that drew its power from the network in which it was embedded. It was never designed to be self-sufficient. And so its fate was inextricably intertwined with that of the larger Indus Civilization, even if it may have appeared, at the beginning, to be insulated from it.

As the city's population boomed in the midst of an environmental crisis, its public-minded values seem to have faltered. Perhaps the drought itself was spiritually or symbolically disruptive to an urban culture that had invested so much in managing water, from its public baths to its drains and sewers, and the weakened monsoon undermined the city's confidence in its ability to cope with this unprecedented challenge. For the first time in seven hundred years, Harappa's social fabric was fraying enough that archaeologists can see evidence of inequality, which seems to have increased alongside the decline.

Trash piled up in once pristine public spaces, and ramshackle houses appeared in the streets. This level of disorder and visible poverty was new to Harappa, and its citizens may have been shocked to see it spreading in the heart of their city. Maybe some of them resented the newcomers who had insisted on coming to a place that no longer had enough to provide for them. Others, perhaps, tried to share what they did have, taking on the civic responsibilities the government was in the midst of vacating. Without knowing more details about Harappa's government, we cannot know if this deterioration in public spaces and services was caused by a political crisis or perhaps arose in its aftermath. We can imagine that food would have eventually stopped arriving in Harappa's markets, as emergency stores and rural surpluses withered to nothing. We can imagine panic and desperation, as apocalypse undermined the integrity of the place where people thought they would be safe.

◉

Gwen Robbins Schug has a lot of tattoos, but one of her favorites depicts the head and torso of a person whose muscles and blood vessels were, after death, scientifically preserved in a nineteenth-century form of plastination. If this seems like an odd choice, it's the kind of thing that Robbins Schug gets excited about. This image she has lovingly inked on her body represents some of the people she has examined during her work as a bioarchaeologist. It's a vivid representation of how intimate bioarchaeology can be: a symbol of their flesh etched onto hers.

By studying bones and other human remains, bioarchaeologists can reconstruct the features and experiences of past people in incredible detail, from how tall they were to what diseases they had to what foods they ate on a regular basis. Bioarchaeology reaches back into a person's own past, learning the stories behind healed injuries, tracing patterns of migration, and determining whether a person had enough to eat as a child. If archaeologists who focus on architecture and artifacts can see decades or centuries of a society's arc at a glance, bioarchaeologists necessarily work on the scale of individual lives.

Robbins Schug wanted to use the tools of bioarchaeology to study how past episodes of climate change had affected the health and well-being of the people who lived through them. She had been working in South Asia since she was a graduate student, and in 2011, she spent six months in Kolkata, India, getting to know the people who had lived and died in Harappa. Many of the human remains excavated from the city are now stored in a laboratory there belonging to the Anthropological Survey of India. The cemeteries where they were originally buried spanned from before, during, and after Harappa's collapse. Robbins Schug would be the first bioarchaeologist to examine them for signs of how apocalypse affected the city's residents.

One cemetery held people who had lived during Harappa's height, from 2450 to 2200 BC (about forty-five hundred to forty-two hundred years ago). Robbins Schug was able to examine sixty-six of them. Their graves and remains spoke to Harappa's high standard of living and apparent commitment to equality. They'd been buried with offerings including ceramic vessels filled with food, mirrors, gold beads, and shell jewelry, but no one had dramatically more or fewer grave goods, nor did anyone receive the kind of rare or exotic offerings that might suggest a higher status during life. They had some cavities in their teeth—a common issue in agricultural societies—and joints that showed the wear and tear of hard work, but the growth patterns of their bones and teeth showed they'd had plenty to eat throughout their lives. Only 4 percent of their skulls showed evidence of violence, in the form of blows to the head. This was enough to make Robbins Schug think Harappa hadn't exactly been a peaceful, cooperative paradise, but neither was it a sign of widespread, systemic violence. Somewhat unexpectedly, two of the individuals in the urban cemetery had advanced leprosy, which, among other skeletal effects, slowly eats away at a person's nasal bones and gives their skull an unusually large and empty nasal cavity. Their inclusion in the same cemetery as people with no signs of the disfiguring disease suggested that, unlike in many places across the ancient world, leprosy wasn't stigmatized in Harappa.

That apparent peace and equality would change as the apocalypse crept into Harappa. One day near the beginning of her stay in Kolkata, Robbins Schug opened a box and lifted out the skull of a young child, around five years old. They had lived and died between 2000 and 1900 BC, at least two hundred years into the 4.2-kiloyear drought. Other major Indus cities had already been abandoned, but Harappa was still hanging on, barely. This child's family might have seen the tail end of Harappa's desperate overpopulation period, or the very beginning of its panicked abandonment, which would be largely complete by 1900 BC. Maybe they lived through and experienced the worst of both.

The child was one of twenty-three people whose remains had been interred in an ossuary just outside Harappa's walls, along with some pieces of pottery and a few animal bones. It seems that their bodies had decayed elsewhere, and afterward, their skulls, as well as one complete skeleton, had been collected and moved to this unusual collective burial. The location, near the city's main sewer drain, and the mortuary treatment they had received were nothing like the people buried in the earlier city cemetery. Those graves were hardly opulent, but they indicated clear care and respect for those laid to rest there. Robbins Schug wasn't sure the same could be said for the jumbled bones and incomplete skeletons of the ossuary.

Examining the child's skull for the first time, Robbins Schug was shocked to notice it was fractured in two places. One crack ran straight up from the forehead and over the top of the skull, and the other was on the back left side of the head. Neither wound showed any sign of healing, making it likely that the child had died of the blows. It disturbed her to think of a child so young being violently killed. How had this been allowed to happen? What kind of world had they been born into? "This is the beginning of something important," she thought.

As Robbins Schug worked her way through the ossuary bones, she discovered the injured child wasn't the only victim of violence buried there. Fully half of the skulls in the ossuary showed signs of violence in the form of blows to the head, compared to the 4 percent in the earlier urban cemetery. Women and children were at the highest risk of injury. The people buried in the ossuary were also clearly much sicker than previous generations of Harappa residents. Almost a quarter of them had advanced leprosy, and 35 percent suffered from some other kind of chronic infection that damaged their skeletons. Even the children didn't have enough to eat; one third of them showed signs of scurvy in the form of porous bones.

Because Robbins Schug had found people with leprosy buried alongside seemingly healthy people in the earlier cemetery, she didn't think the people in the ossuary were interred there as a quarantine measure or because of stigma against people with the disease. More likely, they belonged to a group that existed on the fringes of Harappa's society for other reasons, reasons we may never know, and that exclusion put them at higher risk for violence, deprivation, and disease. It could be that in addition to being buried outside the city walls, they lived there, too, in dilapidated buildings found near their final resting place.

It's possible, even likely, that similar types of social divisions and hierarchies existed in Harappa before the apocalypse, too. The earlier urban cemetery, where all the people were buried with similar offerings and seemed to have enjoyed good health, was nowhere near large enough for all Harappans to be interred there, and some archaeologists have suggested the remains do, in fact, represent a group of the city's elites. Lower-status people might have been buried elsewhere, or perhaps they were cremated. Maybe if archaeologists one day find their remains, their bones will also bear traces of violence and deprivation, and they will force researchers to rethink the prevailing vision of a peaceful and inclusive Harappa. After all, a government in which power is shared can just as easily be an oligarchy as a democracy. No one craft guild, kin group, or neighborhood might have dominated the others, but each could have still contained and enforced stratified social classes that are invisible to us four millennia later.

So it could be that when the apocalypse began around forty-two hundred years ago, its challenges and stressors magnified preexisting inequalities, bringing them to the fore in ways Harappa previously had been able to prevent. Perhaps there had always been tensions between different groups—newcomers and long-term residents, merchants and laborers, migrants from one region or another—and apocalypse heightened their intensity and worsened their consequences.

Or it really could be that apocalypse created entirely new hierarchies in a city that had previously resisted inequality's temptations and prevented its tragedies. As climate change and likely food shortages strained Harappa's resources and ate away at its civic values, those new social divisions could have exploded into truly unprecedented violence. We can't see the precise social lines Harappans drew between groups, and we can't know how they justified these new, or at least intensified, divisions and hierarchies. What we can see is how the deadly consequences of this rising inequality inscribed themselves on people's bones, an incontrovertible record of violence in a once welcoming city now pushed to the edge by apocalypse.

◉

Climate change, then and now, is a slow-moving apocalypse. Life can seem normal for long stretches of time, or maybe just a little more difficult than it had been. One region will be hit hard by drought or food shortages or conflict, and then the next year it will be another. Groups of people who never had enough will find themselves with even less, but the rest of society will rationalize it as an inevitability rather than heed it as the warning it is. Acute disasters strike, and they are terrible, and then they become the new normal as expectations shift. It can take a long time to understand what's happening, or for the effects to compound to the point where they become undeniable. In Harappa, it took about three hundred years from the beginning of the 4.2-kiloyear event for people to see the truth: The city was no longer sustainable. The farmers had nothing left over to feed them. The rain the urban infrastructure had been built to manage had ceased to fall. They had to leave. Now.

By about 1900 BC, seven hundred years after the Indus cities first arose, most people had left Harappa, and it began its transformation from capital to ruin. According to the shifts in the size and location of settlements, it seems that most city dwellers left Harappa and moved to villages. Perhaps these villages were their birthplaces, or their ancestral homes, places that had been gladly drawn into Harappa's economic and cultural web for a time but had existed long before the city and would continue to exist long after. In the villages, people could grow their own food and make their own decisions about how best to cope with a difficult climate. They weren't dependent on someone else's surplus, or infrastructure whose continued functioning depended on the cooperation of tens of thousands of strangers. In the villages, there were no strangers.

Still, it appears that some people in Harappa didn't have anywhere else to go. They might have been descendants of the excluded community of the ossuary, or they might have been another group that suffered from a similarly abject social status and its violent consequences. Or perhaps they moved to the empty city after the previous residents had fled, looking to scavenge what they could. Now the formerly glorious spaces of central Harappa, the public plazas and the opulent baths, were theirs for the taking, but conditions were squalid, and too few people wanted to live there to be able to make meaningful improvements. Harappa's ruins turned into a dangerous place to be. In the remains of twenty-three people buried in the city in the two centuries immediately following its abandonment, Robbins Schug found that almost 40 percent had head injuries, nearly reaching the levels seen in the ossuary. And as in the ossuary, women and children were at the highest risk of violence. In addition, more than a quarter had signs of skeletal damage from some kind of long-term infection, including leprosy and tuberculosis.

As time went on and Harappa decayed further, the health prospects of its residents got even worse. Among fifteen children whose remains dated to two hundred to six hundred years after the city's collapse,

Robbins Schug found that nearly half were malnourished and possibly had scurvy. Some were young enough that their mothers were likely breastfeeding them, and so their remains suggest those women were also severely underfed.

It's possible the brutality and deprivation on display in postapocalyptic Harappa made the descendants of its citizens recoil in fear and disgust if and when they heard rumors of it. Now generations removed from city life, they couldn't imagine what its benefits had been, especially compared to the flexibility, self-determination, and insulation of the villages. But they could still see some of its dangers and downsides, including the legacy of social divisions and exclusions that led to certain people being forced to live among the city's ruins, even now. Long after the climate stabilized and other cultures affected by the 4.2-kiloyear event returned to their old, hierarchical ways of life, descendants of the Indus Civilization rejected their ancestors' urban tradition and the social complexity it required. They did not build another city for one thousand years.

◉

In AD 1347, just over three thousand years after Harappa had been abandoned, Europeans began to hear stories of a mysterious sickness spreading from the east. Its suite of painful and frightening symptoms included fever, vomiting, coughing up blood, black pustules on the skin, and swollen lymph nodes. Death usually came within three days. It was carried to Crimea, the people of western Europe heard, by the armies of the Golden Horde, the western division of the Mongol Empire. During their siege of a Genoese trading outpost, the Mongols were rumored to have turned their dead comrades into weapons by loading their bodies into catapults and launching them over the city walls.

Those who survived long enough to flee the subsequent outbreak carried the pestilence across the Black Sea to Constantinople, one of the medieval world's most prominent and well-connected cities. From there the disease spread to the trading hubs of Sicily and then around the Mediterranean, from Alexandria to Marseille. Eventually it would reach all the way to Ireland, Norway, and perhaps Ethiopia and Ghana.

Various cities tried to enact quarantines and travel bans from those places where the infection was known to be spreading, or at least bar entry to the visibly sick. "But all to no avail," wrote Giovanni Boccaccio in the introduction to *The Decameron*, drawing on his experience in Florence during the Black Death. The disease always found a way in.

Once the plague took hold, a city transformed into a shadow of itself. All the normal urban sounds abruptly ceased as people retreated to their homes in fear; in Padua, the streets were silent except for the wails of mourners who had watched their families and neighbors die. The cathedral in Pistoia, Italy, stopped ringing its bells during funerals to avoid terrifying the living with their sheer number, and the city banned all announcement of or invitation to funerals to avoid public gatherings. "Bodies were here, there and everywhere," Boccaccio wrote of Florence: lying in the streets; rotting inside houses; awaiting collection outside their front doors, where their neighbors had dragged them when the smell became unbearable. Priests and gravediggers rushed through funerals as fast as they could, "lower[ing] the body into the nearest empty grave they could find." Soon they resorted to mass graves dug in churchyards and public plazas, "into which new arrivals were placed in their hundreds, stowed tier upon tier like ships' cargo."

People who experienced the Black Death had no doubt it was the end of the world. Multiple European chroniclers compared it to Noah's flood and the biblical plagues, except worse, because at least those events left *some* people alive. Medieval Christians were convinced God was once again punishing humanity for its sins, and the religious authorities begged people to pray like they had never prayed before. The streets of cities saw both sanctioned religious processions and gruesome displays of public penance by the "flagellants," a leaderless cult that spread across continental Europe and England whose members swarmed churches to whip themselves bloody to dramatically repent for the sins that had caused the plague. But it all seemed for naught as outbreak after outbreak burned through the known world. The Italian lawyer

Gabriele de' Mussis imagined a furious God's response to people's pleas for salvation: "I bid you weep. The time for mercy has passed."

Respect for law and life evaporated as the apocalypse dragged on. "People behaved as though their days were numbered, and treated their belongings and their persons with equal abandon," wrote Boccaccio. The still-healthy turned their backs on the sick; many medieval writers reported, with horror, that even parents refused to care for their dying children. Subsumed by a wave of relentless and universal grief, survivors eventually lost their ability to mourn or feel anything else. Monastic chroniclers in Austria wrote about people determined to "cheer each other up with comfort and merrymaking, so that they were not overwhelmed by depression." After a particularly bad outbreak, villagers insisted on throwing parties and weddings but could only ever arrive at "a sort of half-happiness." All people could do was go through the motions of being alive.

Between 1347 and 1351, the plague killed between 30 and 60 percent of all people in Europe. To the survivors, the disease usually seemed indiscriminate, and the sense that no one was safe no doubt added to the terror. But as in Harappa three millennia earlier, the rupture of apocalypse and the violence it unleashed had its source in fault lines of discrimination and inequality that already ran through society's foundations.

◉

When a construction project necessitated the excavation of a medieval Jewish cemetery in Tàrrega, Spain, archaeologists from the local museum found some unusual graves. Amid the 158 typical individual graves they found and excavated, there were six mass graves, containing the remains of at least seventy people and possibly more. In the mass graves, men, women, and children of all ages had been buried together. Amid the bones, the archaeologists found a few coins dating the burials to around the time of the Black Death.

Unlike the bodies in the mass graves of plague victims found all over

Europe, these people hadn't died of the disease. "Many of the bones showed signs of violence," says Anna Colet, the archaeologist who directed the excavation. She's not a bioarchaeologist and doesn't usually study human remains, but, she says, "even I could see it right away." More than half of the bodies Colet's team excavated had injuries on their skulls or other parts of their skeletons, similar to the cracks and fractures Robbins Schug had observed on the bones from Harappa's ossuary. The wounds were severe and showed no signs of healing, meaning they were fatal. The people in Tàrrega's mass graves had been massacred.

Historical documents spoke of attacks on Jewish communities in Tàrrega and other nearby towns and cities in 1348, including Barcelona. It fit a pattern of attacks that swept across Europe during the Black Death as Christian communities all over the continent accused their Jewish neighbors of poisoning wells and causing the plague. They extracted, through well-documented torture of Jews, confessions of an international conspiracy to use the disease to wipe out all Christians. Fearing the destabilizing social forces that could be unleashed by a populist revolt during a pandemic, Christian religious and political authorities scrambled to protect Jews from extrajudicial killings; Pope Clement VI himself issued a mandate to excommunicate anyone who participated in the violence. But these mandates and laws had little effect. In towns and cities from Spain to Austria, ordinary Christians defied their own church's orders and murdered their Jewish neighbors, often by burning them alive. This vigilante violence could also turn on beggars, travelers, or anyone else deemed an outsider as entire towns roiled themselves into a panic.

In Tàrrega, Christians and Jews had lived side by side with little conflict for decades if not centuries before the plague arrived. But as in Harappa, social divisions erupted into violence during the uncertainty and fear of an apocalypse. The bodies buried in the mass graves didn't show signs of burning, but the attacks were nevertheless shockingly brutal. Most of the injuries were caused by forceful, determined blows with swords, axes, or sickles. Some limbs had been completely severed. Even children had been cut down in what appeared to be an indiscriminate attack that showed no mercy even to the defenseless. One man had an old fracture on one of his legs that hadn't healed properly, which would have made it hard for him to run. He suffered twenty-two blows to his head and body—the most of any body recovered from the mass graves so far.

The archaeologists in Tàrrega found six mass graves, but they could also see the corners or walls of two or possibly three more. Seventy bodies have been recovered so far, but when Jewish survivors formally reported the attack to the Spanish king the following year, they spoke of three hundred people being murdered that day. That may be an overestimate, as only about twelve hundred people total lived in Tàrrega at the time, Colet says. Or it could include Jews from nearby towns who had fled to Tàrrega seeking refuge when their own communities were attacked, only to die as the violence spread.

The attack was intended to destroy Tàrrega's Jewish community, but the archaeologists can tell it didn't succeed. The victims' bodies weren't simply dumped atop one another or otherwise desecrated, as might be expected if the killers had disposed of them. Rather, each body was laid out with the head to the west and the feet to the east, in accordance with Jewish custom. The graves weren't always large enough for everyone to be laid flat, so some bodies were bent at the knees or otherwise contorted to fit in the space, but they weren't piled up or jumbled together, as in Harappa's ossuary. Colet thinks these signs of care mean the victims of the Tàrrega massacre were likely buried by surviving members of the Jewish community, in their own cemetery and following their own rituals to the extent they could.

These survivors found their lives transformed overnight. Accounts of the attack speak of the lucky ones hiding in the homes of friends as their neighbors broke down the gate to the Jewish quarter, hacked people to pieces, and ransacked their houses. Those who escaped with their lives still lost their homes and everything in them. They no doubt feared another attack at any moment. Still, they did what they could. Some of the bodies were buried right away, before decomposition set in; their skeletons remained more or less intact over the following centuries. Other skeletons in the mass graves had decayed into messy clusters of bones, body parts no longer connected where they should have been, indicating the bodies were buried well after death, once decomposition had already begun. It could have been weeks or months, in the high summer of Europe's worst plague year, before they made it to their graves. One account of the massacre says the attackers threw many of the bodies into a cistern; it's possible they were left to decay there until the survivors felt safe enough to collect the dead. It's also possible the survivors themselves hid some of the bodies until the immediate threat of violence had passed. Or perhaps the burials were delayed, as so many were in those years, by the plague itself.

These and other mass graves, especially during plague years, are often understood to be signs of the chaos, desperation, and violence unleashed during apocalypse. They often are those things, of course, especially in the case of the Tàrrega massacre. But mass graves can also be understood as an act of care, solidarity, and community performed by survivors, often while still under threat themselves. Burial customs and funeral rites designed for unexceptional times strain under the pressures of apocalypse. And yet, mass graves show that even under previously unimaginable circumstances, people try their best to maintain a version of the rituals that define their community in life and death.

◉

By the autumn of 1348, the pestilence reached the southern coast of England, and officials in London knew it was only a matter of time before it ravaged its way to the capital. They had heard about the crush of bodies that overwhelmed so many cities and towns on the continent that year. So London, with the benefit of a bit more time, began construction of a massive cemetery, called East Smithfield, as a future site for as many victims as possible to be buried in consecrated ground. Unable to save lives, London tried to save souls. More than one thousand people were buried in East Smithfield over the course of the next two years, with much more care than would have been possible otherwise.

They were only a fraction of those who died, however; the Black Death claimed nearly half of London's eighty thousand inhabitants over a horrific fifteen months.

With that level of mortality, most people, scientists included, have assumed the Black Death was an indiscriminate killer, felling the healthy and the sick, the rich and the poor, the young and the old alike. Chroniclers seemed to have experienced it that way at the time; as a Belgian abbot wrote of the plague years, "no one, rich, middling or poor, was safe, but each one of them spent every day awaiting God's will." But the bioarchaeologist Sharon DeWitte had her doubts. She knew that poverty, age, malnutrition, and frail health increase people's risk of most infectious diseases. Could the Black Death really be an outlier among apocalypses, unaffected by the hierarchies and inequalities of the complex society it collided with? Or did it, like so many others, unfold along preexisting societal cracks?

The confluence of inequality, disease, and violence dates all the way back to Harappa—and Harappa was, very likely, a more equal, clean, and healthy place to live than medieval London. When the Black Death struck, England and other European countries were feudal societies designed to accommodate, perpetuate, and exploit extreme economic and social inequality. King Edward III ruled England, while the aristocracy presided over manors where they lived off the labor of huge numbers of peasants. Inequality wasn't a side effect of feudalism but a necessity.

As DeWitte studied the bones of centuries of medieval Londoners and the historical records about the era in which they lived, she came to understand that rather than arriving as an unprecedented shock, the Black Death was the latest tragedy in a century's worth of crises. In the late thirteenth and early fourteenth centuries—the hundred years or so leading up to the Black Death—England, like most of Europe, had struggled through decades of climatic cooling and erratic weather. Harvests failed and food was scarce. The Great Famine of 1315 to 1317 killed up to 15 percent of the population of England and Wales, a little more than thirty years before the plague would arrive in the same region. Grain prices soared as wages fell, and more and more people were driven into poverty. Household account books and records of payments to workers on English manors show that by the turn of the fourteenth century, 70 percent of English families didn't have enough money or resources to avoid going cold and hungry. Meanwhile, the wealthiest 3 percent of households received 15 percent of the national income.

This environmentally and economically challenging century left its mark on people's health. When DeWitte analyzed the remains of Londoners who had lived in the hundred years before the Black Death and compared them to those from the relatively comfortable eleventh and twelfth centuries, she found those who died just before the plague were shorter and had more grooves on their teeth, a sign that a person's enamel growth was disrupted during childhood because of malnutrition, disease, or other forms of physiological stress. They were also more likely to have died young, after childhoods marked by illness and hunger.

DeWitte also examined the remains of about five hundred Black Death victims buried in East Smithfield, which had been partially excavated during a construction project in the 1980s. She worked in an underground chamber in the Museum of London, where the East Smithfield skeletons had been moved. One at a time, DeWitte carefully laid their bones out on a table, fitting their bodies back together. She examined each person's pelvis for signs of their age and biological sex and measured the length of their arm and leg bones for clues to their height. She looked for a record of a person's past in the enamel grooves on their teeth and on their skulls; childhood anemia can leave holes in the outer layer of bone around the eye sockets and the top of the head. Meanwhile, malnutrition, injury, or disease later in life can cause knobby stubs of bone to grow where they shouldn't. DeWitte painstakingly surveyed each plague victim for these and other signs of hardship during their lives. Like evidence of head trauma in the Harappa ossuary, they were more widespread than DeWitte expected. "When I saw an individual who didn't have a pathological indicator, it was a shock," she says.

DeWitte compiled all this data and used it to calculate the age distribution of people in the cemetery, as well as differences in the life expectancies of those with and without markers of stress on their skeletons. Her models showed people who had already suffered a lifetime of poor health and physiological stress were, in fact, more likely to die during the Black Death than those whose skeletons showed no signs of stress, perhaps because they had enjoyed plenty of resources throughout their lives. DeWitte also found the plague disproportionately killed older adults. That could have been an effect of their age alone, but they also belonged to the generation that had grown up during the hardest years of the Great Famine, setting them up for a lifetime of ill health.

By the time the plague arrived in England, a century of famine and rising inequality had created an abundance of at-risk people, and they were indeed the ones most likely to die when the pestilence swept through their city. Meanwhile, historical records suggest that only 13 percent of English nobility died in 1349.

This wasn't the same kind of acute violence as the Tàrrega massacre or the beaten children in the Harappa ossuary, but it was violence all the same. This kind of violence, the kind that systematically deprived, disadvantaged, and disempowered the poor, was embedded in and enacted by the structure of medieval English society. Apocalypse didn't create the hierarchies and divisions that defined medieval Europe, but it did capitalize on them, and in the process, it revealed their true cost.

◉

As the plague finally receded from European cities and towns by 1351, the survivors were struck by a sudden, palpable emptiness. There was, quite simply, almost no one left. Survivors wandered out of ghost towns, everyone they had ever known taken from them in a matter of months. "We should make new friends," wrote the Italian poet Petrarch, "but how, when the human race is almost wiped out; and why, when it looks to me like the end of the world is at hand?"

The silence permeated cities, towns, and the countryside between them, existing alongside an uncomfortable abundance of resources that proved impossible to manage. In the English countryside, the chronicler Henry Knighton wrote, grain rotted in the fields and farm animals roamed freely and died uncared for, "for there was so great a shortage of servants and laborers that there was no one who knew what needed to be done." Surviving workers looked at all the work that needed doing, and how few of them were still there to do it, and they realized just how essential their labor was. Almost immediately, they began charging higher wages. "If anyone was to hire them he had to submit to their demands, for either his fruit and [grain] would be lost or he had to pander to the arrogance and greed of the workers," Knighton wrote.

Before the Black Death, it was almost impossible for peasants to move away from the land they worked and the lords they served. Afterward, every manor was in desperate need of farmers and workers, who suddenly had their choice of where to live and work. Landowners desperately tried to keep their tenant farmers from moving away by slashing rents and offering higher wages. "By an inversion of the natural order, those who were accustomed to have plenty and those accustomed to suffer want, fell into need on the one hand and into abundance on the other," wrote the English chronicler William Dene.

When it came to wages, poverty, and physical health, the century after the Black Death was the inverse of the century of suffering that preceded it. Following her studies of Black Death victims and their generally poorer health before the epidemic, DeWitte also examined the remains of people of various social classes who died after the plague, who were buried in the cemetery of a London abbey between 1350 and 1538. They were, by and large, much healthier than the people who died during the plague or in the century before it. Both men and women survived to older ages, and men were taller and had fewer of the grooves on their teeth that point toward childhood deprivation. Women were a bit shorter than their pre–Black Death counterparts, but counterintuitively, that might also be a sign of better overall health. Girls tend to stop growing taller around the time they reach menarche, so it's possible the girls born after the plague started their periods at younger ages, enabled by better nutrition and less physical stress. Of course, these improvements in health and living standards came at "an unimaginably high cost" that surely included severe psychological trauma for the survivors, DeWitte says. But they were improvements all the same.

The pre-plague social order—which had made the Black Death as deadly as possible for the poor, and doubly dangerous for Jewish communities targeted for attacks—spent decades defending itself tooth and nail against the forces of change unleashed by the epidemic. As early as 1349, the king of England set forth "the ordinance of laborers," which forced unemployed, landless men and women to accept any job offered to them for the same wages they would have received in 1346, the year before the plague arrived in Europe. If they refused the terms of employment, they would be imprisoned. Potential employers would be fined if they offered higher wages. The ordinance even promised to jail anyone who gave alms to beggars, "so that they will be forced to work for a living." And yet, two years later, in 1351, a frustrated parliament needed to pass another, similar law because workers "[had] no regard to the said ordinance but rather to their own ease and exceptional greed." Commoners ignored that new law, too.

A full forty years after the Black Death swept into Europe, the English government was still scrambling to force the working class back into the pre-plague economic order. In 1388, commoners' freedom and autonomy, born of the staggering losses a generation earlier, were still so vexing to parliament that it amended the 1351 law to make it illegal for workers to travel or move without an official letter attesting to their return date or new offer of employment, compelling craftsmen to do agricultural labor during the harvest, and permanently confining any "beggars unfit to work" to their hometowns. For those who refused, "there shall be a pair of stocks in every town."

These laws, too, are an example of apocalypse turning inequality into violence—the violence of imprisonment, surveillance, and restriction of movement wielded against the poor, the disabled, or anyone else who couldn't or wouldn't participate in the fiction that the Black Death hadn't transformed the known world and the lives of everyone in it. But the fact that parliament was still passing laws intended to curb workers' movements and limit their employment choices four decades and at least one generation after the epidemic implies that the new economic and social possibilities unleashed by the plague were not so easily or quickly suppressed. DeWitte's work shows that the general population's health improvements persisted for at least two hundred years, despite recurrences of plague itself in London. Similar patterns have been found outside of England, as well. According to data from northern Italy, wealth inequality plummeted during the Black Death and didn't reach pre-plague levels again for almost four hundred years.

Still, the "prelates, earls, barons and other great men" of European society were unwaveringly committed to restoring the pre–Black Death world. And in some sense, they achieved their goal of continuity. Unlike in the Indus Valley three thousand years prior, the plague didn't cause governments to disintegrate, states to collapse, and cities to be permanently abandoned. We still speak the same languages, live in many of the same countries, and walk the same city streets that bore witness to the Black Death's unimaginable mortality. Harappa, on the other hand, has lain in ruins for three millennia. No one can read its writing; we don't even know what language its residents spoke. In its ghostly abandonment and unfamiliarity, it can seem like Harappa failed where European societies succeeded in surviving. But embedded in, and somewhat obscured by, that continuity, there is also violence—the violence of a society passing through the fire of apocalypse and refusing to allow itself to be changed.

Chapter 5

HOW SOCIETY COLLAPSES BUT CIVILIZATION SURVIVES

Around forty-five hundred years ago, a young man walked off the first boat he'd ever been on straight into the biggest crowd he'd ever seen. The dock bustled with more kinds of activity than he knew was possible. Crews of men hauled huge slabs of granite off the barges that had carried them to Giza all the way from Egypt's southern frontier, nearly four hundred miles of winding river away. Others hoisted sacks of barley and wheat onto their shoulders, carrying them off to the town's bakeries and breweries. Groups of laborers, who had recently been as green and awed as the young man was, now marched in perfect unison to the chanted rhythm of their work songs, heading off as one to their crews' shifts in the pyramid field. The sound of metal tools striking stone echoed through the streets. Artists toiled in workshops, making pottery for the townspeople to use and figurines destined for tombs. Herds of cattle jostled and lowed as they were driven, unwittingly, toward slaughterhouses. Dozens of animals needed to be killed every day to feed the workers on the nation's most important project.

That sound, the cattle lowing, was one of the few the young man recognized from his life until now. He had grown up in the swampy land of the Nile Delta, where the great river split into many smaller fingers that reached toward the sea. In his town, everyone raised cattle, because they didn't have a choice. The swamps were all but impossible to farm, and they were especially inhospitable to the kind of farming that best served the Authority: the vast fields of barley and wheat that grew so readily along the riverbanks farther south. So the Authority taxed those farms and provinces, collected enormous stores of grain, and shipped some of it to the young man's village, where people had a different role. The Authority had commanded all the families in the village to dedicate themselves to raising cattle for the pyramid town. The meat was for the mess halls of the pyramid crews, who needed all the strength they could get during their months of toil. The king was counting on them to ensure his continued prosperity in the afterlife, which was the same thing as the country counting on them to ensure its future.

The young man had spent years tending his family's herds, overseeing the breeding season and the births that followed, driving the animals from pasture to pasture, and choosing the finest of them to join the Giza-bound herds each year. The animals hardly ever ended up on his family's table; he could count on two hands the number of times he'd tasted beef. Now, though, it was his turn to work on the pyramid and eat in the mess halls where meat from his herds and so many others was cooked and served daily.

Life in the pyramid town was strictly organized. The young man was assigned to a work gang along with the others from his region, and that gang was part of a crew of laborers. Each man was given a bed in the long rows of them in the barracks. They rose early and spent their days hauling stones up huge earthen ramps and levering them into place. Every day, the pyramid reached farther toward the sky, its point destined to be the first place touched each morning by the rays of the reborn sun god. Sometimes the young man caught a glimpse of painters and architects below, doing their more delicate work. They were the experts who lived here year-round and would be buried in their own cemetery in this most sacred and prestigious of places. Workers who died on the job, crushed by stones or falling from the scaffolding, would be buried here, too, though they couldn't hope for the same kinds of tombs even the painters could build for themselves. The young man knew it would be a great honor to rest here for his eternal life, but he still hoped he would be one of the lucky among them who got to go home.

The crews ate together at long tables in huge halls attached to the barracks. Every day there was meat, some of it likely provided by his family's own herds. The bakeries in town churned out unfathomable quantities of beer and bread for them. The young man rarely had a moment to himself. He was always with his gang and their crew. Sometimes the crews would compete to see who could complete a job fastest. His crew was respectable, and he was proud to be part of it. They sang work songs while they were on a shift and off. Their work, and their lives, depended on staying in sync with each other during dangerous tasks.

In the pyramid town, the young man met farmers and potters, carpenters and metalworkers, bakers and porters, hailing from towns and cities all along the length of the nation and beyond. Some had been brought to Giza to perform their usual jobs in service of the king; others, like him, had been conscripted into construction of the monuments, larger than any building they'd seen before or would see again. Some were foreigners from Nubia, Punt, and the desert lands to the east and west. The young man had known other lands existed beyond Egypt's borders, but he never thought he'd meet any of their people, much less work side by side with them. Some of these foreigners had come to Egypt willingly, in search of a place that would reward their expert craftsmanship and refined taste; the styles of pottery and other crafts developed here, near the capital, would go on to be copied throughout the provinces. Others had been taken captive and their labor extracted by force.

And then, after a season, the young man's work requirement was fulfilled, and his sojourn in Giza was over. The flood ended, planting would soon begin for the farmers, and the young man went home to the delta and his herds. Back in his old, familiar life, he would think of his months in the pyramid field, and he would miss it. It had been the most grueling work he'd ever done, every minute of every day regimented and accounted for. Nothing like the quiet, solitary hours he spent in the pastures with his herds. But he had loved the exhaustion, the camaraderie, and the sense of belonging that came from seeing how his crew's stones fit perfectly into the larger whole of the pyramid. The young man knew his work with the herds was just as essential to maintaining Egypt's balance and harmony. The king wouldn't have ordered his village to raise the animals otherwise. But alone in the delta's pastures, he didn't feel overwhelmed by the grandeur of the nation, the divinity of the king, the infallibility of the Nile. He didn't have much occasion to think about those things at all. In the pyramid field, he had finally known what it felt like to be a small part of ensuring Egypt's eternal greatness, and he would be proud of it for the rest of his life.

◉

At the same time that Harappa was experimenting with cooperative government, monumental public works, and social equality, another early state, half a continent away, had risen to great heights by taking the opposite approach. Around forty-five hundred years ago, at the height of pyramid building, Old Kingdom Egypt was one of the richest and most complex societies the world had ever seen, and it was as stratified as Harappa was egalitarian. A divine king ruled from the glorious capital of Memphis. He sat at the top of a sprawling cadre of nobles, priests, artists, architects, bureaucrats, scribes, and local governors, all of whom had a part to play in fulfilling the king's, and thus the state's, needs. Below them were peasant farmers and herders, who grew the crops and raised the animals the central government would redistribute to feed its people and fuel its vast construction projects. Social classes were rigid and hereditary, as strict as anything in medieval England three thousand years later.

Old Kingdom Egypt's social order was designed to take advantage of—and perhaps symbolically reflect—the predictable, reliable, and complementary structure of its natural world. The nation's territory hugged the banks of the Nile, occupying the lush river valley on either side and a bit of the desert beyond. Upper Egypt referred to the south of the country, closer to the Nile's source. Lower Egypt referred to the north, where the river split into tributaries that feed into the Mediterranean Sea. The two regions had once been separate, but around five thousand years ago, the kings of the First Dynasty founded the nation by uniting Upper and Lower Egypt into one complementary whole. The new central government's seat in Memphis, near modern-day Cairo, occupied the hinge point between the two regions, and it made sure their strengths and weaknesses reinforced each other. Ever after, Egypt's highest value would be *maat*, meaning truth, order, harmony, and balance.

Upper Egypt was long and skinny, meandering along with the river. Its wheat and barley fields depended on the annual flood, when the Nile would overflow its banks. Water and silt settled over the farmland of the river valley, irrigating and fertilizing it for the planting season to come. In good years, a surplus of grain was all but guaranteed. People had more than enough to feed their families and build up their household stores, as well as plenty to pay in taxes to the central government, which shipped surplus grain from Upper Egypt all over the country to feed the villages, cities, temples, and palaces, and stockpiled the rest in case of a bad harvest. The abundance of those years protected against the scarcity of the lean ones, which were few and far between.

To the north, Lower Egypt's river delta was swampy and wet all year round, making large-scale grain farming difficult. Instead, villagers there focused on herding cattle, sheep, and goats. They ate grain shipped in from Upper Egypt, as well as their own pigs, which couldn't be herded from place to place. But most of their other livestock was herded more than sixty miles south to Giza, where the animals fed the tens of thousands of workers who were gathered at any given time to build monuments and royal tombs, including the great pyramids.

The pyramids were a manifestation of the king's tremendous spiritual and political power, and they were also a cornerstone of Egypt's economy. At the height of pyramid building, the enterprise likely supported around two hundred and fifty thousand people, or a quarter of Egypt's total population during the Old Kingdom. Every villager who came to work on the pyramids and other royal tombs, or raised cattle to feed those workers, or grew enough grain to fill royal storehouses with

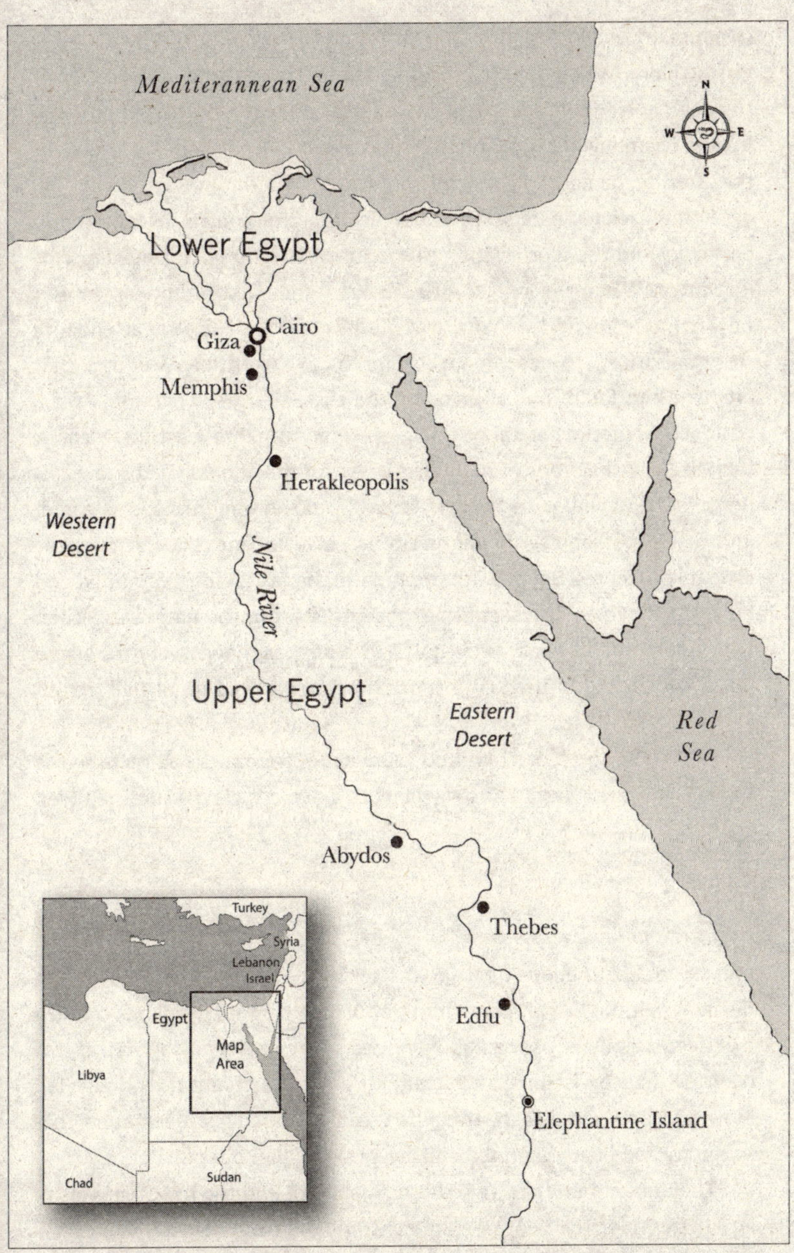

Ancient Egypt during the Old Kingdom

surpluses, played a small role in fulfilling the promise of Egypt's everlasting glory. When the king died, he would travel through the world of the dead to sit alongside the gods and guarantee the continued prosperity and harmony of his country. To make that journey and live forever in the afterlife, he needed a magnificent tomb.

Some archaeologists see this level of state control as inherently despotic, and the glorification of the king could indeed come at a violent price. When the rulers of the dynasty that first united Upper and Lower Egypt died, dozens or even hundreds of their elite attendants were sacrificed to accompany them to the afterlife. Although that practice had fallen out of favor by the time the great pyramids were built, construction of those staggering monuments was not without its risks; the skeletons of many workers entombed near Giza show evidence of heavy labor and broken bones. But the king's status as a god, and his responsibility for maintaining *maat*, meant that most people probably accepted Egypt's inherent inequality as divinely ordained and believed it served the sacred purpose of holding the nation together. Every person had a job, every job had a purpose, and every life had a place within the unified country's complex scaffolding of hierarchies and responsibilities.

And then, forty-two hundred years ago—around the same time the Indus Civilization began to struggle with a dry, erratic climate—it all fell apart.

◉

Ipuwer couldn't believe what he was seeing. Nothing in his life, or even his imagination, had prepared him for the horrors into which his country had descended. For as long as there had been an Egypt, the nation had been defined by its unshakable stability and its commitment to *maat*. Now, three hundred years after the great pyramids had been built, that harmony had been disrupted and Egypt had fallen out of balance.

The annual flood didn't arrive as it should, and the next year wasn't any better. Nor the next nor the next nor the next. Ipuwer, like everyone else, remembered good years and bad. But as a scribe in Memphis, he had access to records stretching back many centuries, and even there he couldn't find any memory of the floods being this low for this long. Wheat and barley withered in the fields of the river valley, and grain surpluses disappeared. There wasn't enough to eat this year, let alone save for the next. The swamps and marshes of the Nile Delta dried up, and the region's herds of cattle grew skinny and sickly. Even the pigs, who would eat anything, couldn't find enough food and water to fill their bellies. The animals started dying, and soon the people did, too.

Sand dunes crept closer and closer to the Nile's banks, turning farmland into desert. Desperate people ransacked the tombs of their ancestors for precious objects they could trade for something to eat. Malnourished women couldn't conceive, and of the babies who were born, many didn't live longer than a few days or months. People who had once celebrated times of good fortune with their neighbors now stole food from them, and then from their own family members. Generosity became an inconceivable luxury. The bloated corpses of the dead, too many to bury, choked the low Nile; when people went to gather drinking water, they had to push the bodies out of the way. Ipuwer had even heard hushed whispers about towns where people were so hungry they had started to eat each other. Some people, driven into hopelessness, walked into the river that had betrayed them and straight into a crocodile's jaws. If this was survival, they didn't want it. Better the afterlife.

The courtiers, scribes, and government officials Ipuwer had worked alongside in Memphis had once been among the richest and most powerful people in Egypt. Now, they were fleeing the palaces and cities. Their comfortable lives had been made possible by their estates' steady output of grain and their brimming storehouses. Once the floods failed, they burned through their stockpiles and found themselves helpless. The peasants who worked for them stopped trying to coax a harvest from the parched land and abandoned the estates without a word of warning. Ipuwer and his peers in the royal court hadn't known how to farm in the best of times, and much less now that the Nile had withdrawn its steady, dependable help. They had spent their lives reading, writing, administering the Authority's storehouses and wealth, tending to the king's body, and keeping his secrets. Such skills had no place in this brutal new reality. There was even talk of the king himself abandoning the capital. Ipuwer was surprised to find he didn't care. The king had failed to restore *maat*, his most important duty. He didn't deserve to even look upon the glorious tombs of his predecessors, much less be buried among those great pyramids.

Dispatches arrived from province after province in the south declaring themselves free of royal rule. These were quickly followed by news of war, as the newly independent regions fought each other for supremacy. The new warlords assumed the trappings and duties once reserved for the king alone. They wrote their names in the royal style, hoarded grain for their towns and allies, and refused to pay taxes or even acknowledge the existence of any leader above them. Ipuwer knew they were wrong to do so, but even he had to admit that since the king wouldn't be offering any help, everyone was on their own.

Violence always hovered at the edge of consciousness, threatening to shatter any fragile local peace. Farmers and herders who had never needed weapons when the flood was high and the state was strong now sought bows and spears. They used them to fend off the hungry and desperate, and when they grew hungry and desperate themselves, they used their weapons to attack other villages and towns. Egyptians had always been buried with their prized possessions; now people were buried with their weapons. Cemeteries swelled as death from hunger and violence swept the land.

Ipuwer had to make sure people remembered this dark age, so that it wouldn't happen again. He started to write down what he saw. In the face of unprecedented hardship and suffering, *maat*, once the moral web that held Egyptian society together, became an impossible ideal. "The land turns round as does a potter's wheel," he wrote. The orderly society of ancient Egypt had devolved into chaos. Everything was upside down.

◉

Ipuwer's *Admonitions of an Egyptian Sage* is one of the most famous ancient documents that purports to depict a societal collapse, and one of the most apocalyptic. Over four millennia, it has helped establish and reinforce our popular vision of collapse as a nightmare, a tragedy, and a worst-case scenario. We conjure visions of death and destruction on a massive scale. We see ruined cities and fallen civilizations decaying into dust. We imagine a postapocalyptic dark age, as the glories of the former world are rejected, abandoned, and forgotten.

Collapse means something far different to archaeologists, however. In 1988, anthropologist Joseph Tainter put forth what would become the most influential definition of the term: Collapse is "a rapid, significant loss of an established level of sociopolitical complexity." In other words, collapse is a political and economic process in which a complex, centralized society quickly disintegrates into smaller, less interconnected pieces.

A society that's growing in complexity will add more and more layers to its political organization, economy, and social hierarchies, as we saw on the north coast of Peru in response to El Niño. In a society that's collapsing, many of those layers will quickly disintegrate and disappear, as we saw when people abandoned Harappa to return to rural village life. An economy that had once supported many specialized jobs—certainly artisans and merchants, and perhaps politicians and urban planners—contracted to primarily agricultural work. Trade networks broke down, and communities became more self-reliant. People went from having many different kinds of lives, often in close proximity to each other, to having mostly the same kind of life, now spread out across an environmentally precarious landscape.

For archaeologists, collapse isn't an annihilation. It's an unraveling. Most ancient and modern states (and especially empires) are already built of smaller political units—cities, provinces, regions, the United States' fifty states—and they will usually collapse into their smaller constituent parts. If the United States were to hypothetically collapse, California, Texas, or New York City might go on existing as independent entities, now no longer connected by or answerable to a larger federal government. Or the boundaries we live within now could be redrawn. Florida could split into city-states like those that made up medieval Italy, or the Dakotas might join up with Montana and Idaho—or merge with the Canadian province of Manitoba or Saskatchewan. When nations dissolve in a collapse, old borders become irrelevant.

As it had for the Indus Civilization, collapse came for Egypt during a prolonged drought associated with the 4.2-kiloyear event, the period when environments all over the world became drier forty-two hundred years ago. In Egypt, the environmental crisis took the form of critically low Nile floods. In a sediment core drilled deep into a lake in the Nile Delta, scientists observed a sharp decline in pollen from grassy wetland plants around forty-two hundred years ago, indicating the normally swampy delta was very dry. Another core taken from a desert lake fed by the Nile showed it nearly disappeared entirely around the same time. Between forty-five hundred and forty-two hundred years ago, the drought caused plants that held riverbank soils in place near one of the Nile's sources in Ethiopia to wither and die. More and more sediment fell into the already low Nile, eventually settling into lagoons in the delta and forming layers that can be seen in paleoclimate cores.

This modern paleoclimate data confirms ancient records from Egypt itself. On a monument known as the Palermo Stone, scribes recorded the height of dozens of Nile floods throughout the Old Kingdom, allowing archaeologists to calculate their average over time. During the First Dynasty, when Egypt was unified under one king, the flood was an average of 7.6 feet high. It fell during the Second and Third Dynasties, swung upward a bit in the Fourth when the great pyramids were built, and by the Fifth—the penultimate dynasty of the Old Kingdom—the average flood had dropped again to 5.5 feet.

The Palermo Stone stops there, but archaeological evidence from Elephantine Island, on ancient Egypt's southern border, shows the water level continued to fall. There, the receding river exposed more and more land over the course of the Old Kingdom, allowing people to build settlements lower and lower on the island, ever closer to the river's banks. The lowest settlement—and, therefore, the lowest water level—is dated to the Sixth Dynasty, the last of the Old Kingdom.

As the flood levels fell, the desert—the world of the dead, in ancient Egyptian cosmology—crept ever closer to the vibrant, green world of the living in the Nile Valley. During the Fifth Dynasty, hunting scenes painted in Egyptian tombs began to include desert animals and landscapes where scenes of farming or religious rituals would have been before, and desiccated desert beetles have been found in Sixth Dynasty tombs. The Sahara Desert expanded, leaving behind the fossilized stumps and roots of long dead trees, as well as the remains of abandoned settlements in what had once been grasslands. Many ancient Egyptian texts themselves mention sand. In his *Admonitions*, Ipuwer wrote, "the desert is throughout the land"; a biography of a local leader described him governing during a time when "the land was in the wind," probably referring to the sand blowing off the encroaching dunes. Several texts from the time also link the appearance of sandbanks and sandbars in and around the Nile to periods of famine, as farming became impossible when the water dropped low enough to expose those river features.

While the life-giving waters of the Nile fell to crisis levels, extreme weather also took the form of infrequent but catastrophically heavy rains that could lead to flash floods. In some tombs from the end of the Old Kingdom, archaeologists have uncovered thick layers of mud deposited by those floods, much like the sediment left behind by El Niño rains around the Peruvian temple pyramids. Ancient Egyptians depended on the predictable floods of the Nile, not the chaos of torrential storms, and they considered rain to be a curse sent by the god of the desert. In some excavations, the mud layers are interspersed with layers of sand, blown in from the expanding Sahara. As the environment grew unpredictable, it pulled Egypt farther and farther away from its foundational balance.

A strong centralized state, like the one that organized the construction of the great pyramids, may have been able to withstand the challenge the low floods posed by throwing its might behind taxation, distribution of grain from its storehouses, and religious rituals aimed at returning order to the Nile's cycles (or at least, increasing people's trust that such a thing was still under the king's control). Egypt's kings certainly would have tried. But by the time the climate change of the

4.2-kiloyear event arrived, political struggles had already weakened the power of the Egyptian monarchy.

Throughout the Old Kingdom, Egyptian politics and culture had revolved around the capital of Memphis. Important positions in the government were filled by members of the royal family, and the governors sent to lead the provinces always returned to be buried near the king. Beyond their political assignments, they had no connection to the region they ruled nor to the people who would fill their posts after them. The job of a governor during most of the Old Kingdom was to ensure that each region did its part to keep the centralized state running smoothly. Everything was in service to the king, the unquestioned head of it all.

But as the Egyptian state grew more and more complex, with more and more layers of bureaucrats and priests and scribes required to manage it, the royal family was forced to loosen its grip on government positions and, with them, direct control of the regions that made up the nation. The king began filling important posts with skilled outsiders rather than his own relatives, ceding control of important regions to people who had less reason to be loyal to his rule. Beginning in the Fifth Dynasty, about a hundred years before the collapse began, princesses started to be married off to high-ranking officials and members of other noble families, elevating their husbands' stature instead of keeping nobles and bureaucrats resolutely below members of the monarchy. Meanwhile, increasingly ambitious governors began to appoint their own sons to fill their positions after their deaths, creating local dynasties that mirrored and rivaled the royal family. They copied the architecture of royal tombs to build their own, now in their home regions instead of near the capital. One particularly presumptuous local leader even started to write his name inside an oval, a style previously reserved only for the nobility; the same man would eventually build himself a pyramid for a tomb. The message was clear: The king was no longer the sole and supreme ruler of Egypt. The governors were closing the gap between them and seizing more and more power for themselves.

By the time Pepy II, the last king of the Sixth Dynasty and of the Old Kingdom itself, took the throne, the king's power had greatly eroded.

He tried everything to rein in his governors, especially in distant Upper Egypt. He alternately granted and took away titles and responsibilities from the southern governors, seemingly oscillating between placating and subordinating them. He created a new office of the southern vizier and required the governors to report to him. He built new grain storehouses in powerful southern cities to collect taxes and assert the central government's presence there. But the governors of Upper Egypt continued to consolidate their power throughout Pepy II's sixty-four long and ineffectual years on the throne. When he finally died, Pepy II left behind a crisis of succession, as potential heirs from at least eight wives vied to rule. None of these "kinglets" of the Seventh Dynasty managed to consolidate power or put a stop to the political chaos. Ancient Egyptian historians remembered it as a time when the state had seventy kings in seventy days.

Into this political crisis came the worst of the low floods. The disruption of the Nile's natural cycles almost certainly made a series of weak kings seem even weaker, as they failed in their divine duty to restore balance to Egypt's environment and their practical responsibility to distribute resources. Fed up, the provinces of Upper Egypt declared themselves free of any king's control. The construction of pyramids and other monuments abruptly ceased, and Egypt's capital soon moved from the glorious city of Memphis to the provincial town of Herakleopolis. Ancient Egyptian historians recorded a break in their lists of kings after the Sixth Dynasty, the last of the Old Kingdom. Socially complex and politically unified Egypt unraveled into smaller, independent parts, with no single ruler governing it all. An already weak central government proved useless at mitigating an environmental crisis. The solution was collapse.

◉

Ankhtifi was no stranger to waging war. Any ruler had to be, in these times of parched earth and famine. And especially a ruler with ambition, which Ankhtifi certainly was. He was an independent upstart, a nobody who had become somebody by stepping up when everyone else was afraid to take charge. With no king to answer to, he controlled his own army and deployed it to his own ends. Some might call him a warlord. He called himself a governor, a general, a leader when people needed one the most.

Ankhtifi kicked off his conquests by taking control of one province in Egypt's far south. Then shortly thereafter he received a divine message from the falcon god Horus that the nearby province of Edfu was in trouble, too. When he arrived with his army, he found Edfu neglected by its ineffectual leader and at war with itself. Ankhtifi quickly reimposed order and forced reconciliation between factions. So many places had fallen into chaos now that Upper Egypt had broken free of the king. But kings, as all of Upper Egypt had seen as drought ravaged their crops and desert sand blew into their towns, couldn't protect people far from their capitals when the cycles of nature broke down. Ankhtifi was no king, and he didn't want to be. He was something new. Something better.

Now he and his soldiers stood outside of the walls of Thebes, one of the most powerful places in Upper Egypt. Ankhtifi had come to do battle and bring Thebes under his control. They would be lucky to have a such a leader, devoted as he was to his people's well-being and creative in his means for achieving it. His army could expertly maintain peace but also stoke fear among provinces far and wide. Thebes should welcome him with open gates and gratitude, Ankhtifi thought. But perhaps it was better to show its people he was worthy of their loyalty by fighting for it.

And yet, no Thebans responded to his challenge. The city walls stayed locked, and everyone inside ignored Ankhtifi's presence. His soldiers roamed the whole province, searching for someone, anyone, to fight, thereby proving their leader's strength. Ankhtifi refused to consider the other possibility, that the army of Thebes didn't take his threat seriously enough to waste its energy on a battle. Other leaders might have seen such disregard as a humiliation worse than defeat. Not Ankhtifi. He knew it was because the Thebans were terrified to lose to him, as they inevitably would—or at least that's how he would tell the story.

Ankhtifi returned to his province, unbowed by his failure to expand his territory this time. Thebes might have eluded his grasp, but conquest wasn't the only way to grow his influence and might. Ankhtifi always welcomed refugees, who would soon become his subjects. His military accomplishments and the power he fought for would mean nothing if he didn't use it to take care of his people. Without him, they would be lost, especially during these times of drought and starvation.

When Ankhtifi died, he left no heir, and the tiny kingdom he amassed in Egypt's far south dissolved as quickly as an unfired clay pot under one of the desert god's rainstorms. His tomb would stand for eternity, however, just like the neglected resting places of the kings near the old capital. He had hired artisans to carve on its pillars the story of his life, all that he had achieved, and the way he wanted to be remembered: "I am the hero without equal," his tomb proclaimed, reverberating deep into the future.

◉

It never would have occurred to the kings of the Old Kingdom to justify their power. They were gods on earth, and their right to authority was divine and unquestioned. They didn't serve Egypt; Egypt served them. The local leaders of the post-collapse era, called the First Intermediate Period, didn't enjoy those privileges. They didn't have a sacred right to their subjects' loyalty and material support. They had to earn it by protecting them from the turmoil of apocalypse.

One of those leaders was Ankhtifi, whom archaeologists know about from his boastful tomb texts, which reveal the new rules for those vying for power in the political vacuum that arose after the unified state of the Old Kingdom broke apart. In this post-collapse world, Ankhtifi had to fight for, defend, and continually legitimize his social and political standing through his actions, not his divine identity. His concerns were decidedly local and material, in sharp contrast to the spiritually focused and geographically distant kings of the Old Kingdom. "I gave bread to the hungry and clothing to the naked; I anointed those who had no cosmetic oil; I gave sandals to the barefooted; I gave a wife to him who had no wife. I took care of the towns of Hefat and Hormer in every [situation of crisis, when] the sky was clouded and the earth [was parched] . . . All of Upper Egypt was dying of hunger and people were eating their children, but I did not allow anybody to die of hunger in this [province]," the tomb texts read.

The writing on the pillars of Ankhtifi's tomb almost certainly exaggerate his personal influence and success, just by nature of the form. But they also represent the emergence of a value system and political ideology that were almost the exact opposite of the Old Kingdom's. For the first time since the formation of the Egyptian state, rulers were answerable to their people, not the other way around.

During the Old Kingdom, the price of a maximally complex, unified Egypt had been extreme inequality and rigid social roles that enforced and maintained the state's political and economic hierarchy. Its collapse revealed other, long-suppressed possibilities for how society might be organized and whom might be allowed to benefit from it. During the First Intermediate Period, people shook off their old roles, with their attendant old rules, and staked claim to new ones. Some people, like Ankhtifi, clawed their way straight into positions of leadership and power, reinventing what those concepts meant in the process. For many others, the change was more subtle, if no less profound.

Archaeologists have long noticed a sharp increase in the number of graves in Egyptian towns and villages during the First Intermediate Period. Until recently, this was taken as evidence of mass mortality during and after the collapse, possibly due to famine and provincial wars like the ones Ankhtifi waged. But some archaeologists have started to see the First Intermediate Period graves differently. Tombs from that era are not only more numerous than their predecessors, they are also much sturdier and better equipped. Perhaps the increase in tombs archaeologists are able to find doesn't mean more people were dying from violence or starvation after the state collapsed. It could mean, instead, that without the strictures and demands of a centralized state, provincial commoners grew richer and more willing and able to assert their preferences, capabilities, and identities in this life and the next. The kinds of people who would have previously been buried in simple pits now had the resources, and the motivations, to build tombs able to survive for four thousand years.

Many of these new provincial tombs bordered on opulent, especially compared to what commoners could hope for before. They were filled with offerings like mirrors, alabaster headrests, gemstone amulets, and gold. Luxuries once reserved only for the tomb of the king and the capital's highest nobles, like funerary spells and dioramas depicting daily activities, became common for regular people across Egypt. Such an abundance of these items implies the existence—even flourishing—of craftspeople all over the provinces who had the time and opportunity to devote to artistic pursuits, rather than just the manufacture of practical objects. It seems that after the collapse, more people all over Egypt were living lives of, if not exactly luxury, then at least comfort and possibility.

Perhaps driven by artisans with more resources and newfound time for their own projects, a previously suppressed creativity exploded in post-collapse Egypt. When the Old Kingdom government was powerful and Egypt was unified, archaeologists find the same artistic styles prevailing throughout the country. As the government collapsed and the First Intermediate Period got underway, artists, architects, and craftspeople across the country began experimenting. Architects started designing and building local tombs that looked nothing like those of Old Kingdom royalty, and painters started decorating them with new kinds of scenes: "files of soldiers and hunters, mercenaries engaged in battle, and religious festivals," as well as the daily tasks of people with more humble occupations, such as spinners and weavers. Potters who had once been limited to making elegant but time-intensive oval-shaped vases, presumably dictated by the tastes of the royal court and capital, now started exploring the full range of forms they could make on the potter's wheel, a relatively new technology in Egypt. In Upper Egypt, pots started to have wide bases, sometimes appearing almost baggy—an easy, efficient shape to throw on the wheel. In Lower Egypt, potters, and their customers, preferred long and thin vessels. Objects, texts, and art made during the First Intermediate Period "exhibit[ed] an astonishing degree of originality and creativity"—even as they were often also "simply ugly and incompetently made." That drop in quality was taken by previous generations of scholars as proof that ancient Egypt's civilization had fallen from its former height. But the proliferation of local styles and new kinds of artwork doesn't have to be a sign of cultural decline. Instead, it may be an emblem of liberation enabled by collapse.

Previously unshakable social roles also began to change after the Old Kingdom's collapse. When Egyptian society was stable, text in women's tombs tended to praise their beauty and other "passive" virtues and emphasize their connection to their husbands and other family members. In the First Intermediate Period, however, a woman named Djehutinakht boasted of ascending the social ladder to become a noblewoman and, like Ankhtifi, took pride in her ability to "[give] bread to the hungry" and otherwise provide for her people. "For the first time," a woman centered her "resources and morality" in the official story of her life. It only took a societal collapse to make it possible.

One group seems to have been especially resilient to the First Intermediate Period's political and environmental challenges: Egyptian commoners. Evidence of their daily lives is difficult to find, as the remains of many villages and towns from the Old Kingdom and First Intermediate Period lie under settlements from later in ancient Egyptian history, or even beneath the current water table. But in the village of Abydos, about two hundred and fifty miles south of Memphis in Upper Egypt, commoners' houses from these periods happen to be covered by just a thin layer of desert sand. Despite being symbolically important as the home of the first kings to unify Egypt—and later, as the center of the Osiris cult, which grew in popularity during the First Intermediate Period—Abydos was also a fairly standard village, occupied mostly by farmers and their families, now precious to archaeologists because it is one of the few such places they can study.

The archaeologist Matthew Douglas Adams, along with a team of expert Egyptian workers, mapped and excavated the remains of nine ancient houses in Abydos to study how commoners experienced the collapse of the Old Kingdom. The workers hauled away basket after basket of sand and sieved it through mesh screens to separate out any artifacts.

Most were broken pieces of pottery—"Millions, billions" of them, Adams remembers, exaggerating only slightly. Once the houses' mud brick walls were exposed and identified, the excavation became much more delicate. Workers sat in the middle of each long-abandoned room and used trowels to scrape away layer after layer of earth, gradually moving back in time. They carefully bagged and labeled every piece of pottery, broken animal bone, and burnt bit of wood and seed, remnants of ancient hearths and the meals people once cooked in them.

What Adams found ran counter to everything the ancient scribe Ipuwer, in his *Admonitions*, said about the First Intermediate Period. Not only did these Abydos residents not suffer from an extreme economic decline as the Old Kingdom collapsed, nothing about their lives seems to have changed much at all. Some houses and storage facilities got smaller over time, which might signal a downturn in their inhabitants' fortunes. But other houses and storerooms got larger. Everyone, from those living in the town's biggest houses to those living in the smallest, had access to goods that arrived in Abydos by trade, such as grinding stones and certain pigments, even after the Old Kingdom government ceased to exist. Abydos never received much outside help, either before or after the collapse; Adams found the broken remains of only a few of the stamped clay seals affixed to shipments of redistributed grain or other resources. The village appears to have mostly taken care of itself, no matter what was happening in the capital or the country at large.

None of this means there wasn't a famine, or at least some hard years, that touched Abydos at the end of the Old Kingdom. Archaeological excavation can reveal much about ancient people's lives, but it usually can't pick out relatively brief changes that happen on the scale of years or even decades. It also can't peer into the minds or hearts of past people, unless they were among the very, very few—like Ipuwer—who wrote down their feelings and perspectives. The people of Abydos may have very well endured some terrible years they never forgot. They may have worried just as much as Ipuwer about the unprecedented loss of unity and harmony in Egypt, and what that political earthquake meant for their lives. But the remains of their houses tell us they never suffered a material or cultural dark age. Perhaps the collapse itself enabled the village's persistence, by empowering local leaders to navigate the apocalypse in ways that would best serve their people instead of the interests of a faraway king.

The villagers of Abydos and places like it may have been at the bottom of Egypt's social order, but that meant they were already equipped with the survival skills they needed to make it through the political apocalypse of a state collapse relatively unscathed. The elites, on the other hand, weren't so lucky. They lived off the labor of others, from the farmers harvesting grain on royal estates to the rotating cadre of workers building the pyramids. And so when Egypt suddenly became less complex—and more equal—in the wake of societal collapse, they had nowhere to turn. "The picture of the state in ancient Egypt has historically been that of the all-powerful king controlling everything, and if you're lucky he'll see to it that you get your little share," Adams says. Everyone else belonged to a "nameless mass of peasantry." But that's merely how the elites "wanted the world to look," and how they depicted it in their texts and art. It doesn't mean it was true.

◉

To Ipuwer, whose *Admonitions* has influenced how generations of scholars think about the First Intermediate Period, the rupture of the state under weak kings was a tragedy that incited almost unspeakable horrors. He conjured images of anarchy, starvation, murder, infanticide, a Nile choked by dead bodies, and suicide by crocodile. These indelible images influenced how ancient Egyptians remembered their own history and shaped what generations of modern Egyptologists expected to find when they studied the First Intermediate Period.

Ipuwer wrote his *Admonitions* as a warning—not about the effects of drought or the agonies of famine but about the loss of kingship and the breakdown of a social hierarchy in which he had been at the top. Scribes like Ipuwer were highborn and spent their lives in the orbit of the king and his court. To him, the true horror of the apocalypse he describes is how elites like himself had fallen, while the fortunes of those beneath them improved. "The highborn are full of lamentations, and the poor are full of joy," he wrote. "Every town saith: 'Let us drive out the powerful from our midst . . . The possessor of wealth now spends the night thirsty . . . he who had no shade is now the possessor of shade, while the erstwhile possessors of shade are now in the full blast of the storm," he wrote, foreshadowing the similar sentiments recorded by elite post–Black Death chroniclers three thousand years later.

By writing about a time when his country had turned upside down, Ipuwer argued for what ancient Egyptian society should look like when it was right side up: hierarchical, authoritarian, and profoundly unequal. To him, the violation and inversion of that social order was in and of itself an apocalypse worthy of being depicted in nightmarish terms, no matter what the actual experience of people like Ankhtifi or the villagers of Abydos had been. But unlike in medieval Europe, where states would not collapse in the wake of an apocalypse, common Egyptians found themselves free of elite control in the First Intermediate Period. Ipuwer's experience didn't reflect their own, and he no longer had any power to impose it upon them.

After about one hundred and fifty years of fragmentation, Egypt was eventually reunited under the kings of the Middle Kingdom. But Egypt wasn't the same country it had been before the collapse, and it never would be again. The middle class stayed influential, cultural and political power permanently shifted to the former provinces, and the new kings strove to justify their rule in ways those of the Old Kingdom never could have imagined. Statues of the new kings show them with what Egyptologist Ellen Morris describes as "careworn brows," eye bags, and "uncommonly large ears," as if they were exhausted by their responsibility to listen to and care for their subjects. Following Ankhtifi's lead, they cast themselves as "good shepherds" capable of tending to the nation—a nation that had learned, in the crucible of collapse, that it could live without a king. It became part of the monarch's job to continually convince his subjects they didn't want to.

As part of that propaganda campaign, Ipuwer's text and others like it were copied and recopied by generations of scribes, preserving the elite perspective on collapse and entrenching it as the only possible reality. The *Admonitions* purported to document a universal dark age, but its true purpose became preserving the power of those who already had it. It vividly shows us what is lost during collapse, but it strenuously ignores all that can be gained.

◉

By the time the people of the village learned they no longer had a king, they'd been on their own for years. The floods had failed, and failed again. They'd scrounged up enough wheat from their meager stalks and dusty storehouses to make it through one year, and then the next. They had nothing left over for the Authority's tax collector, and they prayed to the gods he wouldn't come during these years of famine. He didn't. The people were too relieved to wonder why.

The occasional shipment of grain kept arriving from somewhere, stretching their paltry harvests just long enough to be manageable. Maybe the grain had been sent from the new capital in the north, rumored to house what was left of the royal court. Or maybe it had come from one of the neighboring provinces, somewhere with a new leader who was trying to earn their attention and gratitude and tempt them to join his followers. The villagers appreciated the extra grain, wherever it was coming from. But they preferred to live how they always had: unnoticed and unimportant to anyone with ambitions that extended further than making the best of the next harvest.

Traders still came through the village, and most of the time, the people still had enough to barter for what they needed. From these travelers, they heard rumors about towns where the famine was so bad that people had resorted to cannibalism, suicide, even infanticide. The people shuddered in horror, but they also noticed that those rumors always seemed to be about a town just beyond the end of the traders' routes, places they'd heard about but never seen for themselves.

For years, the Authority didn't command anyone from their village to report to the pyramid fields because, the people eventually realized, there was no Authority anymore, nor would there be any new pyramids. The first generation of young men not to be called up rued their misfortune, devastated to miss this rite of passage and their chance to see the world beyond the village. The next generation barely knew of the tradition. If they thought of it at all, they were relieved not to have to travel through the lawless spaces between provinces as the traders did, happy to never be forced to find out if the stories about not-so-faraway cannibals were true.

Without the demands of the Authority, the people of the village found they had more free time and more space to think about how they wanted to spend it. They were responsible only for themselves, and none of their resources were diverted to support the king and his court. Potters started throwing easier, faster vessel shapes so they could spend more time making miniatures of daily life in the village. Some were intended for the tombs of their friends, and some they made just because they enjoyed it. The villagers were delighted to see themselves and their activities represented in scenes populated by tiny clay figures, as only nobles and bureaucrats had once been. Farmers, with less work to do during the years of low floods, tried their hands at painting. Women, who were better at seeing how to fairly divide up the disappointing harvests, tried their hands at leading. The villagers always told the traders and others who passed through that their lives weren't terribly different with or without a king, before the drought and during it, as members of a unified state or a fractured one. But generations later, they would look at who they had been able to become, and they would realize how much they had changed.

Chapter 6

HOW POSTAPOCALYPTIC SOCIETIES REINVENT THEMSELVES

In 1841, the American diplomat and explorer John Lloyd Stephens set out by cargo ship from New York City, bound for Mexico's Yucatán Peninsula. He had been there briefly about a year before, along with his traveling companion, the British artist Frederick Catherwood, at the end of a tour of Central America and southern Mexico during which they had explored towering pyramids, stone temples, and ancient monuments carved with portraits of ancient kings and gods. In Yucatán, too, "we received vague, but, at the same time, reliable intelligence of the existence of numerous and extensive cities, desolate and in ruins," Stephens wrote. But Catherwood had fallen ill, and they had to return to the United States before they could find and document the region's ruins.

Now they were back in the peninsula, ready to see its ancient wonders for themselves. The expedition would be, Stephens believed, "the most extensive journey ever made by a stranger" in the region. Whereas ancient Egyptian pyramids and Greek temples were well-trodden attractions for European and American tourists by the mid-nineteenth century, the ruins scattered across the Yucatán Peninsula were shrouded in mystery, impossible to reach without the help of local guides and just as difficult to understand.

Over the course of seven months, Stephens and Catherwood would visit the ruins of forty-four cities, including Uxmal, Tulum, and Chichén Itzá. "With but few exceptions, all [these sites] were lost, buried, and unknown," Stephens wrote. The sites were in disrepair, with dense tropical vegetation threatening to topple and subsume even their most impressive buildings. "It has been the fortune of the author to step between them and the entire destruction to which they are destined; and it is his hope to snatch from oblivion these perishing, but still gigantic memorials of a mysterious people." Indeed, these cities wouldn't remain obscure much longer. Stephens's travelogue of the expedition became a bestseller, its texts accompanied by Catherwood's haunting, detailed engravings of abandoned ancient cities half-consumed by forest and jungle.

The last ancient city Stephens and Catherwood visited on their tour was Aké. About twenty miles east of Mérida, the state capital of Yucatán, Aké's ruins sat adjacent to a hacienda that had itself seen better days. "The only shelter we could obtain was a miserable little hut, full of fleas, which no sweeping could clear out. We had considered all our rough work over, but again, and within a day's journey of Mérida, we were in bad straits," Stephens wrote.

The next morning, the hacienda owner and six Maya people who worked there growing corn and raising cattle took the explorers to see Aké's ruins. Even overgrown and crumbling, it was clear that the city had once been impressive, possessing a "rude grandeur, perhaps equal to any that ever existed in the country," Stephens wrote. The buildings had been constructed with unusually enormous stones, and one pyramid was topped with an array of columns, an architectural feature "entirely different from any we had seen." A later foreign visitor would speculate that Aké had been built by giants, but Stephens was more reserved in his theorizing. An early advocate for the idea that contemporary Maya people were the descendants of the ancient pyramid builders, Stephens correctly proposed that Aké's stylistic peculiarities signified that it was older than other sites he and Catherwood had visited.

Clearly Aké and the other Maya sites had once been grand cities, Stephens thought. But no one seemed to know why, or when, they were abandoned. Before he and Catherwood arrived, "the existence of these ruins was entirely unknown" to people in cities as close as Mérida, and the local Maya people who lived around them supposedly had "never bestowed upon them one passing thought" about their possible origins, time period, or ultimate fate. How had these places' histories and achievements—even their locations—been so thoroughly forgotten? Searching for an explanation, Stephens found himself conjuring visions of apocalypse: "Involuntarily we turn for a moment to the frightful scenes of which this now desolate region must have been the theatre; the scenes of blood, agony, and wo[e] which preceded the desolation or abandonment of these cities."

Stephens's romantic accounts of the lost ruins of ancient cities across Central America and southern Mexico, and his conjectures about the violence and upheaval that led to their downfall, were widely read in the nineteenth century and would go on to form the foundations of Maya archaeology. In the nearly two centuries since his travelogues were published, generations of archaeologists have devoted their careers to understanding the apocalypse Stephens could only speculate about. As in ancient Egypt, they've found evidence of a centuries-long political and religious order collapsing during a time of unprecedented drought. But they've also started to understand how Maya people rebuilt and reimagined what society meant, and who it was for, in order to thrive in a postapocalyptic world—including and especially in Aké.

◉

In the year AD 700, it was market day in Aké, and the humid air buzzed with activity. The woman nestled the last steaming tamale into the large clay pot, then strapped the pot to her back using her long colorful shawl. She'd bought the shawl at a previous market day, its vibrant red stripes a reminder it had come all the way from the mountains of the Mixtec people, where women raised tiny insects in their cactus fields and ground them up into a crimson dye. Kings had their palace and temple walls painted with murals containing the pigment, and the woman was delighted to have a little piece of the color for herself, although the shawl was a tool as much as it was an accessory. Nothing she owned was purely decorative. Even the most beautiful things had a practical use.

The woman closed the gate of her family's compound and joined the stream of people walking toward the center of Aké. She chatted with her neighbors about when they thought the rains would start and what they were planting to prepare. As they got closer to the city center, the buildings grew larger and the crowd denser. She greeted friends who lived in other neighborhoods, happy for the chance to run into them. As the earthen paths met the limestone-paved road that connected Aké to other towns and cities, they were joined by traveling merchants and people whose clothing and hairstyles signaled they were from elsewhere. They all walked together to the center of Aké and entered the large plaza flanked by towering pyramids and temples where the king and his priests lived. Other than market days, the woman came to the center only on important holidays, when she and the rest of Aké would gather below the pyramids to watch the king make offerings to the gods and the ancestors. Sometimes the rituals enacted atop the temples were dour and severe—like the days when the king was compelled by tradition or circumstance to pierce his tongue with spines and offer up his own blood—but usually the ceremonies were more joyful and followed by a feast.

The woman found an open spot among the other sellers, spread her shawl on the ground, and placed the tamale pot on top. She would sell or trade as many as she could while people were hungry from their journeys to the plaza—some had walked a lot farther than she had—and use what she acquired to make her own purchases later. People were hungry, and business was brisk. She traded her tamales for cacao beans and bolts of cotton cloth carried by the traveling merchants, which she knew almost anyone in the market would be happy to accept. She also took corn, tomatoes, chiles, and beans, especially from people who also lived in Aké and brought their modest harvest surpluses to trade with.

She glanced over at the pyramid at the base of the plaza and saw the king sitting atop it, in a throne positioned amid its columns. His colorful cape glowed in the shade provided by the thatched roof over his head, and a line of diplomats and even some of the wealthier merchants extended down the pyramid's large stairs, each waiting their turn to show the king of Aké what their town or city had to offer him.

The king and his father before him had overseen the remodeling of many of Aké's older temples, built more than four centuries before. The monarchs had directed their architects and masons to use smaller stones to build new facades. It was the new style, and they wanted their city to look as modern as any other. But the rulers had decided to keep this pyramid as it was, so that its crown of columns and staircase of imposing boulders would serve as a symbol of Aké's antiquity. It may not have been the largest or most powerful city in the region, but it was one of the oldest, and clearly the royal family felt that gave them a certain cachet.

The woman caught a glimpse of a jaguar skin being unfurled in front of the king, and then her eyes drifted to a group of war captives who were bound and kneeling off to the side of the platform. She turned back to her customers, willing away memories of an attack by a rival city she'd seen as a child. Aké's soldiers had repelled the would-be invaders, but her uncle, who'd fought in the battle, had been taken. She'd always wondered if he'd been sold at a market like this one, somewhere far away from home.

After a few hours, the remaining tamales were getting cold, and the woman decided she'd sold enough to fund the rest of her day. She looked for the vendors from the coast selling cakes of salt wrapped in palm leaves, and she bought a few more than she thought she would need before the next market day. She also found a large obsidian blade, mined from a volcano far to the south, which her husband could chip into knives and other tools. With the cacao beans and cotton she had left, and the rest of her tamales, she bought a new serving dish—not strictly necessary for her household, but beautifully painted with an image of the rain god Chaac emerging from the watery depths of the underworld.

The plate came from one of the cities in the south, the trader told her, whose size and sophistication made Aké look like a hamlet. They had more water there, too—rivers, lakes, canals, rain—not just the underground pools people relied on up here, the trader said with a slight shudder. The woman could tell he found the cenotes a bit frightening, the idea that the earth wasn't a solid thing here, that it could give way to the underworld so easily. But she'd always found them miraculous, a divine connection between the worlds that sustained life in this one. Not in the mood for a debate, she told the trader she hoped he could see his city soon and started the walk back home.

◉

Most of the cities Stephens and Catherwood visited, and much of what we tend to think of as ancient Maya culture, flourished during a time known as the Classic period. Between around AD 300 to 900, divine kings who traced their dynastic lines back to gods in the mythological past ruled over Maya city-states like Aké, and the most powerful dynasties conquered and controlled entire networks of towns and cities. The Maya world, which spanned more than 150,000 square miles across what is now southern Mexico, Guatemala, Belize, and Honduras, was never united under the control of a single state or empire, however. Instead, alliances and rivalries between city-states shifted constantly as wars were won or lost, royal families intermarried, monarchs died or were overthrown, and treaties were negotiated and broken.

Scribes and artists recorded much of this history in books, murals, and stone monuments, complete with precise dates and portraits of the major players. Astronomers and priests tracked the movements of the stars and other planets to create a complex system of interlocking calendars that organized various cycles of time. Commoners lived in small houses and neighborhoods scattered around city centers, tending to gardens and farm plots nestled within the surrounding forests. What they couldn't grow or make locally, they acquired at markets. Roads paved with white limestone stucco, called *sacbe'ob*, connected outlying neighborhoods to the plazas and pyramids in their city centers, and a

Key sites in the Maya world

few even longer *sacbe'ob* ran between cities, easing the long journeys of merchants and pilgrims. A nearly twenty-mile-long *sacbe* connected Aké to the ancient city and pilgrimage site of Izamal.

The enormous stones used to build Aké's Pyramid of the Columns indicate it may have been constructed even before the Classic period, as early as between 100 BC and AD 300. It would take until the Early Classic, however, for a full-blown city to grow up around the sacred monument, which happened between the years 300 and 600. Although the building we can call the Pyramid of the Columns retained its original, ancient look, many of Aké's other monumental buildings were remodeled using smaller, easier-to-manage stones starting around 600. The city reached its height around 700, with a population of nineteen thousand.

Like other Classic period cities, Aké was economically prosperous, connected to extensive trade and diplomatic networks, and the religious heart of its community. Everyone from royals to commoners used colorful ceramics intricately decorated with glyphs, human figures, and mythological scenes. Events ranging from market days to religious festivals happened in the city's plaza, and as such it was kept meticulously clean. The spirits of gods and ancestors were believed to inhabit the temples surrounding it, and the succession of divine monarchs who lived alongside them were responsible for keeping Aké—and the rest of the Maya world—in working order through rituals (including sacrifice and bloodletting) that placated the deities and diplomacy that managed Aké's relationship with other city-states, near and far.

The Maya world of the Classic period was a dynamic place. The influence of various city-states grew and shrank; merchants vied with the nobility for wealth and power, established trade routes, and facilitated the transport of goods over long distances; and people moved from place to place with relative ease. But it was also, for the most part, politically, economically, and ideologically stable. That would all change—at first slowly, and then quickly—as an apocalypse rippled up from the south.

At first, the people of Aké would have heard rumors of faraway warfare, in what is now the Petexbatun region of Guatemala, three hundred miles south of Aké. In the mid- to late 700s, when Aké was at its apogee, cities and towns throughout the Petexbatun suddenly turned themselves into walled fortresses, and archaeologists have found evidence that some of the most impressive buildings, even inside the fortifications, were attacked and destroyed. By whom, and why, remain mysterious. The region had plenty of water and doesn't appear to have faced another environmental challenge at the time. Until the war began, the Petexbatun region's population was stable, and there's no evidence of foreign invasion or attempted conquest. Perhaps the low-level tension that typically simmered between Classic Maya city-states boiled over into outright and widespread warfare for reasons we might never know. But by 830, all the cities in the Petexbatun region had collapsed, and their leaders were killed or had fled.

Over the next century or so, the apocalypse slowly spread north and consumed once powerful Classic Maya cities such as Tikal, in northern Guatemala, and Calakmul, in the southern part of the Yucatán Peninsula. Their final years weren't as violent or chaotic as those in the Petexbatun cities, but something made their continued existence untenable all the same. Paleoclimate records from lakes and caves show drought likely hit these southern cities during the ninth century, which perhaps amplified the political instability seeded by the Petexbatun wars, in a classic apocalypse pattern. As in Egypt, a government based on the supernatural power of divine kings may have been particularly vulnerable when the climate proved to be beyond its control. Perhaps, with all the conquests, alliances, and intermarriages, the elite class had grown too large and unwieldy for common farmers to support in a time when food supplies were dwindling. Perhaps there was a popular revolution in philosophy and religion that undermined the justifications for monarchy, evidence of which wasn't preserved as well as portraits of god-kings carved in stone.

As the divine kings of the south fell, their cities did, too. Without the need to glorify all-powerful rulers, the construction of new buildings and monuments stopped. Because Maya artists often engraved their work with precise dates, archaeologists can see when a city's last monument was erected, a final gasp of proven occupation before a site's abandonment. In a handful of Classic Maya cities, archaeologists have found mass graves that some think hold the remains of the former nobility who were massacred in the political transition. But in most places, it appears that the elite class simply left once their hold on power slipped. A city without a divine king didn't have much work for priests or artists, and so they followed. Merchants, especially those who traded in elite and exotic goods, would have made their way to better markets or returned to their homelands as they waited for the next opportunity. Commoners, mostly farmers with household fields, probably would have been able to hold out the longest, if they wanted to. But eventually most people left the old cities, and they fell into ruin.

Whatever news of these crises arrived in Aké—and it must have, especially once refugees started pouring out of the south—its residents may have very well felt protected by their geographic and cultural distance from the chaos. The northern part of the Yucatán Peninsula had always been the driest part of the Maya world, and so its residents would have been used to living with a certain amount of water stress. They would have known how to collect rainfall and conserve the water levels of their artificial reservoirs and natural cenotes, skills that perhaps served them well at the beginning of the dry period. As one southern city after another collapsed, a series of northern capitals, including Uxmal and Chichén Itzá, rose to become the epicenters of Maya politics and culture. Aké, an old city that sat at the terminus of a prestigious and economically crucial *sacbe*, may have been an important ally.

Gradually, however, the strife crept closer and closer to Aké. Uxmal fell around 950, as bellicose Chichén Itzá consolidated its power throughout periodic dry spells in the tenth century. Sometime between 900 and 1000, Aké built a wall that enclosed the temples and palaces of the city center and ran right across the *sacbe*, practically and symbolically cutting the city off from the wider Maya world. Perhaps the wall was meant to protect against attacks from the ambitious Itzás, or perhaps Aké's leadership wanted to exert more control over immigration as more and more refugees wandered a land struggling to produce enough food to feed them.

Still, Aké remained a flourishing city through the tenth century. Even as political power shifted, the climate fluctuated, and the wall went up, the people of Aké probably experienced the apocalypse as something troubling that still hadn't quite arrived. It was always happening somewhere else, to someone else—until suddenly, it happened to them, too. An even more severe and prolonged drought hit between 1000 and 1100, overwhelming even the northern cities' water infrastructure and management. By the end of that century, Aké, Chichén Itzá, and the rest of the cities in the northern Yucatán Peninsula had collapsed and were largely abandoned. Just as had happened in the southern cities a few centuries earlier, the elites left first and most of their subjects dispersed in their wake.

The Classic Maya collapse took far longer and was arguably more complicated than the collapses of Egypt and Harappa. Maya society was certainly socially complex, but it had never been unified into a single state. Until the very end, migrants from one fallen city could find a home in another that was still thriving. And yet, between the years 800 and 1100, life in nearly every part of the Maya world, for people of every social class, was utterly transformed. Divine kingship was resoundingly rejected and its political and religious institutions dismantled. As cities collapsed, old identities and territories dissolved. Architecture and art would never reach the same monumental heights, nor would they ever require the same amount of labor. Ancient trade routes disintegrated and re-formed as shadows of themselves. Scribes and sculptors, for the most part, stopped carving significant dates into stone, creating the eerie sense that Maya history had ended—at least for archaeologists trying to reconstruct the collapse nearly a millennia later.

It hadn't, of course. As in the Indus Valley after the collapse of Harappa, most Maya people moved from cities to villages, many along the peninsula's coast, after there were no more inland cities to try to make a life in. But thatched houses are far more ephemeral than stone pyramids, and material evidence of many of these postapocalyptic communities decayed long ago. Information about how and where most common Maya people remade their lives in a postapocalyptic world has remained so hard to find that past generations of archaeologists didn't bother looking for it—or perhaps they couldn't even imagine there was anything there to find.

◉

Around the year 950, the king of Aké was beginning to worry. It was proving to be another dry year, and the water level in the cenotes continued to fall. His father and grandfather had always assured him the gods would intervene before a drought grew truly dire; as long as he made the correct offerings and sacrifices, they would make sure the city had what it needed. And the king had to admit, the gods had always upheld their end of the bargain. Just enough rain would fall at just the right point in the corn growing season, or groups of traders from the coast would come through more often, bearing enough fish, salt, corn, and beans to tide the city over for a few more weeks and reinvigorate everyone with a market day. Occasionally—but more and more often, the king noticed—the traders would bring captives, too, some of whom he would acquire and later sacrifice to the rain god Chaac atop a temple or at the edge of one of the cenotes. The king didn't enjoy presiding over such ceremonies, but he knew they were necessary to ensure the well-being of Aké, his people, and the current world. Now more than ever, that was what mattered.

Traders had always moved around the peninsula, and the king of Aké was used to hosting visitors, from high-ranking diplomats and their retinues to villagers who used the *sacbe* to come to the city's market days and ceremonies. But now, there were people arriving who had no connection to Aké, or anywhere close by. They had been wandering for a long time, traveling from the lands far to the south. The wanderers said they had once been farmers near the great capitals there, but their cities had fallen into ruin. Their rulers had abandoned them, they said, and eventually everyone else left, too.

The king of Aké suspected many of these wanderers weren't as innocent as they claimed; he'd heard whispers coming from the south of entire royal families being killed by the people they had governed for decades or centuries. But he'd welcomed the wanderers to Aké in any case, if only to show them that authority still existed here in the north. Besides, many of them were just passing through, on their way to the new capital rising to the east, Chichén Itzá. The king wasn't sure how the Itzás were managing to absorb ever more people with ever less water, but he couldn't deny their strategy was working.

More recently, though, people from much closer by had joined the flow of wanderers. They came from the hill country just a few days' walk from Aké, from Uxmal and the cities around it. The king of Aké had never seen the great capitals of the south, but he had been to Uxmal. His family had known the monarchs there for generations, and their noble classes had sometimes intermarried. It was an impressive city, so modern with its geometric art and fashionable devotion to the Feathered Serpent god. Or, he supposed, it had been an impressive city. If the word of the wanderers was to be believed, hardly anyone lived there anymore. The king wondered where the royal family had gone. Maybe to seek protection from the Itzás, in exchange for subordination and a gilded cage in their new capital? Or perhaps to the coast, where their noble lineage would mean nothing in the merchant cities, but at least their remaining wealth would ensure them a comfortable home and a steady supply of food?

The king of Aké hoped he would never have to make such a decision. He couldn't imagine admitting to his ancestors that he could no longer uphold his sacred duty to the city they'd built. He pushed out of his mind gruesome thoughts of what could have compelled the king of Uxmal, and so many others, to do something so unthinkable.

But the king was about to make an unthinkable choice here in Aké, too. He wouldn't leave, but it was clear the chaos was getting closer. City-states that had been allies for generations were now sending soldiers to attack each other, whether in fights for dwindling resources or political differences that had turned heated. The increasing supply of captives in the markets reflected the uptick in violence. To call on the protection of the gods, the king held more and more ceremonies and made them as elaborate as he could. He couldn't afford to provide food for lavish feasts, not with the cenotes this low and the rains this irregular, but he spilled his own blood as a sacrifice at nearly every ritual now, trying to show his subjects he was doing everything he could to help. His ancestors expected nothing less. The decision he was about to make, though, wouldn't have been one any of his predecessors would have been able to imagine. It concerned the *sacbe*.

The *sacbe* had connected Aké to the nearby city of Izamal for as long as anyone could remember. Its paved white surface, kept clean by the constant flow of traffic, gleamed in the sun. When the king of Aké and the neighboring monarchs had disagreed, even fought, about other things, they had always cooperated to maintain the *sacbe*. It ran near countless villages and farms, connecting them to the cities' centers and to each other, and sitting at its terminus conferred undeniable prestige on Aké. By *sacbe* was how many of the traders arrived, and now it also brought wanderers, fleeing whatever was on their heels. If the chaos were to come to Aké, it would arrive on the *sacbe*, the king was sure of it. He would do whatever he could to keep it out.

That was the promise the king made to his people, as he stood atop the Pyramid of the Columns. The crowd didn't fill the plaza like it had in the days of his great-grandfather, but it was still a respectable number, the king thought, and they were all relying on him. *The chaos will not reach us*, he shouted, his voice echoing off the surrounding temples and throughout the plaza. *The wanderers will not steal from us. The Itzás will not attack us. We will build a wall.*

Over the next few months, that's what the people of Aké did. They hauled stones to the city, stacked them firmly to nearly the height of a man, and topped the length of the entire wall with thickets of sharp sticks, enclosing the city center. The fortified wall ran right across the *sacbe*, forcing everyone who would enter the city to pass through small entrances where guards were posted day and night. The new wall encircled the pyramids, the temples, the palaces, and the plazas, all the places where the spirits of the ancestors resided—the places that made Aké the city it was, and the city the king was determined it would remain.

◉

During his first years in Aké, working on excavations led by Mexico's National Institute of Anthropology and History (INAH), the archaeologist Roberto Rosado-Ramirez focused on the city as it existed during the Classic period, when Aké was at its cultural and demographic peak. Most archaeologists studying the ancient Maya do, and between the towering pyramids, stone monuments commemorating historical figures, and lavish royal tombs, they always have plenty to work with. Beginning in 2003, Rosado-Ramirez worked on, and then managed, the first excavations in decades of many of Aké's most monumental buildings. He helped to restore several of the ancient city center's most striking buildings so they could be appreciated by its contemporary visitors—including, recently, me.

Aké is less than an hour's drive from Mérida, where Rosado-Ramirez grew up, but the town still feels like a world apart. No bus routes facilitate commutes to Mérida, and the turnoff from the highway is barely marked. Even Rosado-Ramirez worries he'd missed it, after the coronavirus pandemic forced him to take three years away. But soon we are on the correct one-lane road, driving through a tunnel of green formed by tree branches arching overhead. We're visiting during Yucatán's rainy season, when the region's scrub forest bursts to life. Pendulous, teardrop-shaped birds' nests dangle from the branches, and kaleidoscopes of marigold butterflies flutter ahead of our car. An iguana lounges in the middle of the road, unperturbed by passing bike and motorcycle traffic.

After about fifteen minutes, the forest gives way to the town of Aké. Signs of its past are everywhere. The ruins of a Maya pyramid sit near first base of a community baseball field in the center of town. Modern houses abut the remains of ancient ones, which now take the form of small mounds on the otherwise flat landscape.

Many of the town's men work in a crumbling factory building where for over a century they—and their fathers and grandfathers before them—have processed henequen, a local succulent, into some of the world's strongest rope. Part of the factory's roof caved in during a hurricane in 1988, and the damage was too extensive to repair, but about half of the building is still accessible. The equipment inside is so old that replacement parts are occasionally purchased from owners of historic henequen machines otherwise on display as museum pieces.

There to meet us at the baseball field are Vicente Cocon López and his son Gerardo. Cocon López is Rosado-Ramirez's closest friend and collaborator in Aké. Rosado-Ramirez has known Gerardo, now in his twenties, since he was in elementary school; he'd been working as the project's unofficial photographer for many years. Soon it feels like the whole town is flocking to Rosado-Ramirez as if he were a firefly flashing its beacon. Many of Aké's men have worked with him on excavations over the years, assisting with all the digging, scraping, hauling, and sifting that resembles nothing so much as a construction project in reverse. Rosado-Ramirez hasn't seen any of them in years, and they're eager to fill him in about their new babies and grandchildren, recent marriages in their families, and the continued good luck of the stray dog that hung around their excavation and was later adopted by one of the guys. Eventually Rosado-Ramirez extricates himself from the catching up, promising longer conversations later. As most of the men head to work in the henequen factory, Cocon López and his son accompany us to the core of the town's archaeological site, where some of ancient Aké's largest palaces, temples, and other monumental buildings still stand.

The four of us climb the enormous stairs to the top of the Pyramid of the Columns, now cleared of vegetation and restored to something like its former glory thanks to INAH's work. The ascent requires taking huge steps that leave me short of breath. The pyramid is clearly designed to be both accessible and imposing, and the craftsmanship is impeccable. Cocon López, who has an impressive eye for construction techniques both ancient and modern, makes sure I notice how all the stones in the staircase are roughly the same size—an indication of the incredible amount of labor and skill its ancient builders brought to it.

When it comes to the Classic Mayas' architectural skills, "all you have to know is that these structures are still standing, and our buildings today fall down in five years," Rosado-Ramirez says. Even the pillars on top of the Pyramid of the Columns—the type of feature that is usually the quickest to crumble—have survived for millennia. Which is why the only outlier stood out to Rosado-Ramirez and got him thinking.

On top of the pyramid, just one of the more than thirty columns has been fully knocked down, and it doesn't look like an accident. Its constituent stones aren't haphazardly scattered, as would happen if it had collapsed on its own, but are instead gathered and stacked to form the base of a small square room. Archaeologists first documented the room in the 1980s, and they identified it as a shrine built much later than the original pyramid. In the centuries after Aké was abandoned, they said, pilgrims would occasionally visit the ruins and leave offerings in the shrine. The ceramics they left date to the period known as the Postclassic, which stretched from 1100 to the first European invasion of Yucatán in 1550.

None of those archaeologists thought Aké could still have been inhabited after the abandonment. The Postclassic offerings, which included ceramics, incense burners, and at least one burial, were consistently found in the debris that blanketed the pyramids, indicating that the old buildings were already decaying into disrepair by the time people placed them there. No one would dare do something like knock down one of the pillars on top of the Pyramid of the Columns if Aké had still been home to a community. And why would anyone be living there? Its buildings were crumbling, its roads were overgrown, its leaders had fled. It was, in short, a ruin.

After years and years of getting to know the current inhabitants of Aké, however, that interpretation no longer sat right with Rosado-Ramirez. All of his experience as an archaeologist had taught him to focus on monumental structures like pyramids. Without functioning monumental architecture, most of his training said, an ancient city couldn't be considered inhabited. But if Rosado-Ramirez applied the same rule to present-day Aké, he realized he'd be forced to conclude that the town had been abandoned in the early to mid-twentieth century, when the henequen factory buildings stopped being maintained or remodeled. But here we are, well into the twenty-first century, talking with people who had called Aké home for their whole lives, and whose children and grandchildren likely would, too. Buildings that looked like ruins from the outside still house old but functioning machinery, and people go to work in them every day. The town is smaller than it had been, and it's arguably poorer and more isolated than at the height of the henequen industry in the early twentieth century. But Aké still exists. It isn't abandoned. People still live there, and Rosado-Ramirez knows them all.

As INAH's large-scale Classic period excavations he was working on came to an end, Rosado-Ramirez started trying to see ancient Aké through the lens of modern Aké. Had it been completely abandoned after the apocalypse, or did it remain the home of a different kind of community? If anyone could help him find more evidence of postapocalyptic construction, it was Cocon López, who knew the site better than anyone and was skilled at spotting subtle variations in building patterns and materials. Without the backing of a grant or a government-funded excavation, Rosado-Ramirez started trekking out to Aké on Saturdays to walk the site with Cocon López and see what they could find. "We didn't even have money for water," Rosado-Ramirez remembers.

Cocon López scouted the site during the week, often following old metal tracks laid down during the boom days to move henequen in horse-drawn carts, and drew maps to guide their joint exploration on the weekends. In jumbles of old stones that, to me, are barely legible as the remains of buildings, Cocon López could see the entire timeline of old Aké and how later people interacted with and repurposed what came before. He and Rosado-Ramirez found small structures built with a mix of the huge stones of Aké's earliest urban phase and the smaller stones of the Late Classic period, meaning the new structures were built after both—and after Aké was supposed to have been abandoned. They also found Postclassic shrines not just on top of the Pyramid of the Columns but perched on or near the ruins of five other Classic period buildings, too.

The project became Rosado-Ramirez's doctoral dissertation, and the team expanded to include many of Aké's men. After years of excavating pyramids, identifying artifacts, and working on INAH restoration projects, they had become archaeological experts in their own right, and Rosado-Ramirez valued their intimate knowledge of Aké's past and present as he searched for the subtle signs of commoner lives that so many past archaeologists had overlooked. With his local team's help, Rosado-Ramirez identified the remains of ninety-six small houses within the monumental core of old Aké and excavated eighteen of them. These buildings, most often found clustered together in groups of six or so around a shared patio, were filled with ceramic styles popular in the Postclassic period, and they occupied locations—including the city's once pristinely empty central plaza—where commoners would have never been allowed to live before the collapse. Perhaps they had moved inside Aké's wall for protection during an unstable time, or perhaps they wanted to define their new community by using an old border, one that they suddenly found themselves on the other side of. Rosado-Ramirez estimates that between 170 and 380 people continued living among the ruins of Aké during the Postclassic period. The upper end of that estimate is almost exactly how many people live in Aké today.

◉

Around the year 1050, a man stepped into the center of Aké's plaza. He had never seen it so empty. Throughout his entire life, he had come here for markets, ceremonies, and celebrations. At those events, everyone he knew, and many he didn't, came to the plaza, even when perhaps they should have stayed home to care for their struggling crops. But they had been determined to face the crisis together—at least at the beginning. The elders had lived through droughts before, and they advised their families on what crops could survive, how to make a meager harvest last longer, and what to trade at the markets when they seemingly had nothing to spare. The king resurrected rituals last practiced by his grandfather and great-grandfather, calling on Chaac to restore the yearly rains. But it only got worse. Never had a drought lasted this long or sent the water levels in the cenotes this low.

At first, market days filled in the gaps. Food and other resources still arrived by canoe from the highlands to the west, and traders still carried them from the coastal ports to the inland cities. The man had never liked the dried fish the traders brought. He preferred deer and rabbit, especially when he hunted the meat himself in the forests around the city. But he hadn't seen any deer or rabbits near Aké in years; the animals couldn't live without water, either. So he had learned to like dried fish. He and his wife got used to digging for yuca, using amaranth when before they would have used corn, and trekking ever deeper into the forest to find palm trees from which they could cut the edible hearts. They became accustomed to treating every bean and corn kernel, when they were lucky enough to have them, as though made of precious jade.

In the empty plaza, the man looked up at the Pyramid of the Columns, thinking of all the ceremonies and offerings he'd seen performed on top of it, and of how pointless they had turned out to be. The columns were still standing strong, but the thatched roof that had protected the king and priests from the sun was beginning to sag and splinter. It didn't matter; there was no need for it anymore. At the beginning of the drought, he and his neighbors found solace watching the king's rituals. Surely, after this offering or that ceremony, the bad years couldn't possibly go on. Surely the gods would finally be appeased. But as time passed and the rains didn't come, the people of Aké reluctantly began to suspect the gods and the ancestors had abandoned the king and those he protected. The king's rituals—more and more frequent, and more and more desperate, attended by more and more priests, who needed to be provided with more and more food—weren't turning things around. They only seemed to make them worse.

Traders and wanderers told the people of Aké that their king wasn't alone in being forsaken. People across the peninsula were leaving their cities. Even the powerful Itzás were rumored to be struggling. It undermined everything the man believed about power and rulership. Kings were supposed to be divine themselves, intrinsically connected to the gods who had created the world and all the ancestors who had shaped it into what it was. If the king lost that connection, what was the basis of his power? Why should they, the farmers, continue to send food to the royal court? Why should they attend ineffectual ceremonies when they could be out harvesting hearts of palm or searching for a hidden cenote, however small, that might still have water in it? If all the kings had lost their divinity, as the wanderers said, why should there be kings at all?

The man had been troubled by these thoughts and by similar sentiments his neighbors whispered about. But he also felt thrilled by them. He considered them every time he attended a ritual in the plaza, noting how the crowds grew smaller and smaller. He remembered them when the priests came to his farm early one morning, and his wife wept as they took their last ears of corn as tribute. He dwelled on them when he began stripping bark from trees for food, following instructions his great-grandfather, who had lived through the last drought, had given him as a child. *I hope you'll never have to do this,* his great-grandfather had said. *But you must know how, in case.* That first night the man fed his children bark, he quietly slipped out of his family compound to join the midnight meeting of those who had decided they could no longer live under this king and were preparing to act.

They were too slow, however, in deciding what that action would be. Some wanted a new king. Others wanted to replace one ruler with a council that would govern the city, like they'd heard the Itzás had in their capital. But the Itzás also had an army, control of a port on the coast, and a network of vassal cities sending them tribute. And even then, some wanderers carried news that the capital was struggling to keep people from moving away as the drought dragged on. The man wasn't sure what news to believe, but he also wasn't sure it mattered. Aké had none of the advantages of Chichén Itzá, and what did it matter if an empty city had a council or a king?

While they argued, word of their midnight meetings must have reached the palace. When the man and his neighbors arrived in the city center for the next ceremony—they had to continue attending, to keep up appearances—they quickly realized there would be no ceremony. The king was gone. He had fled in the night, along with the royal family and many of the priests. The gods had abandoned him, and now the king had abandoned Aké. The man was surprised at his fury; after all, he had wanted the king deposed. But he hadn't imagined it happening like this.

Once the royal family fled, there was no more work for the artisans, scribes, and architects who lived within Aké's wall. Soon they were gone, too. The group that had been planning to overthrow the king fractured in the wake of his disappearance. There was no one to organize market days, no one to invite trading delegations from other cities, and no one to speak on behalf Aké in front of the gods. A handful of traders continued to pass through the city on their regular routes, but fewer and fewer bothered as Aké grew poorer and poorer. Without priests to lead large ceremonies, people began conducting their own rituals at home. No one bothered to patrol the wall or guard the entrances to the city. What could invaders want with Aké now?

The man used to believe that after the king was gone, the gods would turn their favor toward Aké once again. But that didn't happen. The crops continued to die, the animals didn't return, the cenotes dwindled even further, and the rains still evaded them. It felt like every day, another neighbor and their family left the city, joining the flow of wanderers. The man and his wife talked about leaving, but it never felt like the right time to go. Two of their children were still too young to walk very far, and both parents were too weak from hunger to carry them.

Besides, it wasn't clear there was anywhere else to go. The closest coastal cities had faltered, and they didn't know if Chichén Itzá was still standing. Neither of them had family in the villages. The man feared they had waited too long to make a decision, which left them no choice but to wait even longer. Aké grew emptier with every day that passed, but it also felt more and more impossible to leave.

The man had come to the plaza to see what he could scavenge from the pyramids. The royal family had taken as much jade and jewelry as they could carry when they fled, but the man knew from past visits that they had left behind many intricate clay figurines in now-useless royal shrines, all their serving ware and storage pots, and carved statues of past rulers. The man was more than willing to take all of it and more to trade the next time someone came through Aké with food. He had even chipped away pieces of the colorful murals that decorated the interiors of the palace rooms. Who was here to stop him? Even in his neighborhood outside the wall, he'd seen no one besides his family for weeks.

But today, there was someone else in the plaza: an older couple, doing their best to gather loose stones from the pyramid's quickly deteriorating staircase and arrange them in the shape of a new, much smaller house. The man recognized the couple from market days; they had also lived outside the wall, but on the other side of the city from his family. As he walked over, he could tell they were just as surprised and relieved to see another person as he was.

As the man helped push the stones into their new positions, the couple told them their grown children had already fled Aké with their families, and there had been no one left in their neighborhood. *We told them to go,* the older woman said. *But it felt so lonely in that house.*

The man went home and talked to his wife. They wouldn't be moving far, he assured her. Just to the other side of the wall, close to the plaza. There was plenty of material to build a new house there, maybe even a nicer one. The soils in the city center had never been planted, and maybe they were more fertile than their exhausted field. And there were other people there, other people who had stayed.

The next day, they and their children moved inside the wall.

◉

After descending the Pyramid of the Columns, Rosado-Ramirez, Cocon López, and I walk across old Aké's plaza and into a part of the site where forest has been allowed to grow. We arrive at what looks, to me, like a pile of stones chaotically clustered together on a small overgrown mound. But here, too, Rosado-Ramirez and Cocon López can see things I can't. "This was one of the things that made me say, 'Okay, we're not that crazy,'" Rosado-Ramirez says.

Much of the stone pile is made up of the rubble left behind when a Classic period pyramid crumbled to pieces. Over the years, decades, and then centuries, its stones came loose and tumbled down the sides, blanketing the building in its own debris. But Rosado-Ramirez and Cocon López point out that not all of the stones in the pile had fallen haphazardly. Some of the largest blocks are planted vertically in the ground, creating a kind of wall that contains the rubble. Smaller stones are wedged horizontally into the debris to create rough stairs up to the top of the ruin, where a small shrine had been built. The purposeful position of the stones shows that the shrine and the improvised staircase were built deliberately, Rosado-Ramirez says, likely to commemorate, protect, and preserve a kind of access to the old pyramid long after it had lost its original form.

Like this new kind of staircase, the vast majority of the postapocalyptic construction in Aké was done with materials left over from the monumental core of the old city. Common people built the foundations of their small houses with stones repurposed from pyramids. They arranged pieces of monuments covered in carved glyphs—once made for Aké's most elite spaces—inside their humble houses and patios as altars and decoration. Rosado-Ramirez and Cocon López found some of the huge stone blocks from the early pyramids in domestic spaces with grooves worn down their centers; people had taken them home and turned them into grinding stones for corn, a vital tool in every Maya household. The new Postclassic shrines were all on or near old Classic period buildings, built from the rubble of the pyramids themselves. Like Aké's postapocalyptic community itself, they were much smaller and less imposing than their predecessors. But still, they were there.

Historically, archaeologists might have deemed the people of postapocalypse Aké to be squatters, leeching off the material wealth of the old city with no respect for its history. It's also possible that if Rosado-Ramirez finds more of their graves, their remains will reveal that they lived in a postapocalypse riddled with violence and disease, as Robbins Schug saw in the ruins of Harappa. But when Rosado-Ramirez considered how Aké's postapocalyptic community interacted with the ruins around them, he didn't see people who didn't care about what the city had been or who were struggling for basic survival. The central places they chose to live and the way they both utilized and protected the city's material remains suggested that they were people who knew Aké's history, its geography, and its landmarks and spent much of their time and resources figuring out creative ways to maintain their connection to them. He saw people who likely believed they lived not in a time of scarcity and conflict but of abundance and belonging.

It's unlikely that outsiders who moved in later would have taken such care with signs of Aké's past, or even have understood how to do so. In Copán, a major Classic Maya capital in Honduras, Postclassic people also reused material from the abandoned city in new constructions. In the walls of their new buildings, they positioned the old stones' glyphs, portraits, and other carvings with their blank, uncarved sides facing out, rendering their decorations invisible and meaningless. They also seem to have raided Classic period royal tombs for trade goods instead of for use in local shrines like the one on top of Aké's Pyramid of the Columns. Archaeologists think this indicates that the city was reoccupied by a community from elsewhere, and the new residents chose to maintain a certain distance from the Copán of the past.

In Aké, on the other hand, Postclassic people prominently displayed carved glyphs and other emblems of the city's glorious past in their homes. They continued to honor the old palaces and temples—and the spirits and ancestors that dwelled within them—with shrines, offerings, and even burials. They anchored themselves in the city's history and used its ruins to define themselves as people who continued to belong there. Contemporary Maya people believe ancient ruins are not empty but rather homes for gods, ancestors, and forest spirits. Perhaps the people of postapocalyptic Aké never thought of their city as abandoned, even though it had undoubtedly changed.

People like them—farmers, commoners, peasants—would have once lived on the outskirts of Aké, with little say in its political, economic, or religious life. During the Classic period, everything from diplomacy to prayer would have flowed through the king. Now, in this new, post-apocalyptic world, they were the ones who decided what Aké was and how to live in it. They would have been the ones who invited the traders who continued to travel the peninsula, bringing goods from the new capital, Mayapán, coalescing south of Aké. They would have diplomatically managed Aké's relationship with Mayapán and the countless other towns that dotted the decentralized, post-collapse peninsula. They had to invent ways to practice their religion without the help of a king, redesigning rituals so they could be performed in the small shrines Rosado-Ramirez found and at family altars in their homes. They were the ones who lived in the city center, the most important people in Aké.

◉

For over four hundred years, this smaller, more egalitarian, more flexible, and more resilient Postclassic lifestyle worked for the Maya people of the Yucatán Peninsula. Even after the drought ended and the environment stabilized, they never again agreed to the rule of a divine king. They had tried living in that kind of ultra-stratified complex society, and it had failed them, catastrophically. It made their cities vulnerable, their politics fragile, and their religion powerless when apocalypse struck. Why would they take that kind of risk again?

Instead, the Maya of the northern Yucatán Peninsula built a different kind of capital, starting around 1100. Mayapán wasn't the seat of a god-king but rather the meeting place for a confederacy comprised of representatives from powerful families and polities across the peninsula. Isotopes in the bones of people buried there show that the city attracted people from far and wide, both commoners and elites. Perhaps that's where the rulers of Aké ended up after they fled, as junior members of Mayapán's council.

Like Aké at the end of its first phase of life, Mayapán built a city wall. Unlike Aké, its enclosed center was densely occupied with both monumental buildings and commoner neighborhoods. Mayapán was home to several imposing pyramids, but no single central plaza like the one in front of Aké's Pyramid of the Columns. No one person or group controlled Mayapán, and so they didn't need a massive public space where their followers could gather to hear their proclamations. Politics happened in the compounds of the council's most powerful constituencies, and religious practices were more personal, with altars and incense burners inside people's homes. Without the need to glorify individual rulers, scribes wrote books instead of carving history into stone monuments, and architects designed pyramids that were much easier to build. Unlike in megalithic Aké of the Early Classic, people in Postclassic Mayapán didn't need to spend their time shaping and precisely arranging huge stone blocks into elegant, perfect staircases and palace walls to comply with royal tastes. Instead, they built pyramids from jumbles of smaller stones, which were then covered in stucco and painted with colorful murals. Most of those murals have long since faded away, exposing the stone foundations beneath. When explorers and archaeologists, like John Lloyd Stephens, visited these ruins centuries later, Mayapán's monumental architecture looked messier and less refined than its Classic period counterparts. But at the time, it would have been just as beautiful and imposing, albeit in a different way.

A trader could walk the twenty-five miles between Mayapán and Aké in a day or two, and Rosado-Ramirez found many of Mayapán's signature ceramics, including incense burners, in postapocalyptic Aké. For about three hundred and fifty years, the village within the ruins sat comfortably in the orbit of the capital where power was shared. Then, around 1400, drought struck again, and Mayapán, too, collapsed. According to surviving Maya texts, it was largely abandoned by 1441. Its confederacy and council government had likely been a reaction to the inequality and failure of divine kingship, but the Maya of the Yucatán Peninsula were now learning that any kind of centralized power, even when it was shared, could succumb in the face of an environmental challenge that required the kind of flexibility and adaptation that only smaller communities were capable of. As in the Indus Valley and along the Nile River three thousand years before, the Postclassic Maya learned it was villages, where people could act quickly and cooperate face-to-face, that would keep them safe, and they created and sustained such small communities before and after Mayapán fell.

The people of postapocalyptic Aké likely felt the stress of this new drought, but they didn't have to leave their homes or remake their lives. They were already living in the safest, most adaptable way they knew. Unlike Egypt, which centralized again as soon as it could after the First Intermediate Period, or post–Black Death England, where the powerful insisted that nothing about the structure of their society needed to change in the wake of apocalypse, the Postclassic Maya continued to reject divine kingship, maximally complex states, and, after Mayapán, centralized power. But their past was anything but lost or forgotten. People rebuilt and reimagined their communities with the help of everything their ancestors left behind, while also, perhaps, vowing not to repeat their mistakes.

◉

One day in the year 1400, a child let go of a rope and dropped down into the heart of the old temple. The remains of a vaulted stone roof extended over his head. Sunlight trickled through the hole he'd slipped through, dimly illuminating the small room. It had once connected to other rooms; the child could make out the outline of a doorway in one of the walls. But the doorway was blocked by rubble, and the child could tell the spaces beyond it had caved in long ago. Still, this chamber looked sturdy enough. The large stones of its walls fit together snuggly, and his parents had told him the remains of the roof had never once budged, even during hurricanes. Sometimes when the child went exploring in these old places, he had to get out as soon as he spotted a crumbling support wall or felt a tremor as the stones deeper in the collapsed building shifted. His older brother had taught him it was never worth staying in a place like that, no matter what treasures he might find. But this room felt safe, so he had a chance to look around.

The child ran his hand along one of the walls and over patches of faded paint, the reds and blues still standing out against the stone. He wondered who had painted them and where all the pigments had come from. His aunt was a talented artist, but she never had such colors to work with, nor did she have much time to decorate walls when she could be painting pottery to be traded in Mayapán. On the wall, the child could make out fragments of feet, hands, parts of faces, and colorful clothing, but none of the figures were complete. Much of the stucco on which the murals were painted had chipped off with time, taking pieces of the images with it. Or perhaps previous explorers had broken off parts to take home with them, the child thought. He'd seen pieces of old paintings in the patio of his grandmother's house, but she didn't know which building they came from. Her father, who had brought home the fragments when she was a child, had told her they were portraits of their ancestors. And so she had cared for them throughout her long life, keeping them clean, leaving them offerings, and burning incense at their feet. Maybe his great-grandfather had visited this old building, too, the child thought.

The child walked around the room until he came to the blocked doorway. He crouched down and started picking through the loose stones. Some of them were so huge he couldn't move them; others were wedged into the pile in ways he didn't dare disturb, lest the rubble come crashing down on top of him. But there were plenty of smaller stones lying free, and many had carvings on them. Some had jagged edges, and the child fit them back together. He soon found they were part of a larger statue that had been broken apart. The child thought it must have fallen over and cracked into pieces. He couldn't imagine anyone he knew destroying such a thing on purpose, knowing it was the work of their ancestors. The old city gave them more than enough material to build their homes and their shrines; they repurposed, but they didn't destroy. Since the statue was already in pieces, however, the child knew it was all right to see if there was anything he could take home.

He picked up and tossed away several pieces on which the carvings were incomplete. No images or even patterns, just meaningless textures.

Finally, he picked up a stone etched with the image of a hand grasping a fish. No one in Aké could read the old writing, but the knowledge of what this glyph meant had survived. It was Aké's name.

The child tucked the carved stone into the long piece of fabric he'd turned into a bag and draped over one shoulder. In its place, he left a tamale he'd brought as an offering to the spirits that lived in the building, a gesture of thanks for letting him visit and for giving him the name glyph.

The child scrambled back up the rope and out through the hole near the ceiling. He untied the rope from the tree trunk where he'd anchored it and tucked it into his bag with the carving. He picked his way down the crude stone path people had laid to the top of this building, its original staircase buried long ago. In the rainy season the building looked like a hill, overgrown with tangles of vines and other vegetation. But the child, along with everyone else in Aké, knew it wasn't.

The child followed the dirt paths among the old buried buildings and the newer houses people lived in now, weaving his way back to the big plaza. His family lived on the edge of it, using some of the flat ground as a garden. His mother was grinding corn out on the kitchen patio. She was still getting used to the new grinding stone's slopes and angles; his father had recently brought it home after it had fallen to the ground in front of one of the pyramids.

The child presented the carving to his mother, who smiled and took him inside to place it on their altar. She let him light the incense to welcome the name glyph and the spirit of the person who had carved it. By building the old city, the ancestors had given them everything they needed. They had given them the new Aké.

PART 3: NEW WORLDS

Chapter 7

HOW THE APOCALYPSE OF COLONIALISM HAS HIDDEN IN PLAIN SIGHT

By the late fifteenth century, people around the world had millennia of experience coping with apocalypses. From ancient Egypt periodically unifying and collapsing, Europeans economically regrouping after the Black Death, and the descendants of Harappans and the Classic Maya rejecting the brittleness of socially complex cities for life in smaller communities, people had developed their own traditions of weathering apocalyptic challenges and harnessing their potential for transformation. Each apocalypse was unique and often unexpected, but histories and myths told all over the world, stretching all the way back to the Great Drowning and perhaps beyond, contained countless stories of survival.

Then, in 1492, the world changed forever. A potent combination of human ingenuity and human cruelty ignited the first truly global apocalypse, threatening the lives of hundreds of millions of people and turning long-held beliefs about nature, community, and survival on their heads. This new apocalypse had everything: political upheaval, unchecked violence, environmental degradation, spiritual chaos, and mass mortality from new diseases, all on a scale never before seen or even imagined. And it started as soon as Christopher Columbus stepped onto the Caribbean island of Hispaniola, thinking it was India.

Like all apocalypses, European colonialism was a transformation, and it affected every society it touched. By connecting the entire planet for the first time, it sparked new identities, built new markets, reinvented cuisines, and remade social, political, and economic hierarchies. It also resulted in the deaths of hundreds of millions of people, the enslavement of millions more, and the attempted destruction of millennia-old communities and cultures. European colonialism created the world we live in today, and yet the true story of what happened, and how it made us who we are, has been distorted at every turn by those who continue to benefit from history's greatest apocalypse.

Over the past five hundred years, colonialism has successfully disguised itself as cultural and moral progress, hidden behind a mask of modernity, and laundered its tragedies as destiny. The official narratives told and retold by empires, and the settler colonial states they spawned, have warped what can be seen of the past in order to convince us that what happened was not an apocalypse, with all its complications and reverberations, but an inevitability whose details and meaning were settled long ago. Those stories, now the basis of the history so many of us learn, try to convince us that the modern world was a predetermined destination, the only possible outcome of the progress we have benefited from and should be grateful for.

To understand European colonialism as the apocalypse it was and is, we must go back to the beginning, before the lie of inevitability had a chance to permeate history, and rewrite the stories many of us think we know to include the perspectives that have been left out, suppressed, or erased. Only then can we appreciate the contingency, agency, uncertainty, resilience, and creativity that were just as inherent to the apocalypse of colonialism as they were to any other.

There are so many of these stories that can and should be told—and that have never stopped being told by people usually ignored by those in power. But here we'll focus on just one, the one I know best, and the one that logistically and ideologically wrote the script for so many of the others that would follow. It's the story that first got me thinking about apocalypses, the transformations they unleash, and how we misunderstand their power: the invasion and conquest of the Aztec Empire and its capital, Tenochtitlan. My life exists in the shadow of this particular colonial apocalypse, in ways I am still learning to see and understand, because it was this apocalypse that created Mexico City, the place I call home.

◉

In April 1519, Moctezuma gathered with his advisers in Tenochtitlan's sacred precinct. The ambassadors had returned from the coast and their first official meeting with the foreigners. Of course there had been unofficial encounters before, for many years. Spies had always been among the frequent travelers along the merchant roads that reached to every corner of the empire and beyond, and intelligence had raced back to Tenochtitlan each time the ships were spotted. The empire had ears and eyes at every landfall long before the foreigners even knew the empire existed. When Moctezuma found out the Maya of Cozumel had enslaved two foreigners who survived a shipwreck eight years before, he had considered sending emissaries to buy them and bring them to Tenochtitlan. It was only fitting the foreigners should belong to him, he who had filled his zoo with every kind of bird and beast, he who received tribute from more lands than his predecessors could have imagined. But Moctezuma had neither the need nor the desire to antagonize any Maya group, which could destabilize diplomatic and trade relations with their brethren throughout the southeast. If those foreigners had come, more would surely follow.

Now they had. Moctezuma sent ambassadors to their camp on the east coast to show them that the Mexica of Tenochtitlan were the most powerful group in this land, with riches to spare as lavish gifts. The foreigners were their guests from the moment they set foot on the beach. Moctezuma had a golden sun, a silver moon, jade, god costumes, and the finest featherwork and textiles the capital's craftspeople could make sent with the ambassadors. If this is what Moctezuma had to give away, he imagined the foreigners thinking, what more could he possess?

The ambassadors returned aghast. The foreigners were filthy, bedraggled, barbaric. They reeked of the sea, the close quarters of the ships that had brought them to the coast, and the blood crusted on their unwashed garments, a remnant of the battles they'd already fought with the first communities they'd met. When had they last bathed? They lived so closely with their animals, even climbing on the backs of the ones that looked like monstrous deer. They devoured the food prepared for them by their slave women, who'd been given to them as part of a peace settlement by the coastal groups they'd defeated, with the unseemly desperation of the starving.

The foreigners all but ignored the feathers, the jade, and the god costumes, but their eyes shone with blatant lust when presented with trinkets made of gold and silver. Worse, they ignited the tail of one of their long metal cylinders and set off an explosion right next to the ambassadors, with no warning at all. They laughed when the ambassadors jumped and shouted with surprise. Even the Tlaxcalteca, the empire's archenemies, received ambassadors from Tenochtitlan with more respect. It was disgraceful, the ambassadors said. How could Moctezuma even consider inviting these uncivilized barbarians to the capital? Their very presence would pollute its order and beauty.

Moctezuma's advisers agreed. It would be folly to further engage with the foreigners, who had, within a matter of weeks, already proven themselves violent, greedy, and disrespectful. How could Moctezuma dream of deigning to speak to them? *I will do more than speak to them,* Moctezuma said. *I will possess them.* For he was consumed by his own kind of greed—an insatiable hunger for knowledge, novelty, and discovery. These men came from lands he hadn't known existed, wearing strange clothes, worshipping a foreign god, and riding unknown animals. Moctezuma wanted—needed—to acquire them. His collections already held wolves, jaguars, and eagles. How much more dangerous could some unwashed men be?

◉

Tenochtitlan was founded in 1325 by the Mexica, a group that arrived in what is now central Mexico after a centuries-long migration from lands to the north. The Valley of Mexico was dominated by a series of interconnected lakes, around which people had lived and farmed for millennia. When the Mexica arrived as relative latecomers, they were relegated to a swampy island where farming was difficult. They ate fish, algae, bird eggs, crayfish, and insects, and they also adopted the difficult but effective agricultural technique of building artificial islands called chinampas, which could be planted with beans, squash, corn, chiles, and other crops. In keeping with their origins as wanderers, the Mexica prided themselves on their adaptability and resilience. They would come to think of their island home as divinely destined; according to myth, the god Huitzilopochtli signaled that they should settle there by sending an eagle to land in front of them. (The Mexican flag's emblem of an eagle eating a snake atop a nopal cactus has its roots in this omen.)

Most people in the area, including the Mexica, spoke a language called Nahuatl, but each town or city had its own political identity, and the Mexica found themselves navigating a complex web of alliances and animosities that long predated their arrival in the valley. During their wanderings and after, they often worked as mercenaries for more powerful communities, until, more often than not, those communities came to see the Mexica's military strength as a threat and expelled them.

The difficulty of farming Tenochtitlan's muddy, boggy land could have put the Mexica at a disadvantage in a world where calendars, cuisine, and wealth all centered on corn and its growing cycle. But instead, their willingness to make do with small chinampas and less appealing but year-round foods like algae and fish made them excellent lieutenants for communities who had to devote more time to farming. The Mexica, used to taking full advantage of what little they had, moving from place to place, and, perhaps, prioritizing warfare and politics over planting and harvesting, turned their unconventional lifestyle into an asset for their richer but less flexible allies, including Azcapotzalco, an older lakeshore town that dominated the valley around the turn of the fifteenth century. When the death of Azcapotzalco's powerful king set off a succession crisis in 1426, the Mexica were able to maneuver themselves into control of the valley, as the principal leaders of an alliance with two lakeside communities. By the early 1430s, Tenochtitlan, Texcoco,

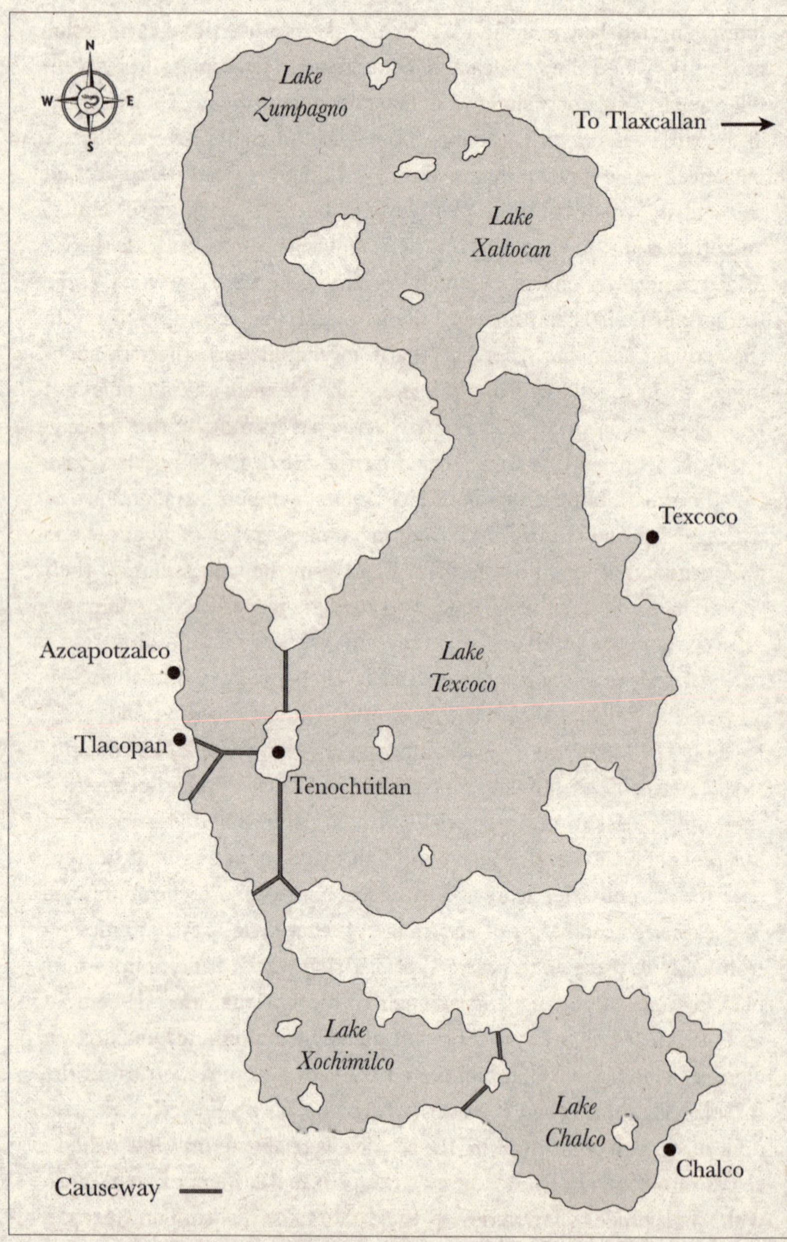

Tenochtitlan and the surrounding lakes in AD 1519

and Tlacopan had formed what would come to be called the Triple Alliance—now more familiarly known as the Aztec Empire.

Within just a few generations, the Mexica had gone from vassal state to imperial rulers, and Tenochtitlan grew from a ramshackle village in an environmentally precarious place to the heart of one of the largest metropolitan areas in the world, eclipsing medieval London and Rome. In addition to the chinampa gardens, the Mexica built dikes and levees for flood control, aqueducts to supply the city with drinking water, causeways to bring people and goods over the lake and into the capital, and streets and canals to navigate the dense, amphibious urban environment. Every neighborhood had its own noble family, interlocking into a complex political power structure led by Tenochtitlan's *huey tlatoani*, or Great Speaker. The core of the city, home to the grandest temples, palaces, and gardens in the entire empire, was considered sacred. Remembering his first glimpse of Tenochtitlan, Spanish conquistador Bernal Díaz del Castillo later wrote, "These great towns and [temples] and buildings rising from the water, all made of stone, seemed like an enchanted vision . . . some of our soldiers asked whether it was not all a dream."

Like all expansionist empires, however, the Triple Alliance had enemies. Some communities successfully fought off the Triple Alliance's soldiers in battle, while others unhappily acquiesced to their rule. The most famous, and arguably most successful, of the imperial resisters was Tlaxcallan, an unusually decentralized and equitable republic not even one hundred miles to the east of Tenochtitlan. The Mexica and the Tlaxcalteca shared a language, a religion, and an ancestral origin as hunter-gatherers in the north who had migrated to become farmers and urbanites in their current homelands. But Tlaxcallan had always done things differently. Their capital had no center but was stitched together out of cooperating neighborhoods. Senators and commoners alike lived near the most important temples, and no one accumulated significantly more wealth than their neighbors. Positions in their government were open to anyone who could endure two years of physical and spiritual trials rather than power running through noble bloodlines, as it did in Tenochtitlan. For nearly one hundred years, Tlaxcallan was surrounded by Aztec territory, and the Triple Alliance imposed trade embargoes and regularly attacked the republic, to no avail. Tlaxcallan was never conquered, instead serving as a bastion of independence for Tenochtitlan's enemies—including, eventually, the Spanish invaders.

Still, by the time the company led by Hernando Cortés arrived on the Gulf Coast of Mexico in the spring of 1519, the Aztec Empire was more powerful than it had ever been. For almost ninety years, the Triple Alliance had conquered and subjugated communities throughout central and southern Mexico; the empire reaped the wealth of their tribute and controlled some of Mesoamerica's most important trade routes. Imperial tribute took the form of food, cotton, seashells, and precious materials like jade and cacao. It could also take the form of enslaved people. Some of the enslaved spent the rest of their lives working for noble families; though their children were guaranteed freedom, the practice of capturing, owning, and distributing human beings inevitably disrupted communities and sowed resentment. Others, including most soldiers captured in battle with Mexica forces, were destined to be sacrificed.

At the time of European contact, not all Indigenous Americans were imperialists or imperial subjects, of course. The Inca Empire dominated the Andes, moving people and goods around to best suit the needs of its sun king. But Maya groups, as well as communities throughout the Mississippi River Valley and eastern North America, had previously experimented with large, stratified societies governed by divine rulers, and they had resoundingly rejected them in the wake of the climate-driven collapse of their capitals. Indigenous nations on the North American East Coast formed democratic coalitions, while those in the Pacific Northwest built a culture based around extreme wealth inequality and the performative generosity of the rich. In what would become the southwestern United States, farmers harnessed technologies like irrigation canals and agricultural terraces to spread across the desert. In California, people rejected the agriculture and hierarchies of their neighbors and intentionally remained egalitarian hunter-gatherers. No Indigenous nation ever existed in a prelapsarian past, unchanged and unchanging since time immemorial. They had their own histories, hierarchies, politics, economies, and strategies for managing the benefits and drawbacks of social complexity.

And so when the Mexica met the invading Europeans, they were just as powerful, sophisticated, and modern as the foreigners and the countries they came from. The Aztecs and the Spaniards all lived in the same sixteenth century, and their respective ancestors had developed and embraced many of the same technologies and cultural practices, from agriculture to empire, despite living an ocean apart. In 1519, the Mexica were scholars, artists, poets, philosophers, priests, nobles, commoners, soldiers, and farmers. They were savvy political actors whose imperial ambitions both expanded their power and fueled resistance to their control. And it was that political landscape, already cut through with the kinds of fault lines of anger, resentment, and violence that apocalypse can reveal and activate, that the Spanish invaders walked into and managed to exploit. But the foreigners were also frequently being exploited themselves, by people whose history and motivations they never quite understood. The Europeans would come to think of the Tlaxcalteca as their greatest allies and the key to their eventual victory—never realizing the Tlaxcalteca saw them as pawns.

◉

In the fall of 1519, Xicotencatl the Elder saw an opportunity. He was a respected leader in Tlaxcallan's senate, and for his entire long life, Tlaxcallan had been holding off the Mexica. It had been getting harder during Moctezuma's reign, as the young emperor sought to expand the Mexica's power into new territories and increase their control over places they had already conquered. Moctezuma's thirst for tribute was unquenchable, and his zoo, gardens, and palaces were bursting with animals, plants, and precious objects from all over the empire. His government had also increased its demand for people to be sacrificed in ceremonies at the Great Temple. Xicotencatl knew some sacrifices were necessary to nourish the gods and sustain the universe. Every year during the war season, he and Tlaxcallan's other senators negotiated with the Mexica the terms of the battles where each city would take captives. Soldiers were hardly ever killed on the field. Their deaths required more honor, more respect. The ceremonies guaranteed their deaths served a greater purpose.

But in recent years, the number of sacrifices in Tenochtitlan had steadily grown as Moctezuma and his priests consolidated their power. Tenochtitlan's *tzompantli*, the rack where the skulls of the sacrificed were hung with honor, had risen to nearly the height of two men. Xicotencatl had heard rumors of representatives from unconquered territories being spirited to Tenochtitlan in secret to witness the ceremonies, after which they were promised their young men would be spared the same fate if they surrendered to Mexica rule. Moctezuma and his council only sometimes kept that promise. Tlaxcallan had never been given any such choice, but Xicotencatl knew his people would never surrender even if they were.

But Tlaxcallan was now surrounded by land under Mexica control. The trade embargoes were growing harsher, and Tlaxcallan had to rely on its local resources more than ever. Much of the senate's time was spent organizing feasts to efficiently distribute food to everyone who needed it. Tlaxcallan had enough resources and allies to survive for a long time yet, but Xicotencatl knew the Triple Alliance would make it as difficult as possible. Moctezuma clearly felt that the continued existence of an independent state so close to the heart of his empire sent a dangerous message to the Mexica's farther-flung territories. Tlaxcallan, with its open government and decentralized city plan, was proof that power could be spread out, distributed, shared. Tlaxcallan showed that the need for an emperor was a lie.

Tlaxcallan's sustained, successful resistance to Mexica hegemony became more of a threat the more powerful the empire grew, and Xicotencatl knew Moctezuma was willing to spend more of that power destroying them. Tenochtitlan had just convinced the nearby holy city of Cholula to abandon their long alliance with Tlaxcallan in favor of imperial support and protection. The senate was furious, but there was little they could do. If they sent soldiers to attack Cholula, what might the Mexica do in response? Could Tlaxcallan withstand their retaliation?

Were the Mexica plotting a reason to destroy them once and for all, by coaxing them into a battle they couldn't win and, given Cholula's long history as a sacred place, might dangerously diminish Tlaxcallan's standing with its own allies?

But now these foreigners had arrived—a new enemy with unknown capabilities and shortcomings. The foreigners had landed on the east coast, where Xicotencatl knew they had already done battle with, and defeated, the soldiers of several local lords. The senate's spies said the foreigners had their eyes on Tenochtitlan's wealth, and their goal was to invade the city and take Moctezuma captive. The defeated local lords on the coast had also deduced as much. Those lords were vassals of the Triple Alliance, but Xicotencatl knew that many of them resented the empire's tribute demands. The vassal lords didn't have the strength to resist Mexica rule, with or without the foreigners' help. Instead, they brought the foreigners to the one place that could conceivably stand against the empire: Tlaxcallan.

Xicotencatl scoffed at the ridiculous notion that the foreigners were capable of capturing Moctezuma or taking control of his city on their own. There were so few of them, and so many were already sick or injured. But the foreigners had surprising and fearful ways of fighting—swinging their swords from the backs of the animals the Tlaxcalteca now knew were called horses, setting off explosions inside guns and cannons, commanding their war dogs to tear their enemies to bits. They killed people right on the field of battle, often in the most brutal and tortuous ways. If Xicotencatl and the other senators could convince the foreigners to do Tlaxcallan's bidding, it could tip the balance of the long war with the Mexica in their favor. But only if the rumors about the foreigners' capacity for violence proved to be true.

Tlaxcallan had to test the foreigners first, and so Tlaxcalteca soldiers attacked their company. The foreigners held their own, and Xicotencatl saw that his spies' intelligence about their ways of fighting had been correct. Xicotencatl also knew that Moctezuma's greed was matched only by his curiosity. If Tlaxcallan sent an army to march on Tenochtitlan, the entire valley would rise up in defense of the capital before they arrived at the lakeshore. But if Tlaxcallan sent their army along with the foreigners, Moctezuma could never resist meeting them. He'd have to let them into the city.

Not everyone in the senate agreed with Xicotencatl's assessment. His son, who had fought in the battle against the foreigners, said they were vicious, bloodthirsty, and had no respect for human life. No one could deny that, especially after they had broken the rules of war and launched a surprise attack against Tlaxcallan at night, targeting not soldiers who had come to meet them in battle but citizens sleeping in their homes. After that, Xicotencatl's son said, it was clear that the foreigners would never stop with Tenochtitlan, that they would one day turn on Tlaxcallan, that it was a mistake to ally with people whose relations were unknown and whose actions couldn't be predicted. Instead of absorbing the foreigners into its forces, Tlaxcallan must destroy them to protect its future.

But Tlaxcallan needed friends more than it needed another enemy, and Xicotencatl's son was overruled. Besides, Xicotencatl thought, they would make sure the foreigners were amenable to Tlaxcallan's power and priorities by first leading them in an attack on traitorous Cholula. The foreigners understood nothing about the political landscape they had walked into, and they didn't seem to want to. Their only priority was to steal Moctezuma's treasures and install their crosses wherever they went. Xicotencatl hadn't minded playing along with their ceremonies, which meant nothing to him but seemed to make the foreigners more trusting and agreeable. Their capacity for violence may have been unprecedented, but it was also easily manipulated. Tlaxcallan would wield the foreigners like a weapon against its enemies and with them become more powerful than Tenochtitlan could have ever dreamed.

◉

By the time a nineteen-year-old Cortés sailed from Spain to the new colony of Hispaniola in 1504, what historian Matthew Restall calls Spanish "conquest procedures" were already developing a legalistic veneer to justify the seizure of land and enslavement of people. Would-be conquistadors had to formally found a town on the land they wished to control, and they were obliged to read a formal request for submission to the area's Indigenous inhabitants, who were no doubt bewildered because this presentation was invariably delivered in Spanish. Ideally the invaders could then seize the uncomprehending community's leader (or the person they thought was the leader), along with other convenient prisoners, and subject them to gruesome, theatrical torture and death to frighten the rest of the population into obedience. Common techniques included cutting off Indigenous people's hands or arms, burning them alive, setting dogs on them, and targeting women, children, and the elderly for massacres. Afterward, the corpses might be sent home to their families.

The invaders' goal, usually, was to "subdue and exploit [Indigenous people] as a more or less compliant labor force" on colonial estates, the foundation of the wealth conquistadors hoped to generate. Preexisting Spanish law allowed colonists to enslave "cannibals," and so invaders from Christopher Columbus on quickly wrote home about having found such monstrous humans and witnessed their hideous practices. Rather than a description of the Indigenous religions and traditions of warfare the invaders actually saw, cannibal was "the term they use to make free people into slaves," wrote Bartolomé de las Casas, an early Spanish colonist who would later renounce his Caribbean estate and become the most influential sixteenth century European voice against the abuse of Indigenous Americans.

Cortés and his company followed many of these "conquest procedures" upon landing on the Gulf Coast of Mexico, including attacking local communities and founding the town of Veracruz. Cortés also intensified the "cannibal" propaganda campaign after he began to witness Mesoamerican state and religious violence, which he immediately cast as "horrible, abominable, and deserving punishment." "They take many boys or girls, and even grown men and women, and in the presence of those idols they open their breasts, while they are alive, and take out the hearts and entrails, and burn the said entrails and hearts before the idols, offering that smoke in sacrifice to them," wrote Cortés in his first letter back to the Spanish king and queen, in July 1519. "Some of us who have seen this say that it is the most terrible and frightful thing to behold that has ever been seen." To read his and other conquistador accounts of the invasion is to hear about near-daily human sacrifices in blood-spattered temples in almost every city, town, and village they visited. The descriptions would only grow more lurid once the company arrived in Tenochtitlan, where Cortés reported seeing idols made of ground corn and seeds "mixed with one another, and kneaded with the hearts' blood of human beings . . . When these are finished the priests offer them more hearts, which have likewise been sacrificed, and besmear the faces with the blood."

In reality, Aztec human sacrifice is best understood not as an occult, demonic ritual regularly practiced by any village priest, but as a form of state violence intertwined with that state's rules of war. Mesoamerican soldiers aimed to capture their enemies, not kill them on the battlefield; their deaths would come later in ceremonies believed to ensure the continuation of the universe. These public executions served military, political, and religious purposes. All communities believed these ceremonies maintained the cycles of time, but they were also a way for the most powerful states to exert control and dominance over their vassals. By the early sixteenth century, the Triple Alliance was the dominant military power in Mesoamerica, and so the vast majority of the executions took place in Tenochtitlan, as displays of the empire's political and religious power.

Dying as a sacrifice ensured a person an honored place in the afterlife, sparing them the unpleasant underworld journey most people could expect. Captives taken by Mexica soldiers would often live in the capital for months or years before being ritually killed atop the city's Great Temple. The actual executions were usually swift, as obsidian blades were sharper than today's surgical steel and the priests had extensive anatomical knowledge. Scenes of heart removal sound gruesome and frightfully bloody to our modern sensibilities, but the method was arguably more humane than the public executions taking place in Europe at the same time, in which heretics and criminals were burned alive, drawn and quartered, or torn apart by dogs, all in front of ecstatic crowds—the same methods of torture and execution that were already being applied in the Caribbean. In Tenochtitlan, the skulls of the sacrificed were cleaned and hung in rows on the city's *tzompantli*, a monument to religious renewal and an unmistakable sign of the Mexica's political domination. In many contemporaneous European cities, ramparts and gates were adorned with the decapitated heads and rotting bodies of the executed, a similar if even grislier reminder of the cost of stepping out of line.

I don't draw these comparisons to excuse Mexica state violence, which the empire wielded as a brutal reminder of its hegemony. I highlight them to remind us that this is the case for all state violence—and especially imperial violence—in the past and the present. By exaggerating the scale, horror, and singularity of the public executions they witnessed or heard about in Tenochtitlan and Mesoamerica more broadly, the Spanish invaders cast the Mexica and other Indigenous groups as barbarians, idolaters, sodomites, and cannibals, and therefore deserving of any and all violence inflicted upon them. "Now let Your Royal Highnesses consider if they ought not to prevent so great an evil and crime," Cortés wrote about human sacrifice in his first letter, while he was still seeking the crown's official permission to launch a conquest effort on the mainland.

Following the conquistadors' lead, invaders and colonists throughout the Americas would go on to exaggerate Indigenous violence and warfare as far more savage, merciless, and gruesome than European practices—and then use their hyperboles to justify, and obscure, any and all of their own atrocities. In 1622, after enduring more than a decade of English raids, intrusions, attacks, and theft, the Powhatans launched a counterassault on England's Virginia colony, killing nearly one third of the colonists with the settlers' own weapons. "That fatal Friday morning, there fell under the bloody and barbarous hands of that perfidious and inhumane people, contrary to all laws of God and men, of Nature and Nations, three hundred forty-seven men, and women, and children . . . [C]onquering [the Powhatans] is much more easier than of civilizing them by fair means," the English would write in the colony's records. Only twelve years earlier, the people of Jamestown had barely survived a terrible winter by eating their own dead.

◉

On November 8, 1519, Marina stood on Tenochtitlan's southern causeway between two men, and two worlds. One of the men was the most powerful person in the empire, the *huey tlatoani* of the Mexica, the Great Speaker, the leader and representative of the empire that had once turned her into a slave. The other was a foreigner who knew how to leverage his novelty into power. He would have kept her a slave if she hadn't proven useful, and she knew he would turn her into one again if she stopped.

Marina had been given to the foreigners as a gift seven months before. She hadn't resisted; she'd learned long ago there was no point. Her duties wouldn't be so different from those she'd been performing among the Chontal Maya for many years, ever since she'd been given to Mexica merchants as a part of her community's desperate negotiations to avoid war with the empire, who had then sold her in Maya territory. The foreigners needed women to grind corn and make tortillas; kill, pluck, and cook turkeys; shape tamales and tuck them into corn husks. They also needed women who could nurse, cure illnesses, and heal wounds; they already had so many wounds. And then there was the other thing, the inevitable thing, the thing that would eventually leave Marina with a child who would first and foremost belong to its father, whoever that turned out to be.

They'd given her a Maya name when she was first enslaved, and now she had a new name in the new language, too: Marina. Her original name had stopped mattering long ago. The Chontal men, and now the Spanish ones, only cared about what she could give them. She was interchangeable: a woman, a slave, a cook, a healer, a concubine. No matter how fully she devoted herself to those roles, or how skilled she grew at their duties, she, like her name, would always be replaceable.

When the ambassadors arrived at their camp on the coast, Marina knew immediately who had sent them. It was Moctezuma, the man who ruled the empire that had traded her life away. Only he would have the resources and the cunning to send such an extravagant gift to the foreigners. The ambassadors greeted the foreigners with all the linguistic flourishes of high Nahuatl. They wanted to intimidate, but they also wanted to communicate.

The foreigners had a translator already, one of their own who had been shipwrecked years earlier and had learned Yucatec Mayan during his time as a slave in the peninsula. He could communicate well enough with those who spoke Chontal Mayan, a related language, although not perfectly. In her time with the foreigners, Marina had already noticed him struggling, as had many of the women. So many of them knew what it felt like to be forced to learn a new language under duress, but they didn't know how it felt to be rescued and welcomed back into their own.

So when Marina once again heard her own language, Nahuatl, she almost couldn't believe she still understood it. Especially since the ambassadors were speaking the noble form of the language, with its own grammar and strict stylistic rules. Marina, like other girls who lived in the orbit of noble households, had learned it in preparation for her intended marriage, through which alliances would be reinforced and bloodlines intertwined. It was an imagined future Marina never got to live. But here was the language of power she had been promised, being spoken in her presence so many years after any remnant of power had been stripped away from her.

Marina tried to ignore the ambassadors as she focused on grinding corn. She tried to let their words flow past her comprehension as she had done so many times among the Chontal Maya. But Nahuatl lived in her heart, next to her original name, and she couldn't choose not to listen. She heard the ambassadors presenting their lavish gifts, meticulously noting where in the empire each had come from and how many artisans had contributed to each sculpture or piece of featherwork. She heard them extending an invitation from the *huey tlatoani* himself to visit Tenochtitlan, where more splendors awaited. She heard their confusion and offense when the foreigners reached greedily for the gold and silver and ignored the jade, textiles, and intricate god costumes sewn in the royal workshops for the most important ceremonies. She could tell that the translator understood none of it, and she could tell that tensions were rising.

He said it would be a great honor for Moctezuma to receive your company in Tenochtitlan. The words slipped out in Chontal Mayan before Marina could stop them. She had meant to stay invisible and let anonymity protect her in this volatile situation. She almost hoped the translator hadn't understood her. But he had. He grabbed her by the arm and hauled her to the center of the group, demanding she help him talk to the ambassadors. And suddenly there it was, the language of power, flowing from her lips again.

She wondered if in another life, if she hadn't been traded away by her family to appease the empire, she could have been married to one of these ambassadors. But as the months passed and the foreigners started their journey toward the capital, she realized she had stumbled into much more power in her new life. She wasn't married to an ambassador. She *was* an ambassador. The leader of the foreigners needed her, and he forbade his men from touching her. If Marina fell pregnant and had a child—or worse, died during the birth—she wouldn't be available to translate. Soon she and the other translator worked out a system: She would translate from Nahuatl to Mayan, and he from Mayan to the foreign tongue. She could tell he didn't always understand her, and so she started learning Spanish, too. That was the language of power among the foreigners, and she knew if she didn't speak it, she might not be able to hold on to her new position for long.

Working with the other translator, and then on her own, Marina spoke the foreigners' words to the fierce Tlaxcalteca, the embattled Cholulans, and every other community they met, and she spoke their words back to the foreigners. When she could tell that one side or the other wouldn't like a message she was delivering, she judged when to throw in threats of force and when to soften demands into diplomatic requests. She was, she sometimes thought, the only one who knew what all these men were really thinking, and what they really wanted. She was the one who decided whether they understood each other, and how well. She was the one who decided what would happen next.

Her reputation traveled along with news of the foreigners, and the leaders of every community they traveled through sought her out first. In recognition of her importance, they added the Nahuatl honorific "tzin" to the end of her Spanish name, and soon Marina became Malintzin—another new name. Of all the costumes Marina had been forced to wear, all the identities she'd been forced to assume, Malintzin was the one that could finally protect her. Marina had been anonymous and disposable, but Malintzin was indispensable. Malintzin was known.

And so Marina found herself on the southern causeway leading into Tenochtitlan, listening as Moctezuma addressed the foreigners in high Nahuatl, with its required displays of humility. He was their humble servant, he would be honored to gift them the splendors of the capital, he had never received such impressive guests. Marina knew, according to the florid linguistic conventions of the nobility, that his speech was meant to convey the opposite. It was meant to show just how powerful Moctezuma was to be able to extend such generosity to the foreigners, and to place them forever in his debt.

But in that moment, Marina translated his words literally. She saw the surprise and ambition spread across Cortés's face as she told him Moctezuma was offering him the city and everything in it. The Mexica didn't deserve her diplomacy, not after they had taken away her future. They didn't deserve the protection they never would have thought she had the power to bestow. She didn't trust the foreigners, but she hated the empire. Moctezuma may have been *huey tlatoani*, Marina thought, but if there was a great speaker among them on the causeway that day, it was her.

◉

One of the most pervasive "myths of the Spanish conquest," to borrow Restall's words, is that a few hundred Spanish soldiers were able to take down one of the most powerful empires in the world. The conquistadors are remembered as both wily underdogs who overcame impossible odds and preordained victors whose technological and cultural superiority made their triumph inevitable. The Indigenous people they met are stereotyped as enemies and victims, their communities destined to be destroyed.

In reality, it wasn't European cunning, weapons, technology, religion, or even disease that made it possible to defeat the Aztec Empire. It was the thousands of Indigenous soldiers, including and especially the Tlaxcalteca, who allied with the Europeans and fought alongside them. Unhappy with the Triple Alliance's hegemony, the Tlaxcalteca invited the invading Spaniards into an alliance and arguably directed at least some of the battles that followed, such as the attack on Cholula. The conquistadors claimed responsibility for instigating the massacre in their accounts of the war, but it was the Tlaxcalteca who had reason to attack the holy city, as Cholula had recently broken its alliance with Tlaxcallan. The Spaniards were never seen as uniquely frightening or invincible foes, but they were unpredictable wild cards with different technologies, different rules of war, and no preexisting allegiances. The Tlaxcalteca, marginalized in a political world dominated by the Aztec Empire, had little to lose and much to gain by allying with those who had no qualms about using unprecedented violence to destroy that world.

Other Indigenous groups stood unwavering in their opposition to the invaders, and still others continually changed their position as political power structures shifted and transformed around them. In Mexico and throughout the Americas, there was no one way Indigenous groups reacted to the arrival of the foreigners, just as there was no single "Native American" identity that existed before the creation of colonial states and the new racial hierarchies they invented and enforced. The Mexica were distinct from the Tlaxcalteca, and both were different from the Maya groups in the southeast, who in turn were different from each other. Political and social identities were created and sustained at the level of the local community, not anything resembling the modern nation-state, much less an entire continent. Class differences also permeated those local communities, especially in Mesoamerica, dividing nobles, commoners, and enslaved people into distinct social strata while also binding them together in a web of interdependent roles.

The Spaniards could not have won the war against the Aztec Empire without their Indigenous allies fighting alongside them, advising them on strategy, and providing them with shelter and reinforcements after defeats. (They also received help from the many Africans, enslaved and free, who were among their company, as well as enslaved Indigenous people they had brought from the Caribbean.) These alliances were far more decisive than the novel weapons the foreigners used. The Mexica and other Indigenous soldiers fought with spears, bows and arrows, slingshots, and clubs spiked with razor-sharp obsidian blades, whereas the Spaniards had horses, steel swords, crossbows, canons, and guns. Horses and anything that exploded with gunpowder would have surprised and frightened people who had never seen them before, at least at the beginning of the invasion. But in the extensive documentation of the Spanish-Aztec war by authors on both sides, "At no point do the [Indigenous] warriors seem to have been awestruck or paralyzed with fear by the strangers' weapons," writes historian Camilla Townsend.

And with good reason. Sixteenth-century guns were slow to load—some models "could only fire once every 10 minutes"—and notoriously inaccurate, "making them more of a psychological than tactical advantage," writes archaeologist David Carballo. Horses could be decisive in battles that took place on large areas of open ground, but not in the tight spaces and confined routes of urban warfare, which would eventually determine the outcome of the war. Steel blades lasted longer than obsidian ones, but the Spanish-Tlaxcalteca forces used plenty of obsidian, too, especially if they couldn't recover their used steel spear points and arrowheads after battle. Most conquistadors weren't wealthy or well-equipped enough to have full metal armor, but many came to outfit themselves in the cotton-quilted armor used by Mesoamerican soldiers, which offered strong protection against obsidian weapons. Both Indigenous and European fighters quickly adapted to the weapons used by the other and took advantage of the other side's technological weaknesses whenever possible.

It is true, however, that the Spaniards brought with them a dangerous new type of war: total war. European armies had for centuries set out to kill their enemies—often seen as a racial or religious "other"—on the battlefield in order to seize direct control of their territory. This ran counter to Mesoamerican rules of war, which called for taking captives in ritualized battles and allowing the victor to extract tribute from those it defeated. "The key aspect of Spanish power during the conquest was precisely their excessive capacity for violence," writes historian Federico Navarrete Linares. Their willingness to "murder enemy leaders, mutilate ambassadors, rape women, and massacre unarmed populations" shocked their Indigenous enemies and allies alike and no doubt played a role in convincing some in those communities, including Tlaxcallan, to become their allies in the first place. The invaders' readiness to engage in a new kind of violence challenged Mesoamerican conceptions of what war was for and what it could achieve.

◉

After entering the Mexica capital in November 1519, the Spanish invaders stayed in Tenochtitlan for eight months. Colonial accounts often elide the length and detail of such periods of uneasy coexistence, preferring to gloss over the negotiations, translations, misunderstandings, and accidents that reveal how little was actually under European control. In Tenochtitlan, although the conquistadors claimed to have taken Moctezuma captive as soon as they entered the city, all accounts document the *huey tlatoani* going about his regular business, receiving royal visitors, spending time in his gardens and zoo, and overseeing religious ceremonies. It's much more likely Moctezuma was the one keeping the Spaniards prisoner, under the guise of hosting them as honored guests. He confined them to the lavish quarters of his father's palace, watching them closely the whole time. He accompanied them on excursions to the Great Temple, his hunting zoo, and the city's most impressive market, and he offered them gifts of gold and jade from his personal storehouse. Everything was a distraction, and a test.

This period of confinement and relative inaction in the capital allowed Cortés's past to catch up with him. When he arrived in Mexico and began to claim land for Spain, he had been defying orders from Cuba's colonial governor, who was the only one licensed by the crown to explore and conquer Mesoamerica. By leapfrogging several levels of colonial hierarchy and claiming authority over the new territory for himself, Cortés threatened to cut Cuba's governor and many other powerful officials out of the hoped-for—although still largely imaginary—conquest spoils, as well as the political prestige that accompanied them. Cortés made no secret of this rebellion and even sent men to argue his case directly to the king of Spain. As the legal case dragged on, the frustrated governor sent one thousand men from Cuba to Mexico in the spring of 1520 with orders to arrest Cortés and, effectively, begin the conquest process anew.

Moctezuma allowed Cortés and some of his Spanish and Indigenous soldiers—as well as the translator Malintzin—to leave Tenochtitlan to meet the new arrivals from Cuba on the coast. It's possible that after months of careful observation, Moctezuma had come to understand that there were factions among the foreigners and trouble between Cortés and his superior. He might have suspected that the men on the new ships, loaded with weapons, had come to subdue Cortés. If Moctezuma allowed Cortés to go to the coast, the Spaniard might not be allowed to return, which may have suited the *huey tlatoani*.

But after a few weeks of bribery, and then fighting, Cortés's forces took the leader of the new expedition captive and absorbed his troops into their own company. This provided the small Spanish force with a much-needed infusion of energy, supplies, horses, and men, although it's unlikely a small increase in the number of foreigners returning to the city would have altered the balance of power in Tenochtitlan, where Moctezuma remained firmly in control and every male citizen was trained for war.

In the absence of Cortés's command and Malintzin's diplomatic skills, however, the foreigners who had remained in Tenochtitlan broke the precarious peace in the capital with yet another unprecedented show of violence. Tenochtitlan's residents were enjoying a religious festival to mark the end of the dry season, and the Spaniards were invited to watch a ceremonial dance honoring two of the Mexica's most important gods, which likely would have traditionally culminated in sacrifices. But instead of watching as the polite guests they were expected to be, the foreigners interrupted the ceremony, trapped the priests and spectators inside a courtyard, and massacred them all. As Mexica soldiers rallied to fight back, the Spaniards retreated inside their palace complex. They remained there for weeks as the city outside prepared for war with the foreigners, who had finally tipped their hand and crossed the line from guests to enemies.

It was during this volatile period that Cortés returned to the city with his army, enlivened by fresh men from Cuba, and that Moctezuma died. The details of his death remain hazy to this day. What is known is that after the massacre of Mexica nobles and priests by the Spaniards who had remained in the city, the invaders finally managed to take the *huey tlatoani* and his court captive. At some point Moctezuma ascended to the roof of the palace-turned-fortress, apparently to address his subjects who had gathered outside. The people were angry about the massacre, and they were throwing stones. One of those stones may or may not have hit Moctezuma in the head, and the blow may or may not have killed him. Restall thinks this wound—or even the rumor of such a wound—provided the perfect cover for the Spanish forces to murder Moctezuma and blame it on his own people. The invaders unquestionably killed the other Mexica nobles they held prisoner at the same time.

The Spaniards and their allies knew they had to escape the city as soon as possible. On June 30, 1520, under the cover of night, they gathered as much treasure as they could carry and fled along the causeway toward the western shore of the lake. There the Mexica, led by Moctezuma's brother Cuitláhuac, were ready for them. Soon the water was choked with the bodies of men, horses, and the boxes of supplies and treasure the Spaniards were attempting to carry out of the city. Cortés escaped across the causeway, but the Mexica killed approximately six hundred Europeans, including many of the fresh new arrivals from Cuba, along with more than one thousand Tlaxcalteca and other Indigenous allies. Those who escaped made haste back to the safety of Tlaxcallan.

The Mexica fared much better in the battle, but the city bore its scars. Canals, bridges, and other infrastructure were severely damaged, and the Mexica were still mourning those killed in the massacre and the unrest that followed, including Moctezuma. Although Tenochtitlan's council quickly elected Cuitláhuac as the next *huey tlatoani*, the political transition took place amid great trauma and uncertainty. For the Mexica, this was likely the first moment they experienced the arrival of the foreigners as anything approaching apocalyptic. Attacked in their own city for the first time and reeling from the sudden loss of the leader who had kept a volatile situation under control for over a year, the Mexica were just now beginning to understand that they faced a threat capable of upending their lives, identities, and place in the world.

◉

Cuitláhuac missed his brother. All he could think during his election and inauguration as Tenochtitlan's new *huey tlatoani* was that Moctezuma should still be here, occupying the role he was born for and had so capably filled. Moctezuma should have been the one to the direct the assault on the foreigners and their allies as the cowards tried to flee the city. Maybe if he had been, none of them would have escaped.

But Cuitláhuac was now the new Great Speaker, and with the surviving foreigners licking their wounds in Tlaxcallan, his primary responsibility shifted away from planning the next battle and toward directing the reconstruction of the city. The canals were a delicate system and needed to be repaired as soon as possible, and planting in the chinampas should have been underway but had been delayed by battle preparations. Wars were traditionally fought in the dry season, while the rainy season was dedicated to farming. But even though the rains had begun, Cuitláhuac made sure Tenochtitlan's men maintained their military training regimen. It was clearer than ever the foreigners didn't respect any rules, most especially when and where war should happen. Cuitláhuac knew he and his men would have to adapt to this new, less predictable way of fighting.

But the foreigners left something behind in Tenochtitlan, something that undermined Cuitláhuac's plans for the city's recovery. A disease started to spread just a few weeks after the foreigners were driven out. People fell ill with fever, vomiting, unbearable pain, and a frightening rash whose red spots soon filled with pus. The healers had never seen such marks before. Nearly one third of those who fell ill died, and those who survived were left covered in scars, and some blind. People couldn't take care of each other, let alone train for future battles or reconstruct what had been damaged in the fighting. Those who had been injured—which included some of the Mexica's strongest soldiers—were especially susceptible in their weakened state.

Cuitláhuac still wished his brother were here, but at the same time he was relieved Moctezuma had not lived to see this, Tenochtitlan's darkest night. He was pushing himself to the edge trying to hold the Triple Alliance together and direct the work that could be done to repair the city, but so little progress could be made, given the illness immobilizing his people. Cuitláhuac went to bed exhausted and achy, hoping it was just the weeks of exertion taking their toll. But in the morning he noticed the first spots of a rash on his leg. He wanted to believe he would be one of the ones to survive, but he suspected that was impossible. There would be no relief for him or his people while the foreigners were still in the land, deploying their most powerful weapon: chaos.

◉

Back in April 1520, when Cortés went to intercept the new arrivals from Cuba, he had received a great gift, although he didn't know it at the time. In addition to the fresh men, horses, and several ships' worth of supplies, the new arrivals brought along a passenger they might not have been aware of: smallpox.

Legend holds the infected was an enslaved African, although in truth it could have been anyone. It could have traveled from the Caribbean as "a scab in a blanket," or in the body of a living person who didn't develop symptoms until after they arrived. Wherever it came from, the disease raced back to Tenochtitlan along with the panicked Cortés and his troops. Even if someone had been sick, wounds, infections, and diseases were a common part of the conquistador experience, and Cortés had just received news of the massacre at the festival. He wouldn't have let an outbreak slow him down.

Although the Spaniards were decisively driven out of Tenochtitlan, the virus had already gained a foothold in the capital. The invaders also carried it to every town they passed through during their retreat, including their safe haven of Tlaxcallan. Smallpox began to spread like wildfire throughout the Valley of Mexico and beyond. Some Europeans also fell dreadfully ill, but the disease was completely new, and thus far more dangerous, to the people of Mesoamerica. Its fever and painful pustules quickly amassed on bodies, leaping from town to town and city to city, infecting the invaders' enemies and allies alike. In Tenochtitlan, the new *huey tlatoani* Cuitláhuac succumbed to the disease after only eighty days of rule, along with thousands of his citizens. In one postconquest account of the epidemic written in Nahuatl, the authors wrote, "There was indeed perishing . . . No longer could [the sick people] move, no longer could they bestir themselves, no longer could they raise themselves . . . Indeed many people died of [the pustules], and many just died of hunger. There was death from hunger; there was no one to take care of another; there was no one to attend to another."

Today, colonial epidemics like these are largely blamed for devastating Indigenous communities after their first contacts with Europeans. These diseases were materially, psychologically, and generationally destructive, as the Black Death had been in Europe. But just as during the Black Death, violence, abuse, and social hierarchies played a determinative role in this apocalypse, multiplying and worsening the diseases' biological effects. Many Indigenous people fell ill with these new diseases under circumstances that precipitously increased mortality rates and made it much harder for their communities to recover after the epidemic passed.

Tenochtitlan, Tlaxcallan, and the surrounding cities first faced smallpox during wartime, and the disease killed both Mexica and Tlaxcalteca political leaders, amplifying fear and uncertainty during an already unpredictable and harrowing time. Later epidemics in what would become Mexico, Peru, the United States, and beyond tore through Indigenous communities confined to crowded missions and, later, reservations; forced into backbreaking labor on plantations and mines; terrorized by slave-raiding and other attacks by colonists; cut off from their traditional food sources; removed from their ancestral land; and deprived of basic sanitation. Bioarchaeological studies of Indigenous people buried on missions and in other colonial contexts in Florida, Peru, the U.S. Southwest, and California show many of the signs of lifelong ill health and malnourishment that Black Death bioarchaeologist Sharon DeWitte found predisposed people to dying of plague in London.

Archaeologists working in the United States and Canada haven't found much evidence of epidemics striking Indigenous communities before direct contact with European colonists. But one known case underlines the decisive role that colonial violence played in multiplying these diseases' destruction elsewhere in the continent. The Awahnichi were hunter-gatherers who lived in California's Yosemite Valley. In the 1850s, an Awahnichi leader named Tenaya told an American miner and militia volunteer about a "black sickness"—likely smallpox—that swept through his community before they had met white settlers. The disease probably arrived with Indigenous people fleeing the state's disease-ridden Catholic missions, run by Spanish priests. The archaeologist Kathleen Hull excavated in the Yosemite Valley and analyzed data on the number of Awahnichi villages occupied, the amount of debris created by manufacturing obsidian tools, and changes in controlled burns as revealed by tree ring data. A sudden drop in those indicators of human presence suggested that the Awahnichi experienced a 30 percent population decline around 1800—the standard, worldwide mortality rate from smallpox until it was eradicated in the 1980s.

Before the epidemic struck, the Awahnichi numbered only about three hundred; the death of about ninety people would have been devastating. But unlike the Mexica, hit with smallpox between all-out battles for their city's survival, or the Indigenous captives on missions, sickened within the context of squalid living conditions and horrific abuse, the Awahnichi could—and did—recover. They employed a strategy they had likely used many times over the centuries, to deal with catastrophes ranging from drought to volcanic eruptions: seeking help from their neighbors, who welcomed them into a temporary disaster community. Tenaya told the militia volunteer that after the black sickness, the Awahnichi left their traditional home and moved to the eastern side of the Sierra Nevada mountains to the territory of the Kutzadika'a, or Mono Paiute, people. There, the Awahnichi found support and, in the longer term, an opportunity to rebuild their community through intermarriage. Tenaya himself was the son of an Awahnichi leader who had witnessed the epidemic and a Mono Paiute woman.

After about twenty years, the Awahnichi moved back to their valley homeland, their numbers bolstered and their culture preserved. In her artifact and tree ring data, Hull can see the Awahnichi's sudden departure, but also their return. The epidemic would have been an enormous blow to the Awahnichi. But because they were not yet living under the strictures of colonial rule, they were able to use their own traditions of resilience to recover and even grow. After their return to the Yosemite Valley, they became a safe haven for other Indigenous people fleeing the disruptions of the nascent California gold rush.

But even for those Indigenous communities who lost staggering numbers of people while struggling to defend themselves and their land against colonial incursions, epidemics did not inevitably doom Native nations to long-term cultural, political, or even demographic decline, as so many of us have been taught to believe. In the 1630s, smallpox swept through the Indigenous nations of eastern North America as they were adjusting to the relatively new presence of English, Dutch, and French settlers in their territories. "I have seen maladies in the country before, but never have I seen anything like this," said one Wyandot leader during the epidemic. Afterward, the Iroquois, united in a political alliance called the Five Nations League, had lost almost half their people and found themselves "horribly exposed" amid English, Dutch, and French colonies, writes historian Pekka Hämäläinen. And so, they declared war—specifically, a series of "mourning wars" aimed at transforming other Indigenous communities into Iroquois through capture and ritual adoption, thereby restoring the Five Nations' political strength and the world's spiritual balance. Smallpox and its devastation "triggered the most explosive Indigenous expansion since the migrations across the length of the hemisphere," Hämäläinen writes, as the Iroquois invaded new territory and took control of colonial trade relations, and other nations fled west to escape their attacks. Fifty years after half their people died of smallpox, the Five Nations "were at the height of the power." Apocalyptic colonial epidemics destabilized the world as it had once been, and they opened up new, previously unimaginable possibilities as the affected communities built a different kind of future.

◉

In 1520 and 1521, the Mexica of Tenochtitlan were not yet living under the systematic deprivation and violence of a colonial state. But even though they had emerged victorious from their first official battle with the invaders, they soon found themselves facing the worst version of the Europeans' new kind of total war: a prolonged siege.

As the Spaniards recovered and regrouped in Tlaxcallan, they threatened and periodically attacked nearby towns, frightening many of them into abandoning their support of the Mexica. Ships full of men, horses, and supplies continued to arrive from the Caribbean, allowing the Spaniards to recover their resources and strength in a way the Mexica couldn't, as they struggled to return to day-to-day life after the smallpox epidemic. Remembering how they had been hemmed in by the canals and causeways of Tenochtitlan, the Spaniards used some of their new supplies to build small ships they could sail on the city's lake. They found the perfect place from which to launch their naval attacks when the lakeside city of Texcoco, formerly second-in-command of the Triple Alliance, switched its allegiance away from the Mexica after a group of Texcocan nobles who had been sidelined by Moctezuma sought the Spaniards' help in deposing the dead *huey tlatoani*'s nephew from their throne. Afterward, the new rulers of Texcoco returned the favor by fighting by the Europeans' side as they launched their assault on Tenochtitlan.

At the beginning of the six-month-long siege, the Spaniards and their allies destroyed the aqueduct that carried fresh water into the Mexica capital. They also continually attempted to fill in the city's canals, in order to create more open space that they could control with horses. The Mexica fought back, widening canals wherever they could, attacking the Spanish ships from scores of canoes, and sneaking food across the lake by night. They drove pointed stakes into the lakebed to impale the ships from below. They killed many Europeans, including in the public executions they had always used to terrify their enemies, and they once came extremely close to taking Cortés captive. But as a noble from Texcoco told Cortés when spirits flagged after his close call, "There are so many thousand bands of warriors in the city that they are bound to eat up all the provisions they have, and the water they are now drinking is brackish, for it comes from pools they themselves have dug. They are catching the rainwater and making do with that. But if you stop their food and water, how can they go on? They will suffer worse from hunger than from war."

Thanks to the Mexica's ingenious environmental engineering, it had been nearly a century since Tenochtitlan's once precarious position in the lake had felt like a threat. But now, with their canals and aqueducts destroyed, their homes razed, and their food supplies dwindling, all the harshness and isolation of their island home returned. Meanwhile, the Spaniards and their allies had access to the functionally unlimited resources of the entire valley, as well as what had arrived from the Caribbean. Slowly the Mexica forces retreated to the city center, and then finally to Tlatelolco, Tenochtitlan's semi-independent sister city on the north shore of the same island. After three months of brutal fighting, the new *huey tlatoani*, Cuauhtémoc, boarded a canoe with his wife and set off to surrender to the foreigners.

◉

One afternoon early in a recent rainy season, I took the metro to Mexico City's Historic Center, commonly known as the Centro, for a tour of postapocalyptic Tenochtitlan. I boarded at the station named after Cuauhtémoc and marked with an icon of a fierce eagle head. Four stops later I arrived at one of the Centro's busiest public transit hubs and joined the flow of commuters walking past a patio occupied by a squat stone rectangle topped by a circular platform, rising about twelve feet high. It's a small shrine dedicated to Ehécatl, the Aztec god of wind, uncovered during construction of the metro in 1967. Mexico's National Institute of Anthropology and History (INAH), which manages the research and preservation of the country's national patrimony, once called the shrine its "smallest, but most visited, archaeological site."

I transferred to another train headed to the heart of both the fallen empire and the modern nation. I surfaced in the Zócalo, an enormous plaza that once sat amid the most important Mexica temples and palaces and is now flanked by the Metropolitan Cathedral and the National Palace, the seat of Mexico's federal government. I skirted the eastern edge of the cathedral, which butts up against the ruins of Tenochtitlan's Great Temple, known today as the Templo Mayor. I turned left down a pedestrian street and sat down at a café behind the cathedral as rain clouds gathered overhead. A few minutes later I was joined by Raúl Barrera Rodríguez, the archaeologist in charge of the program that's excavated much of what's known of Tenochtitlan's sacred core.

As the shrine in the metro station attests, it's impossible to dig anywhere in downtown Mexico City without finding the ruins of the Aztec capital that preceded it. But archaeology here isn't as straightforward as excavating somewhere like the Maya city of Aké or the ancient Egyptian town of Abydos. Today, those places are rural towns that occupy a fraction of the older cities' footprints, so it's not hard to find an interesting place to dig that's also minimally disruptive of current residents' daily lives. But ever since the Mexica settled on the island that would become Tenochtitlan, this area has been a densely packed urban core and the seat of political, religious, and economic power for three successive states: the Aztec Empire, colonial New Spain, and modern Mexico. Newer phases of the city's life cover and obscure older ones. Countless historically significant sites, from the remains of Moctezuma's gardens to the graves of Mexico's earliest Catholic officials, lie underneath present-day streets, homes, and shops whose activity can't be interrupted by an excavation. Plus, many of the colonial buildings on top of Tenochtitlan are also considered historic, including the cathedral; clearing them away just to see what's underneath is out of the question.

Barrera Rodríguez and the other archaeologists who work in the heart of downtown Mexico City usually can't determine where they excavate. Archaeology here must be opportunistic, piggybacking on construction projects or taking advantage of the restoration or demolition of damaged buildings. This work is referred to as salvage archaeology or rescue archaeology, as excavation teams are called in to document and save what they can before it would otherwise be destroyed. Salvage is important and necessary work the world over, and it's often the only chance archaeologists have to look underneath still-functioning cities. (London's East Smithfield cemetery of Black Death victims, for example, was excavated during a construction project.) Still, salvage archaeology is rarely a scientist's first choice. They would prefer to formulate their research questions first and then go in search of excavation sites that have a good chance of answering them. During salvage, archaeologists interested in ancient palace life and elite politics might end up meticulously collecting the remains of seeds embedded in an abandoned farm field, or those who want to investigate the deep past of one particular town or neighborhood might find themselves moving quickly and more shallowly along the planned route of a new highway or train.

Barrera Rodríguez, the director of INAH's Urban Archaeology Program, doesn't share many of the worries of the typical salvage archaeologist. Despite the constraints on where they can excavate and how long projects can last, the scientists of the Urban Archaeology Program are almost always guaranteed to find something significant every time their trowels touch earth. Even the most important discovery in Mexico

City archaeology was made accidentally: The razed ruins of the Templo Mayor were rediscovered in 1978 when electrical workers digging under an intersection in the Centro stumbled upon an enormous stone disc carved with the image of the Aztec moon goddess Coyolxauhqui. The monument stretched ten feet across and weighed nearly eight tons. It was strikingly intact, except for a single crack running across its diameter that cut the goddess's torso in half. As archaeologists dug below the city streets around Coyolxauhqui's body, they found the Templo Mayor's still-sturdy stone walls, staircases flanked by sculptures of serpents, rooms decorated with brightly painted murals, and offerings of obsidian blades, seashells, corals, animal bones, and human skulls. Most people had believed that what was left of the Templo Mayor lay directly under the Metropolitan Cathedral, not quite lost but forever inaccessible. But it was actually next door to the church, not underneath. Today, visitors can walk through the remains of the Templo Mayor's nested stone facades, each representing a new construction phase, undertaken by a new Mexica emperor, to expand the temple's size and grandeur.

I first met Barrera Rodríguez after his team made a similar rediscovery during the restoration of a colonial building just a few doors down from the café where we currently sat: the remains of Tenochtitlan's *tzompantli*, the imposing ceremonial rack where the skulls of executed soldiers and sacrificed captives were displayed. Some conquistadors and colonial priests wrote about the *tzompantli*, but historians and archaeologists were hesitant to trust their descriptions because of their well-documented propensity for exaggerating the horrors of the Mexica's ritual executions. After nearly five hundred years without any sign of the *tzompantli*, some researchers wondered if it had existed at all. Still, when Barrera Rodríguez and his team began finding hundreds of skull fragments underneath the building's colonial floor, they had enough historical information to be certain of what they had found.

Unlike many archaeologists, Barrera Rodríguez and other researchers working in Tenochtitlan and central Mexico can enrich their work with information from a plethora of historical documents, including Indigenous and European maps, postconquest histories written in Nahuatl by Indigenous scholars, and the letters and testimonies sent to the Spanish king by various conquistadors. But these sources aren't always trustworthy, and they are never transparent. Documents written by Europeans "aren't eyewitness accounts" in the way we would understand such things today, says Restall. For example, *The Conquest of New Spain* by Bernal Díaz del Castillo is one of the most famous firsthand accounts of the Spanish-Aztec war. It was also written decades after the war it purports to depict as an appeal to the king, after Díaz felt he had been unjustly deprived of his rightful share of conquest spoils. His account, and thousands of similar documents stored in archives, almost certainly record purposeful exaggerations, misremembered details, and false or invented memories. At the same time, Restall says, "there are sentences in [Díaz's account] that are as close as we can get to accurate descriptions of exactly what happened. The problem is, we don't know what those sentences are. And we don't know how many [there are]. It could be one hundred. It could be ten. It could be one thousand sentences that are absolutely spot-on accurate . . . We don't know."

But conquistador propaganda is easier to spot than the doubts and biases that infuse the Indigenous written sources. In the decades after the conquest, the children and grandchildren of the Indigenous elite wrote historical annals in their native language of Nahuatl. They combined earlier glyph- and pictograph-based Nahuatl writing with an alphabetization of the language introduced by colonial priests. These annals and codices preserve much of Mexica and Tlaxcalteca history, culture, and traditions from before and after the arrival of Europeans. Their authors were Indigenous, but they were also raised Catholic and trained in new convent schools with an eye toward becoming priests. Some wrote their annals in collaboration with Spanish friars, focusing on information these European Catholics, and their church, wanted to know in order to more effectively evangelize Indigenous communities. Other annals appear to have been self-directed and intended solely for an Indigenous audience, using "rich and evocative" language to record their own history, not respond to European questionnaires.

These Indigenous scribes and authors were people who "desperately needed to come to terms with the conquest," writes Townsend, and their own dual identities within the society it created. They still occupied the city's upper echelons of social class and education, but their status as Indigenous put them at ever increasing risk for abuse, exploitation, and excessive taxation under New Spain's emerging racial caste system that attempted to organize and rank the many different kinds of people who now coexisted in Mexico City—not only Spaniards, Indigenous Americans, and enslaved and free Africans, but the children of all the possible unions between them. There were parts of their history that many postconquest Indigenous and mestizo scholars wanted to disavow—their ancestors' "pagan" religion, for example—and other parts they wanted to preserve and protect, such as the accomplishments of the Mexica emperors and their grandparents' memories of the Spanish-Aztec war. The Nahuatl annals weren't propaganda in the same way conquistador accounts were, but they, too, had agendas, only some of which scholars can decipher today.

Archaeology has its biases and agendas, too. Barrera Rodríguez's work in the Centro focuses on Tenochtitlan's sacred core, which contained the city's richest palaces and grandest temples, and where commoners may have visited but wouldn't have lived. The Aztec material his team finds receives more research attention than the colonial artifacts above it (although they are excavated and cataloged as well). Because of the limitations of salvage work, their excavations are often confined to the footprint of one modern building at a time and can't be extended to follow interesting finds. Much of the *tzompantli*, for example, remains unexcavated under the present-day pedestrian street and the back patio of the cathedral, even though archaeologists know it's there.

In Mexico City, neither archaeology nor history has a monopoly on truth about the past. Artifacts and documents fill in each other's gaps but also sometimes clash, generating productive questions and debates. When it comes to understanding the apocalypse of conquest and colonialism, Indigenous annals and conquistador testimonies can provide incredible detail, including names, dates, the personalities of the major players, and their emotions during such a transformative time. But there's at least one thing Barrera Rodríguez can see in his excavations that went unrecorded elsewhere: how Tenochtitlan's Indigenous commoners resisted the erasure of their city.

A few doors down from the café where we met is the Spanish Cultural Center, one of the first places Barrera Rodríguez worked after becoming the director of the Urban Archaeology Program. As part of a renovation, the cultural center wanted to add underground parking. "I like it when they tell me they want to build a parking lot," Barrera Rodríguez said with a sly smile. "It'll go well for us."

When Barrera Rodríguez's team begins an excavation, they start by digging through the debris of modern life—discarded plastic, concrete, old drain pipes, and messes of electrical cables. Then come the metal and glass of the early twentieth and late nineteenth centuries, then the porcelain and glazed, painted pottery of the colonial period. Decorative styles and manufacturing processes change as they tunnel back in time, marking the beginning and end of different eras. As the team reaches the transitional period immediately after the conquest, they sometimes find hybrid ceramic forms, such as plates supported by three legs, an Indigenous style, but decorated with images of European plants. And then, eventually, they hit the basalt slab floors and orange-and-black ceramics characteristic of the Mexica city.

Digging under the cultural center, Barrera Rodríguez and his team found a staircase leading up to a large rectangular patio dotted with the bases of sturdy columns that once supported a roof and divided the space into three or four rooms. The building was most likely the calmecac: the imperial school, described by postconquest Indigenous scholars, where the children of the Mexica elite studied philosophy, religion, political science, astronomy, and warfare. "The underground parking lot idea was canceled," Barrera Rodríguez said, and he and others at INAH worked with the cultural center to figure out a new building design that would protect the ruins. Now, the site is a public museum in the building's basement. It was the first stop on our tour.

The calmecac ruins sat in the middle of a hushed, darkened room, surrounded by vitrines holding excavated artifacts ranging from a wooden tool for planting corn on Tenochtitlan's chinampas to a rusty

Smith and Wesson handgun from the nineteenth or early twentieth century. The room's lighting highlights the patio where young Mexica nobles were once educated in their history and their responsibility to sustain Tenochtitlan's power and beauty long into the future. That vision was forever altered by the war that reduced the calmecac and the rest of the city's sacred core to rubble. According to Díaz, during the siege "[Cortés] had ordered that all houses should be pulled down and burnt and the bridged channels filled up . . . every building we captured was razed to the ground."

In the years immediately following the Mexica surrender, Tenochtitlan was a wasteland, and the surviving conquistadors decamped to a nearby lakeshore town called Coyoacán (now its own Mexico City neighborhood). Many didn't want to return to the ruined island and hoped to start fresh by establishing their colonial capital elsewhere. But in the end Cortés ordered the new city be built "in the heart of what had been Tenochtitlan," Barrera Rodríguez said. Leaving the former imperial capital in ruins would inevitably remind the Mexica of who they had been and what they had lost. "I think Cortés was terrified Tenochtitlan would return"—that its former citizens would resurrect the past capital and the power it stood for, if given the opportunity. And so, Barrera Rodríguez said, Tenochtitlan had to be "erased."

The Mexica commoners who survived the war and remained in Tenochtitlan after the surrender were compelled to participate in that painful labor. "They were forced to destroy their temples with their own hands. And with their own hands, they were forced to construct the new houses of the colonial city," Barrera Rodríguez said. Here in the calmecac, however, he found a sign the Mexica didn't simply capitulate to the Spaniards' demands. They may not have had the strength or the numbers to invite another war by openly refusing to participate in the colonial agenda, but they could still protect pieces of the city they had known. Barrera Rodríguez gestured to the now empty space above the calmecac patio. "Here's where they hid them," he said.

Before Barrera Rodríguez's excavation, a jumble of earth and stones had covered the patio, filling the narrow space between it and the floor of the colonial house built directly on top. As the team excavated the fill, they found a pit someone had dug into it, right underneath the colonial floor. Inside were nestled the damaged remains of two large statues: one of Mictlantecuhtli, the Mexica god of the underworld, and one of Xiuhtecuhtli, the god of fire. Mictlantecuhtli's face—represented by an exposed skull—was partially chipped off, and Xiuhtecuhtli's body lay in pieces. Barrera Rodríguez knew that the people who built the house, and who would have had the opportunity to bury the statues, were very likely Indigenous workers. The European residents of the new colonial house probably never knew they were there.

Several years later, during their excavations of the *tzompantli*, Barrera Rodríguez's team found something similar in the fill covering the skull rack, which had been smashed to pieces. For the Spanish invaders, the *tzompantli* represented the supposed idolatry and the imperial power of the Mexica, both of which they were trying to do away with. By commanding the Indigenous workers to bury and build over the destroyed skulls, they hoped to neutralize the power of the site. But the people "being forced to make [the *tzompantli*] disappear" in reality took a risk to commemorate it, Barrera Rodríguez said.

Just under the earliest colonial floor, and right above the remains of the *tzompantli*, someone had buried a cluster of ceremonial obsidian knives. At first the team thought they were looking at artifacts from the Mexica period; similar knives commonly turn up in both humble household graves and opulent temple offerings all over Tenochtitlan. But the position of the fill above the *tzompantli*'s smashed remains left no doubt the knives had been buried after it was destroyed, during the first years of New Spain. Someone had laid the *tzompantli* to rest with the same type of offering the Mexica had buried with their dead for centuries.

In the months and years after Cuauhtémoc's surrender, Aztec elites and commoners alike found themselves navigating an apocalyptic world they never could have imagined. When the Triple Alliance conquered a new territory, its main goal was to extract tribute. Its soldiers didn't remain in occupied lands, and local leaders were often allowed to stay in place, as long as they recognized and cooperated with the demands of the larger Aztec power structure. This new empire, however, was determined to expunge all reminders of Mexica power and impose its religion, technology, and culture on its new subjects as quickly as possible. As the colonists raced to reconstruct the urban core of the island in their image, it may have seemed to them like they were succeeding. But the burials and offerings hidden under the new city reveal how much resistance roiled just out of their sight, and likely beyond their comprehension.

I asked Barrera Rodríguez if he believed the Mexica survivors who buried the statues, knives, and so much else still waiting to be discovered thought—or hoped—someone like him would one day find these hidden, protected pieces of Tenochtitlan and bring some of the city they knew back to life.

"Of course," he said.

Chapter 8

HOW SLAVERY CREATED THE MODERN WORLD

Two hundred and fifty years ago, a ship docked at the port of Christiansted, in the Caribbean island of St. Croix. It was carrying the colonial world's most valuable, and least valued, cargo: enslaved Africans. Many had died locked in the hold of the ship during the treacherous and harrowing journey across the Atlantic. Those who survived were immediately marched to Christiansted's scale house, where all imported goods, including human beings, were inspected and processed. St. Croix was then a colony of Denmark, and the colonial government collected its share of taxes on their heads.

After weeks of imprisonment on board the ship—and often even longer in captivity in West Africa, being transported from place to place—none of the enslaved could be called healthy. Vomit and disease, agony and loss, violence and death permeated the stale air they had breathed for months. But their value to the European company that brought them to St. Croix now rested on their ability to labor—or at least, their perceived ability to labor. The slave traders who'd brought them to these shores oiled their skin to create the "illusion of health" and drive up their price. Long-stemmed tobacco pipes were thrust into the hands of women and men alike, their first possession on the island and an induction into the world of colonial traditions and their attendant objects.

The people who appeared to be the healthiest and most highly skilled were bought directly by St. Croix's colonial government and became property of the king of Denmark. These "royal slaves" would stay in Christiansted, living alongside Danish soldiers and laboring as porters, blacksmiths, carpenters, and other skilled professions. Over decades and centuries, the royal slaves built the streets, wharfs, forts, and houses of Christiansted, constructing and maintaining the city that imprisoned them.

Most of the new arrivals were sold to sugar plantations in St. Croix, and some to similar enterprises on other islands. For millennia, sugar had been a luxury good with the price to match. It required massive amounts of water, land, and toil to grow, harvest, and refine sugarcane into the sweet crystals so beloved by anyone lucky enough to try them. But the world was newly globalized, and the tastes, aromas, colors, and luxuries that had once been the special attributes of particular places could now be taken, reproduced, and sold everywhere else. The companies and countries that could both create and satisfy these new cravings, especially for sugar, were all but guaranteed tremendous wealth—if they could produce enough sugar at a low enough cost to turn this luxury into a commodity.

Some of the enslaved Africans sold off the boat in Christiansted were bound for Estate Little Princess, a plantation on St. Croix's northern coast. There, about 140 enslaved Africans were forced into the backbreaking work of clearing the land for sugarcane, planting and harvesting the fields, and then crushing the sugarcane and boiling it down to make processed sugar and rum. They were at constant risk of exhaustion, disease, and injury, especially from the huge machines that crushed the cane and the steaming hot boilers where it was cooked down to a pulp—as well as violence and death inflicted by the enslavers who oversaw and profited from their work. The enslavers kept meticulous records of the enslaved Africans' productivity and output, tallying up the value each person generated for the enslavers' families, companies, and countries, now believed to be the most important fact about their lives.

When they weren't performing these grueling, punishing tasks, the enslaved Africans lived in a village of small houses within sight of the plantation owner's mansion. Their houses were cramped, with two families to each structure. They were built by the enslaved themselves with scavenged stone, coral, and bagasse, the scorched, hardened ash left behind at the end of sugarcane processing. With barely enough space for parents and children all to lie down at night in the limited areas the enslavers set aside for their houses, the enslaved cooked and crafted outside in the tropical heat, always in full view of their enslavers.

But these houses—this plantation—were not only sites of suffering, torture, and deprivation, though they certainly were that. On Estate Little Princess, enslaved Africans married, had children, made friends, and built families under the constant threats of disease, murder, and being sold away. They grew their own food, collected water, shaped and fired new styles of pottery out of local clay, raised livestock, fished, and trapped wild game. They sold their surplus crops and crafts at markets they organized, and they used their earnings to buy items for themselves and their homes. In Estate Little Princess's village, hundreds of enslaved Africans lived all or part of their lives—lives that were just as, if not more, vibrant and complex than those lived by their enslavers, ensconced in their mansion one hundred feet away.

As the years passed in the village, glass bottles would break, ceramic plates and cooking pots would shatter, bones from meals would be tossed away, buttons would come loose and fall off. Precious and mundane possessions alike were lost or cast aside, becoming embedded in the packed-dirt floor of a house or covered by earth outside it. Generation after generation left behind fragments of the objects they'd owned, made, bought, used, chosen, and maybe even loved.

Slavery was abolished in St. Croix and Denmark's other colonies in 1848 after a revolt by the enslaved. But many of the newly freed had nowhere else to go and stayed on Estate Little Princess as paid laborers; the estate continued producing sugar until the 1960s. The land passed through many hands, as had St. Croix itself, and in 1917 the island became a territory of the United States, part of the U.S. Virgin Islands. As the last people finally moved out of the small village houses well into the 1970s, over two centuries of evidence of the lives that were lived there stayed behind, unassuming and undisturbed. Belongings transformed into trash and, gradually, into artifacts.

◉

The apocalypse of European colonialism rearranged lives, communities, identities, economies, and expectations around the world. It destroyed countless futures, while birthing new, or at least newly unrestrained, dreams—of land, power, and, most especially, riches. The wondrous museums and collections of Moctezuma were transported to Europe, fueling the artistic and scientific ambition of the Renaissance. Chocolate came to Europe, tobacco to Asia, silk to Mexico, and horses to the Great Plains. Corn, the Americas' agricultural miracle, went everywhere. Provincial nobodies without inheritances, titles, or opportunities sailed across an ocean and hoped to find new lives of influence, connections, and possibility. Some of them did.

In a world that suddenly seemed to offer the potential for unlimited wealth, few preexisting laws, and destabilized social norms, European colonial powers knew they needed a massive amount of labor to take advantage of these opportunities. And so, they built a newly globalized and racialized slave trade to ensure that the riches would never stop flowing back to them. Slavery had long existed around the world, usually as an outgrowth of a culture's traditions of war and tribute. Everyone from Amazonian villagers to Roman emperors, Mexica nobility to Viking raiders, captured, sold, bought, and held slaves, people taken in battles or traded as resources, stripped of their identities and social connections, and forced into subservience. Colonial slavery, on the other hand, was born of economic exploitation, particularly on European kingdoms' new overseas plantations. The first people to be held captive within what would become the apocalypse of the transatlantic slave trade were Africans sold to Portuguese traders in the mid-1400s and transported to the islands of Cabo Verde, a new Portuguese colony off the coast of Senegal. The islands were uninhabited before the colonists arrived, allowing the Portuguese to turn them into massively profitable agricultural operations dedicated to cotton and sugar through the forced labor of enslaved Africans. Other European powers took note of Portugal's success with the slave plantation model, especially as they, too, began to lay claim to tropical islands, now on the other side of the Atlantic.

Christopher Columbus brought sugarcane to the Caribbean on his second voyage there in 1493. Enslaved Africans soon followed, joining Indigenous captives on Spanish encomiendas, colonial estates that granted settlers parcels of land and entitled them to the forced labor of Indigenous people, who were often violently relocated and separated from their families and communities to live and work on the estates. Spain had developed the encomienda system during the Reconquista, the centuries-long process by which Christian nobles drove Muslim rulers (and later, Jews) out of the Iberian Peninsula. There, encomiendas were a way to distribute conquered Muslim land and property to Christians, and they usually included entitlement to "local, serf-like labor." Spain exported the encomienda model to its colonies, where it blended with the new plantation idea and created a combined African and Indigenous slave labor force to harvest sugar and other cash crops. Bartolomé de las Casas, the influential Spanish priest, wrote fiery accounts condemning the enslavement and systematic abuse of Native Americans he had witnessed in the Caribbean and Mexico. In response, Spain prohibited the formal enslavement of Indigenous people in 1542. But the practice continued for centuries in all but name in Spanish colonies, and it remained legal in others—alongside the universally legal enslavement of Africans.

As more and more Indigenous communities were decimated by malnutrition, overwork, family separation, violence, and disease, increasing numbers of enslaved Africans were imported to the Americas to keep the fragile, growth-obsessed economies of encomiendas, plantations, and entire colonies afloat. Between 1500 and 1875, about 4.8 million enslaved Africans were brought to the Caribbean, compared with about 389,000 brought to the United States in that same time period. The vast majority of them labored on the islands' sugar plantations, like Estate Little Princess in St. Croix.

While not exactly lawless, Caribbean islands were often liminal spaces where it was never quite clear which colonial country was in charge and whose rules and regulations applied at any given time. Islands changed hands frequently, as the results of wars, alliances, and treaties worked out by governments thousands of miles away. That distance and lack of oversight enabled enslavers in Barbados, for example, to import African workers before slavery was officially legal there. Once the profits started rolling in and the enslaved were generating wealth for investors in Europe, no one in power felt the need to look too closely at what was being done to create it. "The rules of society get suspended for the capital yield," says the archaeologist Douglas Armstrong.

British colonists first settled in Barbados in 1627. For the first decade or so, they mostly ran small-scale cotton and tobacco plantations, with indentured Europeans and a smaller number of enslaved Africans supplying the labor. But the colonists, who certainly would have known about the economic success of Portuguese sugar operations and Spanish encomiendas, were after much greater wealth than that. Drawing on technology used on Dutch plantations in Brazil and a significant infusion of capital from Dutch and English investors, the Barbados colonists staked their fortunes on sugar. Thanks to the capital markets of Europe, enslavers in Barbados and elsewhere in the Caribbean "could get all the money necessary to completely outfit an estate, to buy laborers, and to get sugar going within a year, " Armstrong says. "And when you shift to sugar, it changes everything."

These loans were predicated on the astronomically high profit margins enabled by enslaved labor. Not only did enslaved Africans not receive wages, they could be forced to work in inhumane conditions literally until death. Enslavers also spent very little supplying enslaved workers with housing, food, clothing, or any other bare essential of life. The enslaved were expected to procure their own food and material possessions on top of the work they did for the benefit of the enslaver class.

Armstrong's excavations at Trents Plantation in Barbados confirm just how lucrative, and transformative, the switch to sugar was. Near the plantation's mansion, he found trash heaps from before and after Trents started growing sugar. Before sugar, in the 1640s, even the plantation owners had very few material possessions. Most of what they threw out during that time was locally made coarse pottery, interspersed with a few fragments of broken glass bottles and stone jugs, as well as one imported porcelain bowl. Inventories of goods from Trents compiled in this period recorded similar items in similarly sparse numbers. Living on a tiny island far from the power centers of Europe and booming colonial trade hubs like Mexico City, enslavers had to rely mostly on local materials and carefully conserve and reuse the few foreign belongings they'd brought with them or managed to acquire as imports.

After sugar arrived, about fifty years later, the mansion's trash heaps abounded with imported glazed ceramics and porcelain. Locally made pottery was now used only for cooking, labor that would have been done by enslaved Africans. The enslavers remodeled their mansion and threw out mountains of rubble and window glass. Armstrong also found they had discarded many different shapes of crystal wineglasses and tumblers, along with complete glass wine bottles. Before sugar, glass bottles were thrown out only once they broke, presumably after being refilled with water and reused many times. After sugar, glass wine bottles became disposable, as the enslavers could always count on more arriving—and on having the money to buy as many as they liked.

A full century before the Industrial Revolution began in Britain, "you already have full-scale capitalism going on" in Barbados and other Caribbean islands, Armstrong says. "The profitability was so vast . . . and certainly the money was addictive." The influx of wealth sent European countries—and the enormous, militarized corporations they spawned—scrambling for more, and more, and more. More colonies, more products, more profits, more slaves.

In order to meet even half of that lust for wealth, Caribbean plantations also became some of the first companies to industrialize their operations. Sugar was the world's first monocrop, heralding the transition to the industrial agriculture that forms the foundation of today's food supply. Plantations' early experiments with economies of scale, tracking laborers' hours and efficiency, and "turning individuals' lives into energy that's used to generate capital" provided the model for factories that would soon become the economic drivers of Britain and the United States, says archaeologist William White. Steam technology may have arrived in the Caribbean as early as the 1790s for use in sugar refineries and rum distilleries.

To European eyes, Caribbean islands seemed like fertile paradises where almost anything would grow. But the colonists' single-minded focus on industrial agriculture, resource extraction, and constant economic growth continually threatened to decimate island ecologies and everyone who depended on them, enslaved and enslavers alike. Enslaved Africans, the first cogs in the machine of globalized, industrialized capitalism, were made to deforest entire islands, including Barbados and St. Croix, in order to make room for rows of sugarcane. Even more forests were razed to supply enough wood to keep the sugar boilers running day and night. The widespread deforestation exacerbated erosion, which led to landslides when hurricanes hit. Sugar is a notoriously thirsty crop, and the enslaved laboriously altered the course of streams and rivers to divert massive amounts of water to the cane fields. Meanwhile, they were also expected to coax this ravaged landscape into producing most of their own food, in small garden plots called provisioning grounds.

The scale and speed of the ecological transformation on many Caribbean islands was so extreme that the archaeologist Justin Dunnavant calls it "terraforming," the word science fiction writers use to describe the process of making an alien planet habitable. But the new, decidedly apocalyptic environments slavery created were hardly conducive to any kind of life. Enslavers demanded the exploitation of every natural resource they could profit from, and the destruction of the ones they couldn't, confident they could sustain their enterprises indefinitely on money, technology, and resource extraction alone.

As forests were cut down and replaced by sugarcane, droughts grew worse and worse, and groundwater grew scarce. In Dominica, another Caribbean island, archaeologist Mark Hauser found that after the introduction of sugar to the southwestern part of the island in 1763, the wells dug by earlier colonists were filled in or converted to cisterns, suggesting the water table had plummeted below where the wells could reach.

Enslavers and the enslaved alike began relying on captured rainwater. Water collected in cisterns was filtered and directed to the enslavers' mansions and sugar factories. The enslaved relied on water captured in outdoor basins lined with clay, which were frequently polluted by bacteria, mosquitoes, and animal waste, as well as the lead, mercury, and arsenic that permeated the runoff produced by industrial rum distilleries. Visiting European doctors documented outbreaks of stomach ailments, and slave narratives and other testimonies record enslaved Africans' terror of dying of disease. Malnutrition and natural disasters—worsened by the islands' degraded ecologies—also loomed as threats for an early death.

The enslaved were responsible not only for keeping themselves alive in these precarious environments. They were required to keep their enslavers and other colonists alive as well. In the process enslaved Africans were forced to build, operate, and maintain the infrastructure of colonialism and enslavement in which they were trapped. In Christiansted, the archaeologist Alicia Odewale was part of a team that excavated a large urban compound where both Danish soldiers and the so-called "royal slaves" owned by Denmark's king were quartered. In the space occupied by enslaved Africans, she found an abundance of metal tools and artifacts directly related to their skills as carpenters, blacksmiths, barrel makers, masons, and more. The Danish officers' space, on the other hand, yielded "signals of wealth, status, and leisure," such as porcelain and tobacco pipes. "These landless soldiers had no means of survival outside of what their slaves brought in," Odewale writes. The colonists' relationship to the enslaved labor force was "parasitic."

Every day across the colonial Caribbean, enslavers and colonists put their lives, their fortunes, and the very existence of their society in the hands of the people they dehumanized, abused, and exploited. They had created a new world through apocalypse, but, unlike many postapocalyptic societies, it wasn't a logical adaptation to a new climate or a rejection of a political system that no longer served its people. It wasn't more stable, more equal, more cooperative, or more sustainable than what had come before. Instead, slavery created a world where the apocalypse never had to end—could never be allowed to end—as long as it generated profits for the people who had instigated it.

◉

Estate Little Princess in St. Croix is now the headquarters of a non-profit environmental conservancy, covered in vegetation that has been allowed to regrow over much of its once-deforested land. The enslavers' two mansions still stand and are mostly useable as office space, but a much smaller overseer's house is marked by crumbling walls and a few stairs leading to a gaping hole that was once a doorway. The roof has collapsed and filled the inside with debris. Across a clearing, vines reach out from the forest to grow in and around the high stone walls of the still-imposing sugar factory. The inside of the factory, however, is filled with water; at some point in the twentieth century it was turned into an indoor swimming pool. The tall stump of a windmill that once supplied energy for grinding sugarcane still stands beside it.

The archaeologists I'd gone there to visit in 2019, including Dunnavant, White, and Odewale, had left these grand colonial buildings alone. Instead, they worked with conservancy staff to cut trails through the budding tropical forest to reach the remains of the village where enslaved Africans lived. Hardly any of what happened there is preserved in written history. The records from Estate Little Princess and others like it note facts such as the number of enslaved people who lived there, their genders and ages, their places of origin, and occasionally even their names. But slavery's documentary record, though extensive, reveals almost nothing about the daily lives of the enslaved, much less their personalities, preferences, emotions, opinions, hopes, and fears.

A nineteenth-century census conducted by the Danish colonial government documented thirty-eight houses in the estate's village, but many have been demolished, and the archaeologists found the ruins of only five. They focused their excavation on one of the best preserved. The roof was long vanished, but the walls were high enough to show the outlines of some of its doors and windows. Its walls, like those of the four other village houses, were made of stone and chunks of coral harvested from St. Croix's many reefs. Coral was considered the best building material on the island, and so enslaved Africans were sent to collect it. They would canoe out to a reef and use a heavy wooden rod to loosen and break off pieces of the corals below. "The most difficult part was diving down to get it," said Dunnavant, who is a scuba diver. "You're free diving down to sometimes thirty feet or more to lift this coral off the ocean floor." Enslaved divers were also called on to salvage material from shipwrecks—which could have been carrying more enslaved Africans to the island—or do underwater repairs on ships. "It turned into a very skilled practice," Dunnavant said.

At the house, Dunnavant crouched in the earth beside the remains of the stone-and-coral wall, carefully scraping at a shallow, six-and-a-half-foot-long rectangular pit with his trowel. The pit was just outside the house, where residents likely escaped their cramped quarters to do their cooking, possibly leaving behind everything from broken pots to burned plants and bones. He carefully set up the outline of the pit for the excavation crew, which was made up of nineteen middle and high school students from St. Croix. Just on the other side of the same wall, undergraduate students from historically Black colleges and universities dug another, smaller pit inside the house. As two students scraped thin layers of earth into buckets, others sifted it through wire screens and kept a sharp eye out for artifacts caught by the mesh. Because the plantation was much too recent for accurate radiocarbon dating, the archaeologists created a timeline of its occupation by tracing the changing styles of artifacts, such as ceramics and buttons. Missing even one tiny object could mean losing a world of priceless information.

The students alternated days spent excavating with days spent sorting the artifacts they found, the latter under Odewale's guidance. In my years of writing about archaeology, I'd never met someone so excited about every single artifact that came out of the ground. Many archaeologists privately consider excavation to be the most tedious part of their jobs. Even relatively small excavations like the one on Estate Little Princess can yield thousands of artifacts every field season, each of which must be categorized, cleaned, and bagged before fieldwork is over. The hard daily work of digging and sorting doesn't require much creativity. Imagination comes before, when archaeologists survey a past landscape in order to figure out where to dig, and after, when they've got the unearthed artifacts back in the lab to study. Excavation leads to the discovery of material objects, but the discovery of their meanings often comes much later.

Odewale, on the other hand, had a gift for seeing the stories artifacts might tell almost the moment they landed on her sorting table, which was set up in front of the enslavers' mansions. This was no small feat of creativity on Estate Little Princess, where most of the artifacts that emerged from the village were humble in the extreme: fish and pig bones from centuries-old meals, buttons that fell off of clothing, bits of coarse local pottery along with shards of smooth, painted porcelain. As the students emptied bags of artifacts onto plastic trays, Odewale cautioned, "No one has touched these artifacts for two hundred years, so it's really important what happens to them next." She helped the students sort objects by type: glass, bone, metal, ceramic, and the local pottery made from coarse clay and fired in pits covered with brush, called Afro-Crucian ware.

Odewale instructed the students not to wash the fragments of Afro-Crucian ware because they might contain residue from the food once cooked or stored inside. Chemical analyses of those residues could reveal what the enslaved Africans on Estate Little Princess cooked and ate, and how their diets might have changed over time. Even a simple tally of the amount of locally made pottery versus imported ceramics could shed light on the economy of the plantation and the larger island, but there were far too many artifacts of both types to count here. Eventually, every artifact will be entered into a database of material excavated from sites of slavery across North America and the Caribbean, in order to compare the lives of enslaved Africans across place and time.

For now, the students focused on categorizing, cleaning, and bagging the artifacts to facilitate analysis later. Occasionally they had questions about unusual objects, or Odewale herself would notice something on their trays she'd never seen in St. Croix before. The year I visited, it was a pewter spoon. "It's hard to get your hands on [pewter] out here in the Caribbean," Odewale said. It would have been a pricey import, even for the enslavers; Odewale had never found pewter even in urban Christiansted. And yet, the spoon was found among the belongings of the enslaved, on a rural sugar plantation.

Once, archaeologists and historians would have assumed the enslavers bought such items, along with everything else, in their plantations' villages. Enslaved Africans weren't paid wages, so how could they participate in the capitalist economy built from their labor? But further research in archives and the field revealed enslaved Africans in the Caribbean and the southeastern United States did, in fact, buy their possessions. In St. Croix and other Caribbean islands, enslaved Africans—alongside free people of color, traveling peddlers, and poor and middle-class white residents—shopped at Sunday markets often run by free and enslaved Black women. There, enslaved people sold or traded surplus crops from their provisioning grounds or ceramics or other crafts they made, perhaps to people like the royal slaves who didn't have gardens. They used the proceeds to buy other items, including imported porcelain and tobacco pipes. Someone, at some point, bought the pewter spoon. Their identity will remain unknown, as will the reasons behind their decision. But here, amid the detritus of an apocalypse and the creation of so many more, a choice had been made. A preference was expressed. A problem was solved. A desire was fulfilled.

Another of the archaeologists working on Estate Little Princess, Ayana Omilade Flewellen, focused on a specific type of artifact that vividly captures how enslaved Africans expressed their identities: the remains of clothing and jewelry. Any buried cloth would have long since decayed in the tropical environment, but items such as buttons, beads, hook-and-eye fasteners, and perforated shells could still be recovered. The team had found several buttons made from cow bone, but no larger pieces of bone from which they would have been carved. That meant the enslaved Africans who wore these buttons weren't making them but were buying or trading for them at the Sunday markets, either separately or already sewn onto clothing. Flewellen also hoped to see how the adornment practices of enslaved Africans on Estate Little Princess might have conformed with or defied Danish laws dictating who was permitted to wear what kind of fabric, jewelry, and styles on the country's island colonies. In the eighteenth century, Danish slave codes were some of the harshest in existence, "making no mention of any minimal standards of food, clothing, or shelter that should be provided" and permitting punishments including "dismemberment, branding with hot irons, flogging, hanging, and castration." And yet, the only way to truly know how enslaved Africans reacted to laws governing their self-presentation—including if and where they followed them—is to find evidence of what they actually wore.

Back at the sorting table with Odewale, one student held up an unusual artifact, wondering which pile to put it in. It was a small, perfectly round ball, about the size of a chickpea. Odewale rushed over to examine it. The ball was heavy in her palm and looked to have a dark hue beneath the dusting of dirt on its surface. She gasped. "You've got a bullet! That's a musket ball!" she said. It could be evidence of violence against enslaved Africans, or it might be a sign that they were hunting their own wild game—or even planning an uprising or escape.

Odewale was almost ready to put the ball in the metal pile. But first she gently scrubbed its surface with a toothbrush, just to be safe. As the dirt fell away, what emerged wasn't the black surface of a lead bullet but the tan color of local clay. The ball wasn't a bullet after all. It was a solid clay marble, rolled between the hands of someone long ago. The marble might be evidence of children playing, or adults gambling, which Denmark's brutal slave code prohibited. "That's an indication of leisure," Odewale said, a moment set aside for relaxation and fun by people who were officially forbidden to have either. What she saw in the village was "not just people out here working, being forced to labor on this plantation. There are families here, they're connected, and they're making their lives however they can."

But the marble may also have been functional. Odewale knew from oral histories that enslaved Africans dropped spare clay marbles into opaque ceramic water vessels. When the marbles started to clink against the sides of the pot, it was a signal that the water level was getting low. "Innovation!" she cried as she offered this possibility to the students. "I'm telling you, geniuses were out here at work. All we have to do is try and listen."

◉

Asserting identities and creating communities in the slave villages, like people on Estate Little Princess did through their games, inventions, markets, and perhaps clothing, was a type of rebellion against the dehumanizing regime of slavery. Their provisioning grounds also allowed them to exercise control over their diets. On a plantation called Morne Patate in Dominica, Hauser discovered a provisioning ground buried under a still-functioning farm field. His team uncovered and identified seeds and other plant remains from all over the world: corn from the Americas, guava from the Caribbean, barley from Europe, and millet and sorghum, which were staples in Africa. This experimentation with diverse crops led to the creation of a new Caribbean cuisine, guided by the tastes of enslaved Africans.

In their provisioning grounds, the enslaved could also fight back against the environmental destruction they were forced to participate in elsewhere on the islands. As the ones working the land and tending to crops, they would have been intimately aware of how the enslavers' demands affected the islands' ecologies. Planting viney crops like passion fruit in their provisioning grounds held the garden soil in place, counteracting the erosion caused by widespread deforestation. Enslaved Africans were "engineers solving problems not of their own making," says Hauser.

Caribbean geography and politics also provided the conditions for many people to escape enslavement. Enslaved Africans in St. Croix slipped away from plantations to form hidden communities in more rugged parts of the island, and then, once sugar plantations expanded and encroached on previously isolated places, over the sea to neighboring Puerto Rico and other nearby islands. Some might have drifted with ocean currents or swam staggering distances, others smuggled themselves aboard ships with false papers, and still others built their own canoes in secret and rowed to freedom. Slavery was widespread in the Caribbean, and it was still legal in Puerto Rico, but the Spanish government there welcomed escapees from Danish islands like St. Croix in order to undermine one of their imperial rivals and perhaps gather intelligence about the situation in their colonies.

Enslaved Africans who were unable to escape the sugar estates still went to great risk to find places out of their enslavers' sight, where they could build their own communities and work out new ways of being amid the apocalypse of slavery. Such locations aren't marked on any maps or written down in plantation records. They were secrets held close by people whose experiences and private thoughts were usually excluded from written history. Today, archaeologists are often the only ones who can find them—and see them for the spaces of power, agency, and resistance they were.

Armstrong discovered one such secret place on Trents Planation in Barbados. Like on most plantations, there weren't many areas of Trents where enslaved Africans weren't being watched. They were watched in the fields where they planted and harvested sugarcane. They were watched in the steaming-hot factory where the cane was processed into sugar and rum. They were even watched in their houses, which were perched on top of a gully in full view of the enslavers' mansion and factory just across the way. There was just one place the enslaved could, however briefly, evade the prying eyes pervading the plantation: in a cave eighty feet down into the gully itself.

Armstrong had been excavating on Trents for years before he found the cave. He and his team had spent the field season locating and excavating the village where enslaved Africans lived, and they decided to survey the gully, as it offered the only place near the village out of the enslavers' sight. If the archaeologists had noticed that opportunity, surely the enslaved Africans who once lived there would have, too.

Armstrong and a colleague slipped and slid between trees and roots down to the gully floor. There they found a natural shelter created by a rock overhang and obscured by hanging vines—and within the back wall of that shelter, the mouth of a cave about six feet up from the ground. They used hand- and footholds to scramble up the limestone and peer inside. The cave extended about twenty feet into the rock, but it was so low that the archaeologists had to hunch over in order to enter it. Armstrong crawled along the side of the cave, careful not to disturb the floor and the artifacts lying on the surface. With his phone flashlight, he saw animal bones, ash from an extremely old fire, and pieces of iron. Even deeper in the cave, Armstrong and his colleague saw what they immediately realized to be a collection of iron blades.

They realized they had to leave the cave and its artifacts just as they were and return as soon as possible to excavate. But the discovery was so unexpected, so shocking, that once Armstrong emerged from the cave, he had to poke his head back in for another look. Had he really just seen what he thought he'd seen? A secret meeting place? Weapons, hidden just out of sight of the enslavers' mansion? He had.

Subsequent excavations revealed the blades to be at least two hundred years old, and perhaps up to three hundred and fifty or four hundred years old. Many of the weapons started their lives as iron door hinges and other practical objects a long-ago someone had filed into daggers and machetes. A grinding stone, likely taken from the sugar factory to sharpen the blades, was found next to a door hinge crafted into a knife. No one seemed to have lived in the cave—glass bottles, the characteristic domestic trash of the colonial Caribbean and enslaved Africans' primary way of transporting, cooling, and storing scarce water, had been left only in the rock shelter outside.

"Initially I was wondering if they were preparing to engage in the slave rebellion [in Barbados] in 1816," Armstrong says. But excavations showed the iron artifacts were likely left in the cave both before and after that time. Their long time span and the care with which they were placed there made Armstrong think they might have been an offering. The lamb bones supported that interpretation; since they were cooked and eaten far away from any domestic space, perhaps their deaths were sacrifices made as part of a long-ago ritual. The cave, Armstrong concluded, was best understood as a shrine where generations of enslaved Africans practiced a religion they wove out of memory and circumstance, just out of their enslavers' sight.

Blacksmithing and iron working had been practiced in West Africa for centuries before the transatlantic slave trade began, and people there worshipped several gods associated with iron. Transforming metals and turning them into weapons imbued blacksmiths with social and spiritual power, via their connection to the god of iron, Ogun. Ogun had the "ability to reintegrate after disorder, rebalance after instability, and produce something totally new out of heat and violence," writes archaeologist and historian Candice Goucher.

Today, no one knows what the people who made the iron weapons in the Trents Plantation cave were thinking or what they planned to do with them. Maybe they were organizing an uprising, or a series of them, that never happened and thus went unrecorded. Maybe it was a communal supply depot for people beginning their escapes, or who needed a weapon they could disguise as a household object until they were ready to use it. Or, as the sacrificed lamb bones suggest, the cave could have been a kind of chapel to connect with the gods the enslaved had been forced to leave behind, or the new ones they were creating. On this island, at the heart of this new world, perhaps Ogun and his sacred skills took on a new meaning: a god of apocalypse, worshipped by people determined to survive.

Chapter 9

WHY WE'VE STAYED TRAPPED IN THE APOCALYPSE—AND HOW WE CAN FIND OUR WAY OUT

It had been a few decades since the apocalypse, and a new city had risen from the rubble of the old. It was the center of a new empire, the place where people from every corner of the newly mapped globe first met, and where untold riches passed between them and fueled the desire for even more. The new city, with its new opportunities, attracted more and more new people, with new ideas about architecture, religion, cuisine, farming, and government. They wanted to make the new city look and feel like their home, which it now was. Palaces became mansions, temples became churches, and canals became streets.

The people of the old city could still see the shadow of the capital their ancestors had built, as spaces changed hands but not functions; the new markets, plazas, and schools were built atop the old ones, and the lake still surrounded the new city. The old people often lived in the same houses they always had, doing the same jobs they did before. But the new animals trampled the old floating gardens, the causeways and canals still bore the scars of the war, and the new religion strived to blot out everything it could of the old. What it couldn't erase, it would absorb, pretending it had been there all along. The new saints sought followers by disguising themselves as the old gods—or perhaps it was the old gods who slipped into the costumes of saints.

And yet, with every storm of the rainy season, the ghost of the old city made its presence known. A summer day could start out cloudless and bright, the city refreshed by the clean mountain air, every crag of the snowcapped volcanoes visible in the distance. And then, most afternoons, the storm clouds would roll in and turn day to night, sometimes within minutes. The clouds burst open into torrents of rain and hail, and the water sloshed through streets and sometimes into houses. The gardens and canals absorbed what they could, but they had been damaged by the war and the new construction in ways the new people, who had installed themselves as the city's rulers, didn't know how to fix. The storms felt nearly supernatural in their fury, making the old people remember why they had honored their rain god in the old city's greatest temple, and the new people wonder if that demon was punishing them for tearing it down.

Often a storm would end as quickly as it had begun, leaving behind piles of hailstones that looked almost like packed snow under a clear evening sky. But sometimes, the rain would keep going, all afternoon, all night, and into the next day. The lake, which even the old people had never fully tamed, would overflow the tenuous boundaries between itself and the city. Once that happened, the rain had no place to go, and the flood would begin. The water inundated the ground floors of the new people's mansions, and it all but dissolved the adobe houses most of the old people still lived in. It seeped into the foundations of the new churches, palaces, and monasteries, causing them to crack and crumble from within. The causeways that connected the city to the lakeshore would disappear under the water, and the food usually bound for the city's markets would never arrive. The bloated corpses of animals, and sometimes people, floated down the streets. The stagnant, putrid water led to outbreaks of disease.

After a bad flood, the new people who held land outside the city relocated there as they waited for the water to recede, and the old people would call on family and friends in the countryside, reactivating connections that had existed since long before the apocalypse. The old people's wooden and adobe houses suffered more obvious damage than the new stone mansions, but they could also be rebuilt more quickly and completely. The stone palaces and churches were damaged permanently, their outward sturdiness hiding the ways the water had seeped into their very hearts.

But eventually, the people, old and new, always came back to the city. The old people knew they belonged to this island the same way their ancestors had, when they were divinely called to settle there. The new people were drawn back by the wealth and commerce that flowed through the city from every corner of the world. They had staked their futures on the opportunities this new economy provided, in one of the only places where destinies could be written and rewritten. Or perhaps the people, old and new, were forced back by the new rulers, who feared nothing more than losing their grip on this place, which had once been called the navel of the moon and was now the anchor of the new world. If it disappeared, the new empire could easily follow. No matter how many had to suffer, drown, starve, and sacrifice, the city would not—could not—be allowed to fail.

◉

By 1524, enough of Tenochtitlan had been rebuilt and transformed into Mexico City for the Spanish power structure to move back to the island. The new colonial government almost certainly wasn't aware of the way Indigenous people managed to preserve their past in the foundations of the new city that was meant to destroy it. But the Europeans who had declared control of the Valley of Mexico did know they were vastly outnumbered, even after so many Indigenous deaths during the smallpox epidemic and subsequent siege. They needed to work fast if they were to have any hope of building their own capital to replace Tenochtitlan before the Mexica could regroup and rebel.

During our tour of postapocalyptic Tenochtitlan, Raúl Barrera Rodríguez and I left the calmecac ruins and headed to the building next door, which was being converted into a hotel. Underneath will be an even more ambitious underground museum, but when we visited, the whole place was still a construction site. The sounds of clanging and drilling faded as we descended into the basement and back into the past. Here Barrera Rodríguez's team found parts of two ceremonial buildings: a circular wall belonging to the temple of Ehécatl—the wind god whose smaller shrine is in the metro station—and a section of what would have been Tenochtitlan's most important ball court. The Mesoamerican ball game was played all over the region for millennia before Europeans arrived, with players hitting a hard rubber ball with their hips and trying to send it flying through stone hoops hung high on the walls flanking the narrow court. Ball courts range in size and stature, but this one was truly monumental, stretching over one hundred and sixty feet long and housing substantial roofed platforms on either side for spectators, Moctezuma and other Mexica nobles likely among them, to watch the game.

Jutting up from the top of one of those platforms is the base of a European-style house, perched on top of a few feet of fill. It's an obvious architectural interruption of what came before. As the invaders rebuilt the city in their image, a sacred public space designed for ceremony and spectacle became an elite private space intended to enclose and exclude. The raw material of both buildings, however, is the same. Workers took stones from the ball court (or its war-ravaged ruins) and used them to build the walls of the house. During excavations, "it can be hard for us to see the difference between pre-Hispanic and early colonial," Barrera Rodríguez said. "The construction materials are the same stones, the hands doing the labor are the same, the floors are similar." This house atop the ball court, which colonial records suggest once belonged to a man named Juan Engel, is one of the only places where the transition can be seen so starkly.

Another is a few blocks away, under a building running along one side of the Zócalo. Today it's home to a pawnshop, but in 1519 it was the site of the palace compound where Moctezuma housed his foreign guests. Excavating under the modern building, Barrera Rodríguez found the remains of the Mexica-period basalt floor Cortés and his men walked on during their eight months in Tenochtitlan. He also found the remains of the new palace the conquistador had built on top once his forces took over the city. The stones of a razed Mexica palace were used to build a European one atop its ruins, and the same man lived in both.

Barrera Rodríguez found fragments of the vibrant murals that decorated the Mexica palace's walls lying shattered beneath the colonial floor. But he also found a few pieces of the old artwork—a relief of the Feathered Serpent god, and another of an ornate headdress—embedded in the wall of a colonial room. Cortés used them as decoration, just as Moctezuma and his predecessors had. He would have remembered the murals they originally belonged to. Looking at their broken pieces adorning his wall years later, Cortés might have felt a surge of triumph at all he had conquered, or he might have felt wistful for the fantastical city he first knew and the months he spent among its wonders. Even the man who had commanded the erasure of Tenochtitlan couldn't help but commemorate a small piece of what it had been, and perhaps what he had done to it.

Like Postclassic Aké, colonial Mexico City was built from the rubble of apocalypse. Unlike the Classic Maya world or Old Kingdom Egypt, however, Tenochtitlan and the Aztec Empire didn't collapse in the traditional way. The city didn't shrink, the state didn't disintegrate, and the empire didn't fragment. Inequality didn't drop, and social hierarchies didn't turn upside down. After the conquest, the lands and people of one empire merely passed into the hands of another. The capital remained in the same place. Trade routes were maintained and expanded, eventually connecting to lands across both oceans. Spanish men married Indigenous noblewomen, creating a new social and political hierarchy by borrowing the prestige of the old one.

When the Classic Maya world disintegrated four hundred years earlier, it was the collapse itself that created the conditions for recovery. In Aké, people found each other in the ruins. A disaster community transformed itself into, simply, a community through the shared labor and imagination of rebuilding their home not as the place it had been but as the place they needed it to be now. Even though it had very likely been born of fear, uncertainty, and suffering, postapocalyptic Aké blossomed into a place of abundance and possibility, along with countless other Postclassic Maya cities and towns. As in First Intermediate Period Egypt, collapse led to a new kind of freedom and a chance for reinvention and renewal.

The apocalypse of colonialism that had created Mexico City, however, precluded that kind of recovery. The conquistadors and the colonists who followed were too terrified of the possible consequences of what they had done to pause their project of deconstruction and reconstruction even for a moment, much less think about what repairing the old city could look like. Indigenous people were forced to participate in their city's erasure and had little say in the design of the new one. Rather than being able to come together in the rubble to regroup and reimagine, Indigenous communities were continually torn apart by enslavement, rape, forced migration, and disease. As Spain expanded its empire throughout North and South America and across the Pacific to the Philippines, Mexico City became the political, economic, and administrative heart of the Spanish Empire in North America, the node connecting it all. The city's wounds were paved over, and the new world was built on top. But underneath, they never healed.

◉

As the years and decades wore on, and Mexico City grew in importance to the Spanish Empire, a continued threat to its existence became clear: water. It was everywhere in the island city, and it was out of control. Water had been a problem for the Mexica, too, and they hadn't lived in perfect harmony with the lake around them. Tenochtitlan had experienced several devastating floods during its nearly two centuries as the Mexica capital, some of which left behind layers of mud archaeologists like Barrera Rodríguez find in their excavations and use as dating tools, as they can match them up with the precolonial flood years recorded in Indigenous histories. In order to mitigate disaster risk, the Mexica aggressively engineered the lake and its basin by building canals, artificial islands, aqueducts, dikes, causeways, and dams. They aimed to regulate the water, guiding its sometimes intense and dangerous flow to places like the chinampas where it would serve the city's needs instead of threatening its existence.

But Tenochtitlan's hydraulic infrastructure was never completely repaired after Spanish forces attempted to destroy it during the 1521 siege. Many damaged canals were filled in and converted to streets lined with stone monasteries and mansions. Skyrocketing demand for wood in the colonial city deforested the mountains around it, leading to massive amounts of mud and silt sliding into the valley, clogging up what remained of the Mexica water-regulating technologies. European plows loosened sediment, and the hooves of their cattle and sheep trampled the delicate layered soil of the chinampas. "When you put all these things together, it starts to test the limits of pre-Columbian engineering practices," says John López, an architectural historian who studies Mexica and colonial water control strategies in Mexico City. The city that had existed because of the lake now became a city that was continually menaced by the same feature.

Major floods began to hit Mexico City more than twice as often as they had affected the Aztec capital. The precipitation that fell during rainy season storms accumulated too quickly for the city's damaged water infrastructure to accommodate it. Mansions flooded, and colonists "were stranded in the upper floors of their houses, if they still had houses," writes historian Louisa Hoberman. The single-story adobe and wooden homes of the Indigenous lower classes washed away. No food or supplies could make it into the city over the flooded causeways. As the stagnant flood waters grew increasingly polluted in the following days, weeks, and months, the risk of disease exploded. Every rung on the city's socioeconomic ladder was affected, from wealthy property owners to the coerced Indigenous labor force—a disastrous situation for the economy and legitimacy of the entire Spanish Empire. "If Mexico City is flooded, then the whole colonial project is at a standstill," López says. In the aftermath of one such flood, tax revenue from the city plunged by half as the European population fled to cities and towns on higher ground, including Coyoacán, the colonial government's first base after the war, and Puebla, one of the few Spanish settlements not built on top of an Indigenous one.

But the colonial government was determined to maintain its grip on Mexico City (and Tenochtitlan beneath it), and so it grew desperate to solve the flooding problem once and for all. Instead of regulating how water flowed into and out of the city, as the Mexica had done, they decided to get rid of the water entirely. Beginning in the early 1600s, the colonial government hired Europe's finest engineers to drain the water from Mexico City's basin, which had no natural outlet. These engineers designed an eight-mile-long drainage canal and tunnel, called the *desagüe*, to carry water up and over the mountains around Mexico City and feed it into a river that would carry it to the Gulf of Mexico, nearly two hundred miles away. The project cost almost twice as much to build as the Metropolitan Cathedral, and at least forty-seven hundred Indigenous workers—15 percent of the valley's adult Indigenous men—were conscripted into doing the hard labor of constructing it. (No one in charge of the project seems to have considered that these workers might have possessed a wealth of their own hydraulic knowledge applicable to the environment in question.) Two centuries later, the visiting naturalist Alexander von Humboldt would praise the *desagüe* as a marvel of engineering and a triumph of public works, akin to something like the Hoover Dam today.

And yet, it never worked. Mexico City continued to suffer from catastrophic floods throughout the colonial period, even though the *desagüe* was regularly repaired, rebuilt, and expanded over the next three centuries. Its definitive completion was finally announced in 1900, almost three hundred years after its first phase was built, with the inauguration of the city's Grand Drainage Canal, which stretched thirty miles long and was a central feature of dictator Porfirio Díaz's attempts to "modernize"—often a euphemism for "Europeanize"—Mexico City.

As Mexico City desperately tried to get rid of the water it didn't want, it was paradoxically using up the water it needed. As the shrinking lakes created more and more dry land in the valley, millions of people moved to the capital to occupy it. To serve the booming population, more and more water was pumped up from the aquifer underneath the city. At the same time, much of the porous volcanic rock and soil that allowed rainwater to filter back into the aquifer were paved over for ever more development. The parched and desiccated earth of the lakebed began to collapse in on itself. Mexico City—along with its buildings, streets, and infrastructure—started sinking.

The Grand Drainage Canal went with it. Originally intended to funnel water downhill into a tunnel via gravity, the canal now sat below the tunnel's mouth. Pumping stations had to be added to keep the canal functioning, but its capacity was so diminished that multiple other enormous drainage tunnels have been built to supplement it. The latest was completed in 2019, 411 years after the first phase of the *desagüe* was built but no closer to the dream of a city that doesn't regularly flood. In 2021, an abandoned, unusable stretch of the Grand Drainage Canal was turned into a city park, with no water in sight.

Today, Mexico City has both too much water and never enough. Catastrophic floods continue to strike every year during the summer rainy season, turning streets into rivers, damaging homes, sweeping away cars, and killing people, often in the city's poorest neighborhoods. At the same time, water shortages and shutoffs continually plague all but the very richest areas. My apartment building squeaks by—most of the time—by storing what does come through the pipes in an underground cistern. When a nearby leak or a reduction in water pressure means our cistern can't fill up, we ration our supply to three to five hours of running water per day. Meanwhile, in poor neighborhoods on the city's eastern periphery—farthest from the reservoir that now provides at least a quarter of the city's water—residents can't count on municipal water arriving at all. They spend exorbitant amounts of money and time wrangling deliveries from trucks carrying tanks of (often contaminated) water, a situation ripe for corruption and conflict.

Mexico City's water situation has been both an incredible engineering marvel and an unsustainable environmental disaster since drainage began in the early seventeenth century. The apocalypses now on the horizon will only amplify its challenges. Climate change is already leading to "more intense rains, which means more floods, but also more and longer droughts," Ramón Aguirre Díaz, then-director of Mexico City's municipal water system, said in 2017. As the city continues to sink, drainage will keep getting harder at the same time as it becomes steadily less effective.

When the existing drains, pumps, and tunnels fail, as they do somewhere in the metropolitan area nearly every year, emergency services are often slow to arrive, even though the disaster is entirely predictable. In the summer of 2024, the working-class suburb of Chalco was flooded for over a month. The water, polluted with sewage, rose up to five feet in some areas, and residents had to run their own water pumps day and night to keep their houses somewhat livable. Clearing out the water, trash, and sediment "exceeded the capacity of municipal and state teams," Mexico's National Water Commission said. Meanwhile, residents attended meetings promising the construction of a new drainage pipe while their floors were still swamped with sewage.

Prioritizing drainage above all else wasn't simply a bad colonial decision made four hundred years ago. It's a bad colonial decision Mexico City keeps making every day, even as the consequences grow increasingly dire. Still, the dry land created by drainage is where the vast majority of Mexico City lives. It made possible the population boom that turned the capital into one of the largest metropolises in the world. Mexico City is still the political, economic, and cultural heart of its nation. Even after centuries of environmental abuse and degradation—or more precisely, *because of* that abuse and degradation—the lakebed is the foundation of millions of lives, including mine.

It's a shaky foundation, however, and sometimes, it turns deadly.

◉

On September 19, 2017, at 1:14 p.m., I was working in my apartment in Mexico City when I felt a tremor. Within a few seconds I knew it was an earthquake. I was used to quakes in Mexico City feeling like the rocking of a boat, but this shaking was faster, more staccato, and more violent. Furniture jumped around as I dove under my desk and clung to one of its trembling legs. I couldn't remember being in an earthquake this noisy, at least not since I was seven years old and my books fell off my bedroom shelf next to me during Los Angeles's 6.7-magnitude Northridge earthquake. This quake felt more extreme than that one, perhaps because, as an adult who had lived in Mexico City for years, I was fully and immediately aware of the worst that could happen. This was the earthquake I always knew was coming, the one I had been waiting for—and dreading. This was the one that would topple buildings and kill people. Maybe me.

When the shaking finally stopped after an endless minute in our area, and my husband and I got outside, we learned it had been a magnitude 7.1 quake. Cell service was spotty, electricity and gas were out, and it seemed like the entire city was wandering around outside, dazed and unsure if it was safe to go back inside our homes. I would learn later that friends and family outside Mexico City were already seeing horrific television footage of collapsed and damaged buildings, but it would be hours until we caught a glimpse of a working TV or news site. We only knew what was going on in the streets immediately around us, and the scattershot information about building collapses, rescue efforts, and even personal locations people called into radio stations, hoping the hosts would play or read their calls to let their families know where they were. I walked around noting piles of broken glass under empty window frames, building facades that had crumbled into rubble on the street, and people bravely, or foolishly, entering their damaged buildings one last time and leaving with hastily packed suitcases. I tried to memorize which buildings had the worst cracks so that one day, once the visible damage had been plastered over, I wouldn't make the mistake of going inside them.

Eventually we would learn that dozens of buildings had collapsed in Mexico City, including an elementary school, and scores more were damaged. Nearly three hundred people died in the city, and another hundred or so in nearby states, where many small towns were completely leveled. Thousands of people were left homeless, including friends and family. In the aftermath, post-traumatic stress was common; it felt like no one slept or even breathed well for months. I would catch myself bolting for the door at the slightest quiver, only to realize that what I felt was my own heartbeat. The earthquake was all we could think about, and certainly all we could talk about—where we were, what it felt like, who had lost their homes. But we all knew we had been lucky. In the end, it was one of Mexico City's minor apocalypses.

Incredibly, the September 19, 2017, earthquake occurred thirty-seven years to the day after Mexico City's deadliest temblor: the 8.1 quake that struck the city on September 19, 1985. That quake originated off the Pacific coast of the state of Michoacán, two hundred miles away from Mexico City, and the shaking similarly lasted for a staggeringly long minute. Among the hundreds of buildings destroyed were hospitals and schools, along with high-rise apartment buildings, factories, and hotels. In Tlatelolco, a thirteen-story apartment tower in a social housing complex tipped over and toppled to the earth, "like a grounded ship beached in its own rubble," writes Rebecca Solnit. The death toll remains disputed, but it's commonly accepted that at least ten thousand people died.

At first glance, it seems odd that Mexico City should suffer so acutely from earthquakes. It's not particularly close to any major faults; it certainly isn't built on top of one like Los Angeles is. Most of Mexico's earthquakes happen along its Pacific coast, as in 1985; the epicenter of the September 19, 2017, quake, while not on the coast, still wasn't particularly nearby at seventy-five miles away. Still, it was felt nearly as strongly in parts of the city as it was right next to the epicenter. In 1985, the shaking was five times as intense within the city as outside of it. The hundreds of miles of rock between the coast and the city filtered the shock waves into frequencies especially dangerous for buildings six to sixteen stories tall, but it was what happened to those seismic waves once they reached the city that made them so deadly. Under the land that had been Tenochtitlan and its lake, and is now central Mexico City, the sand and clay of the drained lakebed trapped and amplified seismic waves by sending them ricocheting around the basin, growing stronger each time they collided. Geologists often compare Mexico City during an earthquake to a trembling bowl of Jell-O—with a megalopolis teetering on top.

In our postapocalyptic world, the effects of natural disasters are never truly natural. If Mexico City weren't built on unstable ground created by drainage, most quakes would peter out long before they reached us, or at least strike with much less force. If our aquifer hadn't been dangerously depleted after the lake was pumped away, the earth underneath us wouldn't be buckling and sinking. If the lake still existed, the water that is meant to be here wouldn't need to violently force its way back with every rainy season storm.

Other colonized lands have their own version of drainage, the colonial environmental mistake so large its shadow continues to blot out other possibilities, while also ensuring that future disasters and apocalypses morph into the worst versions of themselves. Aboriginal Australian communities had been managing their continent's ecosystems with regular, controlled burning since long before the ancient sea level rise of the Great Drowning. Millennia of anthropogenic fire had created landscapes that made it easy to keep the flames under control, and people trusted their land and ecosystems to know how to best recover, adapt, and flourish after a burn. But when the British colonial government seized Australia, it prohibited cultural burning, which literally and figuratively threatened permanent agricultural settlement and European ideas about private property.

Of course, the colonial government did far more than outlaw cultural burning. It also attempted to sever Aboriginal people's connection with their land and history by killing them, stealing their children for "schooling" and adoption (a practice that continued until the 1970s in Australia and had close analogs in Canada and the United States), and confining them to reservations, among other atrocities. "It was soul-destroying" for Aboriginal people, says Mark Koolmatrie, a Ngarrindjeri elder—and environmentally devastating in a way that made Australia more dangerous for everyone who lives there. Fewer controlled fires means the landscape turns into a tinderbox, ready to ignite at the slightest spark and burn out of control. In January 2020, half of Kangaroo Island, the land and pathway to the afterlife created by Ngurunderi calling in the water to punish his fleeing wives, burned in a disastrous wildfire, as did many other parts of Australia's landscape. Out-of-control bushfires are now a yearly occurrence. "We should have been talking to the elders about how to prevent fire," Koolmatrie says. "But our knowledge system was dismissed."

Similar stories have played out in the Americas, from Canada to the Amazon. In California and the western United States, Indigenous fire control practices were denigrated and outlawed in favor of suppressing wildfires altogether—until landscapes that evolved to burn inevitably burst into unprecedented disasters. On the Great Plains of the United States and Canada, tens of millions of bison were gunned down by nineteenth-century settlers as a way to decimate the health, prosperity, and political power of the Indigenous nations that relied on them. Over the following century and a half, ecosystems that had evolved to nurture bison and be nourished by them in return started to wither in their absence, growing less biodiverse and more vulnerable to drought. In the Caribbean, the environmental precarity created by slavery remains etched into the landscapes of "terraformed" islands. In Dominica, which promotes itself to visitors as the Caribbean's "Nature Island," the aquifers depleted by sugar production in the southwestern part of the island "never came back," says Mark Hauser. And after abolition there, many emancipated laborers were unable to buy land and so were forced to live in dangerous gullies along the shoreline. Their descendants still live there today, directly in the path of landslides and floods during storms, including the devastation caused by Hurricanes Irma and Maria in 2017.

We tell stories of wildfires, superstorms, and the deterioration of beloved landscapes as though they're part of the emerging apocalypse of climate change—a story of the future, not the past. But the modern world, with all its comforts and challenges, miracles and tragedies, is already a postapocalyptic landscape, shaped by the same kind of deep, unhealed wounds that lie beneath Mexico City. Peel back the top layer of our present apocalypses and you'll find another just below it, reaching all the way back to, in my home, the draining of the lake, the floods that made drainage seem like the only solution, the war that Tenochtitlan could never recover from, and the foreign invasion that set off the war. In your home, the layers will look different. But they're there, waiting to be seen for what they've always been.

To think of the modern world as a palimpsest of apocalypses is to see how the mistakes and atrocities of history reverberate into the present in ways that were always contingent and never exactly planned but have nevertheless become inescapable. They've embedded themselves so deeply in our expectations and imaginations that they've come to seem inevitable, even natural. But they weren't then, and they aren't now. If we can understand that we already live in a postapocalypse, we can see that our world was a choice, and it remains a choice. And we can see the possibility of other choices, other worlds.

◉

In recent years, there has been increasing recognition that drainage is a failed and failing strategy for Mexico City, even from the government that continues to fund and expand drainage projects while providing meager aid to its citizens during the inevitable floods. Part of drained Lake Texcoco, recently planned to be paved over to build an international airport, is instead being restored as a wetland and ecological park. The city government has invested in green infrastructure projects and rainwater collection systems in water-stressed neighborhoods. Tiny wetlands have been cultivated along the side of a highway that was once a river, bringing the water out of hiding and filtering away pollution. But solutions remain small, relatively local, and disconnected from each other, and the problem has been compounding for centuries.

At this point, the lacustrine environment of Tenochtitlan will not return exactly as it was, says López. Actually, it cannot return, at least not on anything approaching the time scale of a human life. "You can't reverse five hundred years of building practices and ecological practices overnight," he says. "It may take another five hundred years." For today's residents of Mexico City, the damage of the apocalypse is done.

But as we've seen in Aké, Abydos, the north coast of Peru, and even in the post-collapse villages of the Indus Valley, postapocalyptic landscapes are not wastelands. They can be places of abundance, creativity, and renewal, and they offer their own kinds of gifts. They can give you everything you need, if you are willing to accept it, experiment with it, and use it to see what the world could be instead of just what it no longer is. In a postapocalypse, recovery doesn't mean going back in time. It means building from and with the apocalypse in a way that doesn't try to erase the past but rather to use it to reimagine the future.

The gifts of the postapocalypse are not ones anyone hopes to receive. They are not what we want, what we hope for, what we imagine for our lives. And yet they can be the gateway to previously unimaginable transformations that will go on to define who we are, and what we know ourselves to be capable of, for the rest of our lives. In the postapocalypse, people change. Societies can't help but follow.

After the 1985 Mexico City earthquake, the government's disaster response was woefully lacking, verging on nonexistent. Its own corruption had allowed many substandard buildings to be constructed in the first place. In the Tlatelolco towers, people had been complaining of damage and faulty repairs from an earlier earthquake, and the government ignored them, to devastating consequences. Within minutes of the end of the shaking, people all across the city realized that no official help would be arriving. And so they leapt into action themselves, clearing rubble, rescuing survivors, organizing shelters, setting up street kitchens, and searching for the dead and missing.

In her chronicle of the 1985 earthquake, Mexican journalist Elena Poniatowska interviewed Consuelo Romo Campos, who lost her sister, daughter, and three grandchildren in the Tlatelolco tower collapse. "I lost my only family, everything I had," she said. "I cried alone. Then I said, no, I have to help, I'm not the only one." Weeping, Romo Campos handed out water and food to volunteer rescuers and other waiting families. Soon, she was coordinating legions of others who had come to the devastated neighborhood to help. "I knew what everyone else was feeling, I felt it in my bones, because it was happening to me, too. They were just as destroyed as I was. So I put more and more of my love into my work as a volunteer," doing everything from cooking in a street kitchen to hauling away debris from the skyscraper's collapse.

Also in Tlatelolco, volunteers with no training or equipment crawled into the rubble of the tower and then countless other buildings in the city to search for survivors. Over the following months, those volunteers coalesced into the Topos de Tlatelolco, or the Moles of Tlatelolco, and became an official search-and-rescue team. The Topos now routinely travel to other countries to help after disasters, including the 2004 tsunami in Indonesia and the 2010 earthquake in Haiti. They were on the streets of Mexico City on September 19, 2017, too, joining volunteers from all over the city who raced to the most affected areas and lined up with neighbors to free survivors from collapse sites by passing buckets of rubble from hand to hand.

In both September 19 earthquakes, garment factories were among the buildings to collapse, killing the seamstresses inside. In 2017, the ruins of a clandestine factory employing foreign and possibly undocumented garment workers was one of the first sites to be bulldozed, before anyone could verify how many people had been inside and confirm how many had died. In 1985, at least sixteen hundred garment workers died in collapsed factories, and possibly many more. The survivors first organized to rescue their colleagues, and then to demand the wages they were owed by the factory owners who had put their lives at such risk. "Looking back, the seamstresses pinpoint the day they watched their bosses remove machinery over the bodies and screams of their coworkers as a turning point in their lives," wrote labor organizer Phoebe McKinney. Soon, the seamstresses formed their first union, one of the few labor organizations independent of Mexico's Institutional Revolutionary Party (PRI), which had maintained an iron grip on Mexico's government since 1929 in what's often called "the perfect dictatorship."

The seamstresses, the Topos, the volunteers, the victims—they all found themselves radicalized not only by the PRI government's inaction and the corruption that had led to so many vulnerable buildings, but by their own incredible ability to take action, together. Two years later, because of the political organizing that grew out of the earthquake, Mexico City would win the ability to elect its own Legislative Assembly, the first representative local government it had been allowed under the PRI. The earthquake is widely recognized as the beginning of the end of the PRI dictatorship, as people understood that the one-party government was at least unwilling to, and perhaps incapable of, protecting and helping them in the way they could protect and help each other. Three presidential election cycles after the quake, in the year 2000, the PRI lost the presidency for the first time in seventy-one years. Since then, it has lost four out of five presidential elections.

"This is a city that reinvents itself, that rebuilds itself, out of its destructions. Periodically this city almost disappears and rises again from the rubble. That's our history in Mexico City," Barrera Rodríguez said as we stood in the heart of this apocalyptic city, considering the people who, over and over and over again, refused to let it disappear. They weren't always able to build something better. Sometimes all they could do was hide a sign of their presence and their resistance to the apocalypse in the ruins, for us to find later. Sometimes they built something worse, as the colonial government did when it drained the lake. Sometimes their improvised solutions unexpectedly set history on a new course. But they all gave us the gift of a postapocalyptic city—precarious, flexible, and ready and able to be remade by its people, whenever a crisis comes along to give us the chance.

◉

Today, the north coast of Peru is home to countless fields of sugarcane, rice, and other crops, all set in the heart of the river valleys. It's the same hazard zone where Huaca Cortada and the other temple pyramids sat, before they were abandoned around twenty-nine hundred years ago, after El Niño settled into its current rhythm of appearing once or twice per decade. Despite the recurring flood risk, these low-lying areas are the easiest to irrigate for farming, and agribusinesses—like the temple pyramid builders long before them—have made the most of this efficiency.

But ancient farmers didn't stop there. They extended their canals and their farmland even farther away from the rivers, planting in patches of land that are higher and drier than the valley floors and irrigating up to 40 percent more land than modern farmers use. These areas are called pampas, and today they look like the inhospitable deserts that surround them. But for archaeologists, the remains of ancient life in the pampas are the key to understanding how the people of the north coast adapted to the more frequent El Niño regime.

Archaeologist Ari Caramanica spent five field seasons tracing the outlines of ancient canals etched across the surface of the Pampa de Mocan, part of the Chicama Valley, about fifty miles north of Los Morteros. In the Pampa de Mocan, ancient farmers' canals are still visible right on the surface, protected from being plowed, planted, or built over by the landscape's remoteness and unwelcoming aridity. So are the remains of the fields they irrigated, unused for at least one thousand years but still full of microscopic plant remains, direct evidence of which species once thrived there.

Most of the canals Caramanica mapped connected directly to the river and carried water to flat, cleared farmland, just as she expected. But a significant number of the canals and fields were unlike anything she'd ever seen. Some of the irrigation canals, especially ones that showed signs of long-ago damage, traced back not to the river, as she would have expected, but to the dry streambeds that fill up with floodwater and mud only during El Niño events. These canals led to fields that were purposely sloped, outlined with rocky barriers, and filled with piles of stones—obvious impediments to planting straight rows of corn, these communities' primary crop. Caramanica, who had seen firsthand how modern, large-scale agriculture in the river valleys depended on drawing river water toward flat, even fields of single crops, couldn't get her head around what these strange canals and misshapen, rocky fields were for. But she had no doubt ancient farmers had used them for something: They were filled with the remains of ancient crops, just like their flat, even neighbors, and they accounted for one third of all the fields Caramanica documented. Ceramic styles showed that these peculiar canals and fields first appeared shortly after twenty-nine hundred years ago, when El Niño became much more frequent.

The people of the Pampa de Mocan, or their very recent ancestors, would have lived through the El Niño shift and the abandonment of the temple pyramids. They would have known what it felt like to be thrown into a new, more dangerous environment that their previous societies weren't equipped to handle. The farmers of the Pampa de Mocan looked around at the apocalypse, and they realized, sooner rather than later, that it wasn't going away. When Caramanica looked at the dead-end canals and bizarre, sloping fields through the eyes of people figuring out, yet again, how to live with a new version of El Niño, she could suddenly see what they were for. They were ways to catch—and use—the inevitable floodwaters.

Unlike well-behaved and slow-moving river water, which could be drawn into regular irrigation canals and spread across flat fields with no trouble at all, the flash floods of an El Niño came on fast and furious. The floods not only overflowed standard canals, they ripped apart their embankments. Instead of repairing the canal to its previous state, the ancient farmers took advantage of the destruction to reroute its path not back toward the river but toward a dry streambed. Most of the time there would be no water in the stream or the repaired canal, but during an El Niño they would catch and channel the floodwaters hurtling down from the foothills. Once the water and sediment reached the pampa, the sloped fields and rocky barriers would slow them down, conserving the water and allowing the mud to settle across the peculiar, but now useful, field.

Caramanica saw how well the system worked when she examined the grains of pollen trapped in each layer of earth preserved in an ancient well. In some layers, she found almost only pollen from crops like corn and jicama, pointing to intensive farming in the nearby standard fields. In others, she found an explosion of plants that thrive with lots of water, such as cattail, daisies, and a family of plants related to wild tomatoes. Those layers had to come from El Niño years. But even in the El Niño layers in the well, there was pollen from corn. Despite the floods and rain that destroyed canals and washed away once-productive fields, people continued farming during those years. The floodwater canals and rocky fields had worked. People would get less corn out of a field filled with stones, but they always got some.

Many of Caramanica's ideas were confirmed in 2017, when she personally saw the aftermath of an El Niño in the Chicama Valley. In Peru, this event left one million people homeless in the span of two months. The destruction, while tragic, didn't surprise her. What surprised her was the abundance that followed. The Pampa de Mocan, normally so dry and desolate, exploded with life. Flowers, herbs, legumes, wild tomatoes, and even trees appeared out of nowhere. Caramanica raced to collect samples of the plants, confirming many of them to be the same species or families she'd found in the El Niño layers from the ancient well. The main agricultural industry in the valley, sugarcane, was severely damaged. But farmers planted other crops, including corn and squash, in the standing water the floods left behind, echoing the strategy Caramanica had seen their ancestors using. They got four harvests out of these ephemeral fields, which then disappeared back into the desert as soon as the last of the water evaporated or sank into the earth.

In Peru and elsewhere, El Niño is now considered a disruption to the way the environment should be and the way people should live in it. Recovery means returning to the status quo of a non–El Niño year as quickly as possible. Like drainage in Mexico City, it's a strategy that seems logical under colonial regimes of private property and capitalist resource extraction but has failed since the beginning. "Today the only thing that grows with every El Niño event is the cost of repair," Caramanica says.

Unlike the people who run contemporary agribusinesses—or even the ancient communities who defiantly built their temple pyramids directly in the path of El Niño floods—the people who built the Pampa de Mocan canals didn't see El Niño as a disruption of nature's typical cycle. It *was* nature's typical cycle. They didn't exactly welcome the apocalypse but they did expect it. Rather than trying to control El Niño's force, they built its inevitable destruction into their system, by repurposing damaged canals to carry future floods. The result was a different kind of abundance, but abundance all the same.

Perhaps the people of the Pampa de Mocan never stopped wishing for El Niño to come less often, as they knew it had for their ancestors.

They would have suffered losses—homes, families, communities, ecosystems—and they would have mourned what El Niño took. Maybe they wished, in their prayers and their rituals, that nature would return to the way it had been before. But maybe they didn't. What these ancient farmers left for us was a sign that they learned to live with instability and cataclysms, in all their tragedies and opportunities. They didn't run, or die, or give up. They didn't fail or disappear. They looked straight at the apocalypse, and they built something new.

EPILOGUE

The Beginning

When I started working on what would become this book back in 2018, I thought the kinds of apocalypses I was writing about were still far in the future. Climate change was gathering more and more force by the year, but the pace of its impacts still allowed time for recovery. Politics in the United States and beyond were growing more and more extremist, but state collapse still seemed like a distant possibility. Dangerous pathogens were emerging—SARS, Ebola, bird flu—but global public health infrastructure had always worked well enough to keep them from spreading across the globe. Economic inequality, already entrenched, was growing more pronounced and pernicious, but it still seemed like a backdrop to many people's lives and decisions rather than their driving force. Back then, I knew these trends could and would eventually intertwine into an apocalypse, or possibly many apocalypses. It's why I wanted to write this book, to articulate the stakes I believed our societies would soon face and the opportunities the coming apocalypses would present. But it didn't yet feel, at least to me, like we were living through an event like those I was researching.

Two years later, my assumptions, and all of our lives, would be upended by the coronavirus pandemic, and I ended up writing the vast majority of this book during an apocalypse. It was either perfect timing or the worst timing imaginable. I knew the Before in which I believed I would live the rest of my life was now, suddenly, over, an apocalypse come for me as quickly as for those I was reading and thinking about in our deep past. I spent the height of quarantine talking to archaeologists who had dedicated their careers to studying such events and who still found themselves staggered by what it felt like to live through one. Sharon DeWitte, the Black Death bioarchaeologist, watched in horror as inequality in twenty-first-century America shaped the outcomes of a pandemic just as tragically and inescapably as it had in fourteenth-century London. Roberto Rosado-Ramirez, who studies how the Maya city of Aké regrouped into a village after collapse, felt his world shrink, in a matter of days, from a vibrant, urban, academic, and international community to the four neighbors he could still see. Raúl Barrera Rodríguez's excavations in the Centro paused only for a few months, as he watched Mexico City refuse to succumb to yet another apocalypse.

Grieving for my own world, my own life, my own Before, helped me better understand and imagine how people throughout history reacted to the rapid loss of theirs. Part of that, for me, was mourning the version of this book I didn't get to write. I was heartbroken over the reporting trips I didn't get to take, the people I didn't get to meet, the conversations I didn't get to have. I seethed at the setbacks, both personal and collective, that seemed to interfere with every plan I tried to make, and for so much longer than I thought possible. I despaired for my creativity and my career as I struggled with post-COVID symptoms for months, and then years, after each infection, pre- and post-vaccine. I feared how solidarity and cooperation seemed to decay into hostility and apathy as time went on. I'm still terrified by how much we have already forgotten, and by how deeply we wish we could forget the rest. And yet, I've also spent the last five years reveling in how much my imagination has expanded. I knew apocalypses were transformations and that my purpose in telling these stories was to show how true that has always been. Suddenly, I got to learn what it felt like to transform. It was terrifying, and it was beautiful, and it is still nowhere close to over.

During the pandemic, archaeologists didn't know if or when they would be able to return to the sites they usually study. And so, across the world, they fanned out around their own shuttered cities and towns, looking for artifacts of the apocalypse as they lived through it. They documented signs about social distancing, first handmade and then government issued; caution tape blocking off benches and playgrounds; sidewalks decorated with colorful messages of solidarity; political graffiti infused with righteous anger; discarded and disintegrating gloves, and, later, masks lying on sidewalks and beaches. Museums collected wooden spoons used to bang on pots and pans in celebration of healthcare workers, the plastic trash bags worn by American nurses whose hospitals didn't supply them with personal protective equipment, and the empty vials of the first vaccines to be administered.

Some of these artifacts or interventions in public space were meant to be temporary and ephemeral, like the caution tape and chalk art. Some persist even today, like the occasional lingering sign requiring mask use or social distancing in spaces where few people have done either in years, and long after most official restrictions have been lifted. Some have already entered the archaeological record of landfills and trash deposits, creating a record of our time out of masks and gloves made of plastic, their disposability a feature for protecting us from microbes but a curse for the environment. These objects themselves now have a new life, as trash and pollution that may never fully disappear. But that also means they will persist as artifacts. They will be the things we leave behind.

As the months and years of the pandemic went on and I switched from washable fabric masks to more effective surgical ones and then N-95s, I thought about how preservation would influence what future archaeologists could see of the pandemic. Our panicked, homemade solutions of the beginning would decay while the sturdier, more official equipment of the middle and end would endure to be collected and interpreted. I imagined future archaeologists sifting through ruins and landfills and reaching a layer of elongated plastic swabs and thin plastic rectangles notched with two cutout squares: the debris from COVID rapid tests, their sudden abundance in 2021 as temporally diagnostic as the ash layer left behind by a volcanic eruption. Hopefully, thanks to museum collections, libraries, the internet, and our own passed-down stories, these archaeologists will know what these artifacts mean and be able to match them up with history in the same way Mexico City's archaeologists use layers of mud to identify precolonial flood years. But it's possible, especially millennia from now, that the sudden worldwide appearance of masks, gloves, and rapid tests will be just as mysterious to those who find them as the Maya ruins were to John Lloyd Stephens. Perhaps they will look to the teeth and bones in our generation's mass graves for clues as to what felled us, only then learning that it was the SARS-CoV-2 virus we were trying to protect ourselves from.

Maybe, thanks to the way time and geology can compress decades or centuries into a single archaeological layer, the detritus of the pandemic will be among the final artifacts discovered in some cities and towns before they are abandoned to rising seas, wildfires, superstorms, or simply too-hot temperatures. Future archaeologists might have historical documents to guide them toward how we understood the pandemic and climate change as mostly separate apocalypses, or they might think the ruins they study were abandoned because of a plague, with only a few people hanging on to experience the later climate disaster. They might be able to read the newspapers and government edicts that declared the pandemic over long before material evidence of its destruction ceases. Future archaeologists may think of our written record of the pandemic as vivid but fundamentally untrustworthy propaganda, written by those determined to preserve or resurrect a dangerous and oppressive status quo, like Ipuwer's account of Old Kingdom Egypt's collapse. Maybe, long removed from our everyday context, they will be able to see a certain kind of truth, one that's mostly invisible to us as we live through it: that the pandemic's effects are still rippling through our societies in ways we don't yet understand and can't control, and its shock waves will help shape the apocalypses of the near future.

Apocalypses have always revealed and exploited societies' weak points, from an unsustainable relationship with a changing environment to an overly rigid and oppressive social hierarchy. Because of that, apocalypses are also the best chance our societies have for change. From Neanderthals and *Homo sapiens* collaborating to survive a period of climate instability, to complex civilization springing up from the environmental and social debris left behind by repeated El Niños, to hierarchical states disintegrating into more local, more adaptable pieces in the Indus Valley and along the Nile River, to traumatized workers refusing to return to an exploitative status quo after the Black Death, apocalypse can reveal the failures of old systems and inspire the creation of new ones.

And so, those future archaeologists might also see those pandemic artifacts as a turning point before a society-wide transformation, the signs reminding us to mask up acting something like the final dates carved into stone monuments before the abandonment of Classic Maya cities. They might find themselves arguing over whether the ruins from the twenty-first century represent a tragic mass death event or the renewal that would go on to make their world possible. Perhaps that world will be more just and equal, a grand experiment with a different and more inclusive form of government, as Mayapán once was. Perhaps it will be one where living in vulnerable cities becomes unthinkable, as in the Indus Valley after Harappa, and people prefer inhabiting scattered villages powered by decentralized, local renewable energy. Maybe it will be more destructive and authoritarian, as in early colonial Mexico City, as people trade the risks and uncertainty of our apocalyptic world for something that, like draining the lake, superficially appears to protect them from the fate we suffered.

They would be right about one thing—we have suffered, and we will continue to suffer. But writing this book about apocalypse, during an apocalypse, has shown me that we already have everything we need to adapt to extreme change, if only we let ourselves see the need for change in the first place. Diving into archaeology's new, more interesting ideas about past cataclysms taught me how much our ancestors have already survived and how much their creativity has been misunderstood and even suppressed by how we learn and talk about the past. The material, cultural, and genetic evidence of apocalyptic adaptations apparent from the very beginning of our species and at every point after drove home that people have already faced versions of every challenge looming just over our horizon, and we can learn from what they carried forward and what they were willing to let go—and the consequences of both. Learning to see human history through the lens of apocalypse teaches us that our past is a story of survival, transformation, and reinvention, often in the face of tragedy, loss, and individual and collective pain. That is the story of our time, too, and it will be the story of our future.

It's time to get used to living in, and with, the apocalypse. Whatever is coming, or maybe what is already here, will be the backdrop to the rest of our lives and the lives of countless generations of our descendants. Unlike most of the apocalypses in this book, ours are and will be truly global. In the case of climate change, it might eventually transform our planet into a place unlike any human has ever seen before. But like all people throughout history, we will experience our apocalypses slowly and locally, in the places we already live and love, within the confines of lives that last mere decades. We are the inheritors of a long tradition of adaptation and survival, which is just as formative and powerful as the tradition of social and technological progress that has held so much sway over our modern imaginations. We can harness the energy and potential of apocalypse to create a new world. But first we have to accept that the apocalypse, with all its horrors, is here to stay. Only then can we also see its opportunities, as the ancient builders of the Pampa de Mocan canals once did.

Embracing apocalypse doesn't mean resigning ourselves to the worst-case scenario, or giving up on the idea of progress. It means believing that destruction can be a gateway to that progress, societies can and should change, and endings are also always beginnings. It means recognizing that just because we're used to something doesn't make it right. It means prioritizing values and ways of life that allow us to adapt and change rather than shoring up brittle social structures that crumble at the first hint of challenge or pressure. It means looking forward with clear eyes rather than scrambling backward toward an illusion of safety that has already disappeared or perhaps never really existed. It means mourning what we've lost while also imagining all the things we could create next. It means choosing hope, not instead of fear but alongside it.

◉

The people knew the world was ending, but they couldn't quite believe it. They felt the familiar weather and seasons of their homes grow less and less familiar with each passing year. They heard news of wars that seemed far away but always threatened to spill into their own communities. They saw others fleeing calamity only to be met with violence, forced to scrape together an existence on the outskirts of places that still had enough. The people knew they had to change, but they didn't want to, or they disagreed over how. They feared for their children's futures in a world that was growing increasingly precarious and unstable, not realizing—or wanting to admit—that the apocalypse they were so afraid of had already arrived.

And then, a plague swept across the globe. People died gasping for air in their homes and on the streets, waiting for help from those who were already giving everything they had. Those with the most resources shut themselves away, grateful but uneasy at how little the world seemed to need them. Those who were needed were forced to carry on with nothing to protect themselves. Travel ceased, markets were empty, and the sounds of death and emergency filled the desolate streets. The people struggled to find food and supplies. They wondered how the leaders they had trusted had failed them so horribly. Some people rose up against those leaders, and against the inequalities and oppressions the plague had revealed, looking determinedly toward a different kind of future. Others wanted nothing more than to go back to the past, when they could still pretend they didn't know the truth about the world.

The people lost elders and youths, jobs and homes, relationships and communities. They also lost the belief that tomorrow would always be like today. Some people lost their very selves, as an illness that never seemed to end rendered their bodies and minds frighteningly unfamiliar. Others stayed healthy but still didn't recognize themselves any longer, after everything they'd thought gave their lives meaning evaporated so quickly and completely. The plague brought some communities together and tore others apart. Some people found new values, new communities, and new lives. Some people couldn't bring themselves to trust anyone again.

The people stumbled out of the plague years hoping the worst was over but knowing, now more than ever, that it wasn't. All over the world, the heat, and fires, and floods, and storms became different kinds of plagues, killing the most vulnerable and forcing so many others to flee. The wanderers encountered even more walls and fences, soldiers and guns, prisons and punishment than they had before. And yet, more and more people joined them every year, and from every kind of place, as staying became more dangerous than going.

Storms, fires, droughts, and famines became unlike anything the people had imagined or planned for. Right when one crisis ended, another would begin, deepening the cracks left behind by the ones before. States fractured and empires disintegrated, leaving people to figure out who they were and how to work together without the identities and social structures they were used to. Some people retreated from their neighbors; others attacked them. But most reached out their hands, and many were surprised by who reached back.

There would be other plagues, other storms, other droughts. The sea would swallow cities and all the technology the people had used to stave off the relentless water. Land, ecosystems, and species would disappear, kept alive only in the elders' stories. The people would go back to old ways of life, rediscovering how to hunt, gather, and fish, and they would revolutionize new ones, like powering their communities with energy from the environment around them, not fuels that had to be shipped around the world.

The people would explore the ruins their ancestors left behind, paddling their boats around submerged towers and telling each other what the names of these places had been. They would take what they needed from the ruins, sometimes desperately and sometimes reverentially, or perhaps always a bit of both. The people would venture back into abandoned lands that had grown too hot and dry for farming, but not too hot and dry for different kinds of lives, ones that let the people move when they needed to and follow the weather and resources they preferred.

The people would remember what they needed of the past and forget what they didn't. They would tell stories of ancestors who knew there would be a price to pay and refused to pay it, who had united the globe only to see those connections unraveled by their own greed. But they would also tell stories of ancestors who built wondrous and mysterious ruins, walked the streets of drowned cities, and found ways to survive even when it seemed impossible. The people would feel angry and grateful, mournful and awestruck, as they remembered those ancestors, the ones who were there at the beginning of the world.

ACKNOWLEDGMENTS

This book would not exist without the guidance and encouragement of my agent, Sarah Levitt. I'm grateful every day for her astute editorial eye and her willingness to believe in this book before I did.

Gail Winston brought this book to Harper, and I'm thankful for her wise early edits. Sarah Haugen saw it from first draft to published book and made my arguments immeasurably stronger and my words far more elegant. Thank you, Sarah, for never giving up on me.

At Harper, I'm also grateful for the work of Ezra Kupor, Maya Baran, Becca Putman, Frieda Duggan, Robin Bilardello, Muriel Jorgensen, and Darren Haggar. At Aevitas Creative Management, thank you to Erin Files and Mags Chmielarczyk.

Thank you to John Wyatt Greenlee, who made this book's wonderful maps and was an absolute pleasure to work with.

I owe a debt of gratitude to my colleagues and editors at *Science*, who have taught me how to report and write with rigor, clarity, and compassion over the last twelve years. Thank you especially to Elizabeth Culotta, Tim Appenzeller, Richard Stone, Martin Enserink, and David Grimm. I've learned so much from each of you.

I often can't believe that any scientist agrees to be interviewed by me, and I'm eternally grateful to each and every one who does. I'm so appreciative to everyone I spoke to for this book or who otherwise generously shared their expertise with me over the years: Agustín Fuentes, Guy Middleton, Prudence Rice, John Robb, Rebecca Mendelsohn, David

S. Anderson, Rosie Everett, Tiffiny Tung, Tom Higham, Chris Stringer, Johannes Krause, Paige Madison, Serena Tucci, Ehud Galili, Jim Leary, Patrick Nunn, Vince Gaffney, James Walker, Mark Koolmatrie, Dan Sandweiss, Andrew Somerville, Ana Cecilia Mauricio Llonto, Robert Rosenswig, Ari Caramanica, Jason Nesbitt, Felix Riede, Justin Jennings, Nicola Sharratt, Sara Gonzalez, Gwen Robbins Schug, Cameron Petrie, Sharon DeWitte, Anna Colet, Richard Redding, Miroslav Bárta, Matthew Douglas Adams, Norman Yoffee, Roberto Rosado-Ramirez, Vicente Cocon López, Scott Hutson, Matthew Restall, David Carballo, Kathleen Hull, Enrique Rodríguez-Alegría, Raúl Barrera Rodríguez, Salvador Guilliem Arroyo, John López, Mark Hauser, Alexandra Jones, Alicia Odewale, Justin Dunnavant, Douglas Armstrong, Ayana Omilade Flewellen, and William White.

I couldn't ask for a better group of like-minded science writers than Julia Rosen, Alexandra Witze, Jane C. Hu, Madeline Ostrander, Tiên Nguyễn, Kate Horowitz, Natasha Gilbert, Helen Shen, Rachel Ehrenberg, Antonia Juhasz, Katharine Sanderson, and Laura Sanders. Thank you all for your support and advice about this wild career we've chosen. And thank you to Ashley Bovin for running a virtual co-working group that kept me writing and thinking about this book through some very hard times.

Thank you to my parents, Jan Wildman and Michael Wade, for always supporting my curiosity and sense of adventure. Thank you to my sibling Carrie Wade, for the long phone calls.

Finally, thank you to my husband, Luckez Olmos García. I couldn't have written a single word of this book without your support, and there's no one I would rather face the apocalypse with than you.

NOTES

CHAPTER 1: HOW WE MISUNDERSTOOD THE APOCALYPSE OF HUMAN EXTINCTION

16 "extraordinary form": Hermann Schaaffhausen, "On the Crania of the Most Ancient Races of Man," translated by George Busk, *Natural History Review* series 2, vol. 1, no. 2 (1861).

17 "eminently simial": William King, "The Reputed Fossil Man of the Neanderthal," *Quarterly Journal of Science* 1 (1864): 88–97.

19 "Even the primitives": Quoted in Paige Madison, "Characterized by Darkness: Reconsidering the Origins of the Brutish Neanderthal," *Journal of the History of Biology* 53, no. 4 (2020): 493–519.

19 "Those who observe the fate": Arthur Keith, *The Antiquity of Man* (Williams and Norgate, 1915), 136.

21 the first Neanderthal genome: Richard E. Green et al., "A Draft Sequence of the Neandertal Genome," *Science* 328, no. 5979 (2010): 710–22.

22 evolutionary "phase": Aleš Hrdlička, "The Neanderthal Phase of Man," *Journal of the Royal Anthropological Institute of Great Britain and Ireland* 57 (1927): 249–74.

23 giant camels: Rebecca Wragg Sykes, *Kindred: Neanderthal Life, Love, Death and Art* (Bloomsbury Sigma, 2020), 374–75.

23 gathered shellfish: J. Zilhão et al., "Last Interglacial Iberian Neandertals as Fisher-Hunter-Gatherers," *Science* 367, no. 6485 (2020).

23 prehistoric horses: Wragg Sykes, *Kindred*, 139.

23 cave paintings: Tim Appenzeller, "Europe's First Cave Artists Were Neandertals, Newly Dated Paintings Show," *Science*, February 22, 2018.

23 Neanderthal-specific proteins: Lizzie Wade, "Neandertals Made Their Own Jewelry, New Method Confirms," *Science*, September 16, 2016.

24 the most influential burst: Michael Price, "Neanderthals and Modern Humans Made Babies 47,000 Years Ago," *Science*, May 21, 2024.

24 separate species: Josie Glausiusz, "Were Neanderthals More Than Cousins to *Homo Sapiens*?," *Sapiens*, January 20, 2020.

24 "spread out rather like ripples": Interview with Tom Higham, September 24, 2020.

25 "I was wedded to the idea": Higham interview.

26 the two species overlapped: Tom Higham et al., "The Timing and Spatiotemporal Patterning of Neanderthal Disappearance," *Nature* 512, no. 7514 (2014): 306–309.

26 baby tooth: Michael Price, "Did Neanderthals and Modern Humans Take Turns Living in a French Cave?," *Science*, February 9, 2022.

26 "You can imagine": Higham interview.

26 "fertile ground": Higham interview.

28 cold-loving animals like reindeer: Wragg Sykes, *Kindred*, 221.

28 the climate grew jumpy and unstable: Wragg Sykes, *Kindred*, 374–75.

28 "Things improved for a couple of thousand years": Interview with Chris Stringer, October 14, 2020.

28 "Being welcome at the fires": Wragg Sykes, *Kindred*, 403.

30 "play[ing] dentist": Interview with Johannes Krause, October 16, 2020.

30 "the size of two grains of rice": Svante Pääbo, *Neanderthal Man: In Search of Lost Genomes* (Basic Books, 2014), 313.

30 They named the new group: David Reich et al., "Genetic History of an Archaic Hominin Group from Denisova Cave in Siberia," *Nature* 468, no. 7327 (2010): 1053–60.

31 Denisovan DNA still survives: Sharon R. Browning et al., "Analysis of Human Sequence Data Reveals Two Pulses of Archaic Denisovan Admixture," *Cell* 173, no. 1 (2018): 53–61.e9.

31 Denisovan father and a Neanderthal mother: Viviane Slon et al., "The Genome of the Offspring of a Neanderthal Mother and a Denisovan Father," *Nature* 561, no. 7721 (2018): 113–16.

31 highest habitable altitudes in Tibet: Emilia Huerta-Sánchez et al., "Altitude Adaptation in Tibetans Caused by Introgression of Denisovan-like DNA," *Nature* 512, no. 7513 (2014): 194–97.

31 "It doesn't look like they were in trouble": Stringer interview.

CHAPTER 2: HOW SEA LEVEL RISE SPURRED INGENUITY

39 the last vestiges of Doggerland disappeared: James Walker et al., "The Archaeological Context of Doggerland During the Final Palaeolithic and Mesolithic,"

in *Europe's Lost Frontiers: Volume 1*, edited by Vince Gaffney and Simon Fitch (Archeopress, 2022), 76.

40 Noah's Woods: Clement Reid, *Submerged Forests* (Cambridge University Press, 1913), 1–2.

40 heave up bones: Reid, *Submerged Forests*, 41–42.

40 Sealed inside the peat was a point: Vincent Gaffney, Simon Fitch, and David Smith, *Europe's Lost World: The Rediscovery of Doggerland* (Council for British Archaeology, 2008), 14.

41 carved over thirteen thousand years ago: Geoff Baily et al., "Great Britain: The Intertidal and Underwater Archaeology of Britain's Submerged Landscapes," in *The Archaeology of Europe's Drowned Landscapes*, edited by Geoff Baily et al. (Springer Cham, 2020), 207.

41 "just stood there": Interview with Vince Gaffney, November 30, 2018.

41 "One occasionally gets the feeling": Gaffney et al., *Europe's Lost World*, 42.

42 wooden stakes arranged into fish traps: Ole Grøn and Jørgen Skaarup, "Møllegabet II: A Submerged Mesolithic Site and a 'Boat Burial' from Ærø," *Journal of Danish Archaeology* 10, no. 1 (1991): 38–50.

42 ancient dugout canoes and paddles: Torben Malm, "Excavating Submerged Stone Age Sites in Denmark—the Tybrind Vig Example," https://www.abc.se/~m10354/publ/tybrind.htm.

42 Bryony Coles advocated: Bryony Coles, "Doggerland: A Speculative Survey," *Proceedings of the Prehistoric Society* 64 (1998): 45–81.

45 bounce off sediments and echo back: Gaffney et al., *Europe's Lost World*, 74.

46 map nearly one thousand miles of rivers: Gaffney et al., *Europe's Lost World*, 92.

47 rippling shapes were still preserved: Gaffney et al., *Europe's Lost World*, 96.

47 Doggerlanders switched away from terrestrial sources of food: J. van der Plicht et al., "Surf'n Turf in Doggerland: Dating, Stable Isotopes and Diet of Mesolithic Human Remains from the Southern North Sea," *Journal of Archaeological Science: Reports* 10 (2016): 110–18.

48 plunged vibrating tubes: Tine Missiaen et al., "Targeting the Mesolithic: Interdisciplinary Approaches to Archaeological Prospection in the Brown Bank Area, Southern North Sea," *Quaternary International* 584 (2021): 141–51.

48 The expansion of offshore wind farms: James Walker et al., "Winds of Change: Urgent Challenges and Emerging Opportunities in Submerged Prehistory, a Perspective from the North Sea," *Heritage* 7, no. 4 (2024): 1947–68.

48 dredged up a piece of worked flint: "The First Archaeological Artefacts Found During the Search for Lost Prehistoric Settlements in the North Sea," press release from the University of Bradford, June 11, 2019, https://www.bradford.ac.uk/news/archive/2019/the-first-archaeological-artefacts-found-during-the-search-for-lost-prehistoric-settlements-in-the-north-sea.php.

48 working with volunteer beachcombers: Andrew Curry, "Europe's Lost Frontier," *Science*, January 31, 2020.

49 "It's like magic": Interview with Ehud Galili, December 13, 2019.

49 the remains of a drowned village now called Tel Hreiz: Ehud Galili et al., "A Submerged 7000-year-old Village and Seawall Demonstrate Earliest Known Coastal Defence Against Sea-level Rise," *PLoS ONE* 14, no. 12 (2019).

52 the settlement now called Atlit-Yam: Ehud Galili et al., "Israel: Submerged Prehistoric Sites and Settlements on the Mediterranean Coastline—the Current State of the Art," in *The Archaeology of Europe's Drowned Landscapes*.

53 Ngurunderi's wives had run away: Patrick Nunn, *The Edge of Memory: Ancient Stories, Oral Tradition and the Post-Glacial World* (Bloomsbury Sigma, 2019), 77.

53 *"Prenkulun prakuldun!"—water rise, water fall*: Mark Koolmatrie, personal correspondence, August 10, 2020.

53 on their way to the sky: Neale Draper, "Islands of the Dead? Prehistoric Occupation of Kangaroo Island and Other Southern Offshore Islands and Watercraft Use by Aboriginal Australians," *Quaternary International* 385 (2015): 229–42.

54 an oral history of the Great Drowning: Nunn, *The Edge of Memory*, 77.

54 the flood doesn't end: Interview with Patrick Nunn, February 7, 2020.

55 "dry, dusty, and parched country": Amy L. Roberts et al., "Marine Transgression, Aboriginal Narratives and the Creation of Yorke Peninsula/Guuranda, South Australia," *Journal of Island and Coastal Archaeology* 15, no. 3 (2019): 13.

55 The Yidinjdji people of northeastern Australia remember: Nunn, *The Edge of Memory*, 91.

55 of tree roots: Patrick Nunn, "Responses to Ocean Rise: The Ancestors' Tales," *Cosmos*, June 4, 2019.

55 of spears: Nunn, *The Edge of Memory*, 115.

56 Murujuga's artists began engraving: Jo McDonald, "I Must Go Down to the Seas Again: Or, What Happens When the Sea Comes to You? *Murujuga* Rock Art as an Environmental Indicator for Australia's North-west," *Quaternary International* 385 (2015): 124–35.

56 it was a mainland promontory: Nunn, *The Edge of Memory*, 92.

56 buried at least some of their dead: Jim Leary, *The Remembered Land: Surviving Sea-level Rise After the Last Ice Age* (Bloomsbury, 2015), 72.

57 a nearly seven-thousand-year-old boat burial: Grøn and Skaarup, "Møllegabet II."

57 the bones of a one- or two-year-old child: Galili et al., "Israel: Submerged Prehistoric Sites and Settlements on the Mediterranean Coastline—the Current State of the Art," in *The Archaeology of Europe's Drowned Landscapes*, 469.

57 "a cry to the gods to make it stop": Leary, *The Remembered Land*, 72.

58 they might have been offerings: Leary, *The Remembered Land*, 101.

CHAPTER 3: HOW APOCALYPSE BROUGHT PEOPLE TOGETHER

61 killed 158 people: Ari Caramanica, "Resilience and Resistance in the Peruvian Deserts," *ReVista: Harvard Review of Latin America* 17, no. 3 (2018).

63 "treasure troves of information": Dan Sandweiss, "Oscillations: What Effect Does the Weather Have on the Development of Human Culture?" *Phi Kappa Phi Forum*, Winter issue (2015).

63 "I had never seen oysters in Peru": Interview with Dan Sandweiss, December 1, 2020.

63 "what were you doing in Ecuador?": Conversation reconstructed in Sandweiss interview, 2020.

64 "That was the beginning": Sandweiss interview, 2020.

66 To process what they'd seen: Sandweiss interview, 2020.

66 "radically different": Sandweiss, "Oscillations," 11.

67 picture of when El Niño came and went: Dan Sandweiss and Kirk A. Maasch, "El Nino as Catastrophe on the Peruvian Coast," in *Going Forward by Looking Back: Archaeological Perspectives on Socio-ecological Crisis, Response, and Collapse*, edited by Felix Riede and Payson Sheets (Berghahn Books, 2020), 983.

69 "disasters are extraordinarily generative": Rebecca Solnit, *A Paradise Built in Hell: The Extraordinary Communities That Arise in Disaster* (Penguin Books, 2009), 22.

69 "Suffering and loss are transformed": Solnit, *A Paradise Built in Hell*, 56.

69 "a glimpse of who else we ourselves may be": Solnit, *A Paradise Built in Hell*, 9

69 "the shackles of conventional belief and role": Solnit, *A Paradise Built in Hell*, 97.

69 pre-Columbian Cuba: Jago Cooper, "Fail to Prepare, Then Prepare to Fail: Rethinking Threat, Vulnerability, and Mitigation in the Precolumbian Caribbean," in *Surviving Sudden Environmental Change: Answers from Archaeology*, edited by Jago Cooper and Payson Sheets (University Press of Colorado, 2012).

69 the Kuril Islands: Ben Fitzhugh et al., "Resilience and the Population History of the Kuril Islands, Northwest Pacific: A Study in Complex Human Ecodynamics," *Quaternary International* 419 (2016): 165–93.

70 "every stranger can be spoken to": Solnit, *A Paradise Built in Hell*, 32.

70 "crises and stresses often strengthen social bonds": Solnit, *A Paradise Built in Hell*, 92.

73 "It's like it was frozen in time": Interview with Ana Cecilia Mauricio Llonto, December 9, 2020, my translation from Spanish.

74 one of the most ancient monuments in Peru: Dan Sandweiss et al., "GPR Identification of an Early Monument at Los Morteros in the Peruvian Coastal Desert," *Quaternary Research* 73, no. 3 (2010): 439–48.

76 the oldest adobe monument: Ana Cecilia Mauricio et al., "The Earliest Adobe Monumental Architecture in the Americas," *Proceedings of the National Academy of Sciences* 118, no. 48 (2021).

77 more varied diets: Ann Gibbons, "The Evolution of Diet," *National Geographic*, August 18, 2014.

77 much more free time: James C. Scott, *Against the Grain: A Deep History of the Earliest States* (Yale University Press, 2017), 93.

78 "But they were heading down that path": Mauricio Llonto interview.

78 exploded to staggering sizes: Ruth Shady Solis et al., "Dating Caral, a Preceramic Site in the Supe Valley on the Central Coast of Peru," *Science* 292, no. 5517 (2001): 723–26.

79 grew, splintered, and reorganized: Richard L. Burger and Lucy Salazar, "Monumental Public Complexes and Agricultural Expansion on Peru's Central Coast During the Second Millennium BC," in *Early New World Monumentality*, edited by Richard L. Burger and Robert M. Rosenswig (University Press of Florida, 2012).

79 "The largest and strongest animals": Richard L. Burger, "The Construction of Values During the Peruvian Formative," in *The Construction of Value in the Ancient World*, edited by John K. Papadopoulos and Gary Urton (Cotsen Institute of Archaeology Press, 2012).

79 two separate, powerful groups: Thomas Pozorski and Shelia Pozorski, "Early Complex Society on the North and Central Peruvian Coast: New Archaeological Discoveries and New Insights," *Journal of Archaeological Research* 26, no. 4 (2018): 353–86.

79 "horrible hazard zone": Interview with Jason Nesbitt, December 14, 2020.

80 "take advantage of a crisis": Sandweiss interview, December 20, 2018.

80 "the system would appear to be working": Sandweiss and Maasch, "El Nino as Catastrophe on the Peruvian Coast," 990.

80 a thick layer of mud: Jason Nesbitt, "El Niño and Second-Millennium BC Monument Building at Huaca Cortada (Moche Valley, Peru)," *Antiquity* 90, no. 351 (2016): 638–53.

82 this final, desperate phase: Nesbitt, "El Niño and Second-Millennium BC Monument Building."

83 tear down the pyramid: Pozorski and Pozorski, "Early Complex Society on the North and Central Peruvian Coast."

CHAPTER 4: HOW APOCALYPSES TURN INEQUALITY INTO VIOLENCE

91 have never found a palace: Adam S. Green, "Killing the Priest-King: Addressing Egalitarianism in the Indus Civilization," *Journal of Archaeological Research* 29, no. 2 (2021): 153–202.

91 "much money and thought were lavished": Quoted in Green, "Killing the Priest-King," 154.

92 decipher—or even identify the language of—their writing: Andrew Robinson, "Ancient Civilization: Cracking the Indus Script," *Nature* 526, no. 7574 (2015): 499–501.

92 collaborative city government: Cameron A. Petrie, "Diversity, Variability, Adaptation and 'Fragility' in the Indus Civilization," in *The Evolution of Fragility: Setting the Terms*, edited by Norman Yoffee (McDonald Institute for Archaeological Research, 2019).

92 haven't found vast differences in wealth: Green, "Killing the Priest-King."

92 the 4.2-kiloyear event: Michael Marshall, "Did a Mega Drought Topple Empires 4,200 Years Ago?," *Nature*, January 26, 2022.

93 summer monsoon grew weaker: Petrie et al., "Adaptation to Variable Environments, Resilience to Climate Change: Investigating Land, Water and Settlement in Indus Northwest India," *Current Anthropology* 58, no. 1 (2017): 1–30.

93 "predictably unpredictable": Petrie, "Crisis, What Crisis? Adaptation, Resilience and Transformation in the Indus Civilisation," in *Crisis to Collapse: The Archaeology of Social Breakdown*, edited by Tim Cunningham and Jan Driessen (Presses universitaires de Louvain, 2017).

93 People poured into the city: Petrie, "Diversity, Variability, Adaptation and 'Fragility.'"

94 Trash piled up: Gwen Robbins Schug et al., "A Peaceful Realm? Trauma and Social Differentiation at Harappa," *International Journal of Paleopathology* 2, nos. 2–3 (2012): 136–47.

95 high standard of living: Robbins Schug et al., "A Peaceful Realm?"

96 individuals in the urban cemetery had advanced leprosy: Robbins Schug et al., "Infection, Disease, and Biosocial Processes at the End of the Indus Civilization," *PLoS ONE* 8, no. 12 (2013).

96 "This is the beginning of something important": Interview with Gwen Robbins Schug, August 30, 2021.

97 skulls in the ossuary showed signs of violence: Robbins Schug et al., "A Peaceful Realm?"

97 clearly much sicker than previous generations: Robbins Schug et al., "Infection, Disease, and Biosocial Processes."

97 children didn't have enough to eat: Gwen Robbins Schug and Kelly Elaine Blevins, "The Center Cannot Hold: A Bioarchaeological Perspective on Environmental Crisis in the Second Millennium BCE, South Asia," in *A Companion to South Asia in the Past*, edited by Gwen Robbins Schug and Subhash R. Walimbe (John Wiley & Sons, 2016).

97 represent a group of the city's elites: Jonathan Mark Kenoyer, "Changing Perspectives of the Indus Civilization: New Discoveries and Challenges," *Journal of the Indian Archaeological Society* 41 (2011).

99 most city dwellers left Harappa and moved to villages: Petrie, "Diversity, Variability, Adaptation and 'Fragility.'"

99 almost 40 percent had head injuries: Robbins Schug et al., "A Peaceful Realm?"

99 skeletal damage from some kind of long-term infection: Robbins Schug et al., "Infection, Disease, and Biosocial Processes."

100 nearly half were malnourished: Robbins Schug and Blevins, "The Center Cannot Hold."

100 They did not build another city: Petrie, "Crisis, What Crisis?"

100 loading their bodies into catapults: Gabriele de' Mussis in *The Black Death*, translated and edited by Rosemary Horrox (Manchester University Press, 1994): "The Arrival of the Plague."

101 perhaps Ethiopia and Ghana: Lizzie Wade, "The Black Death May Have Transformed Medieval Societies in Sub-Saharan Africa," *Science*, March 6, 2019.

101 "But all to no avail": Giovanni Boccaccio in Horrox, *The Black Death*: "The Plague in Florence."

101 the wails of mourners: Horrox, *The Black Death*: "The Plague in Padua."

101 stopped ringing its bells: Horrox, *The Black Death*: "Ordinances Against the Spread of Plague, Pistoia, 1348."

101 compared it to Noah's flood: Horrox, *The Black Death*: "The Plague in Padua."

101 whip themselves bloody: Horrox, *The Black Death*: "The Flagellants."

102 "I bid you weep": Gabriele de' Mussis in Horrox, *The Black Death:* "The Arrival of the Plague."

102 "cheer each other up": Horrox, *The Black Death*: "The Plague in Central Europe."

102 coins dating the burials: Anna Colet et al., "The Black Death and Its Consequences for the Jewish Community in Tàrrega: Lessons from History and Archaeology," in *Pandemic Disease in the Medieval World: Rethinking the Black Death*, edited by Monica H. Green (Arc Medieval Press, 2015).

103 "Many of the bones showed signs of violence": Interview with Anna Colet, March 21, 2022, my translation from Spanish.

103 attacks on Jewish communities in Tàrrega: Colet et al., "The Black Death and Its Consequences."

103 accused their Jewish neighbors of poisoning wells: Horrox, *The Black Death*: "Well-Poisoning."

103 Pope Clement VI himself issued a mandate: Horrox, *The Black Death*: "Mandate of Clement VI Concerning the Jews."

103 the attacks were nevertheless shockingly brutal: Colet et al., "The Black Death and Its Consequences."

104 That may be an overestimate: Colet interview.

104 buried by surviving members of the Jewish community: Colet et al., "The Black Death and Its Consequences."

107 more and more people were driven into poverty: Bruce M. S. Campbell, *The Great Transition: Climate, Disease and Society in the Late-Medieval World* (Cambridge University Press, 2016).

107 those who died just before the plague were shorter: Sharon N. DeWitte, "Setting the Stage for Medieval Plague: Pre-Black Death Trends in Survival and Mortality," *American Journal of Physical Anthropology* 158, no. 3 (2015): 441–51.

107 "it was a shock": Interview with Sharon DeWitte, March 7, 2022.

108 more likely to die during the Black Death: DeWitte and James W. Wood, "Selectivity of Black Death Mortality with Respect to Preexisting Health," *Proceedings of the National Academy of Sciences* 105, no. 5 (2008): 1436–41.

108 only 13 percent of English nobility died in 1349: DeWitte and Maryanne Kowaleski, "Black Death Bodies," *Fragments* 6 (2017).

108 "We should make new friends": Horrox, *The Black Death*: "Petrarch on the Death of Friends."

109 "for there was so great a shortage of servants and laborers": Horrox, *The Black Death*: "The Plague According to Henry Knighton."

109 "By an inversion of the natural order": Horrox, *The Black Death:* "The Plague Seen from Rochester."

109 much healthier than the people who died during the plague: Sharon DeWitte, "Stress, Sex, and Plague: Patterns of Developmental Stress and Survival in Pre- and Post-Black Death London," *American Journal of Human Biology* 30, no. 1 (2018).

110 "an unimaginably high cost": DeWitte, "Stress, Sex, and Plague."

110 "so that they will be forced to work for a living": Horrox, *The Black Death*: "The Ordinance of Labourers, 18 June 1349."

110 "[had] no regard to the said ordinance": Horrox, *The Black Death*: "The Statue of Labourers, 1351."

110 "there shall be a pair of stocks in every town": Horrox, *The Black Death*: "Additions to the Statue of Labourers, 1388."

111 wealth inequality plummeted during the Black Death: Guido Alfani, "Economic Inequality in Preindustrial Times: Europe and Beyond," *Journal of Economic Literature* 59, no. 1 (2021): 3–44.

111 "prelates, earls, barons and other great men": Horrox, *The Black Death*: "The Statue of Labourers, 1351."

CHAPTER 5: HOW SOCIETY COLLAPSES BUT CIVILIZATION SURVIVES

113 Life in the pyramid town: Mark Lehner, "The Pyramid Age Settlement of the Southern Mount at Giza," *Journal of the American Research Center in Egypt* 39 (2002): 27–74.

113 work gang: Mark Lehner, "Labor and the Pyramids: The Heit el-Ghurab 'Workers Town' at Giza," in *Labor in the Ancient World*, edited by Piotr Steinkeller and Michael Hudson (ISLET-Verlag, 2015).

116 herding cattle, sheep, and goats: Richard W. Redding, "A Tale of Two Sites: Old Kingdom Subsistence Economy and the Infrastructure of Pyramid Construction," in *Archaeozoology of the Near East X*, edited by Bea De Cupere, Veerle Linseele, and Sheila Hamilton-Dyer (Peeters, 2013).

116 likely supported around two hundred and fifty thousand people: Miroslav Bárta, *Analyzing Collapse: The Rise and Fall of the Old Kingdom* (American University in Cairo Press, 2019).

118 inherently despotic: Toby Wilkinson, *The Rise and Fall of Ancient Egypt* (Random House, 2010).

118 elite attendants were sacrificed: Ellen Morris, "Ancient Egyptian Exceptionalism: Fragility, Flexibility and the Art of Not Collapsing," in *The Evolution of Fragility* (University of Cambridge Press, 2019).

118 workers entombed near Giza: Zahi Hawass, "The Discovery of the Tombs of the Pyramid Builders at Giza," 1997, http://www.guardians.net/hawass/buildtomb.htm.

120 "The land turns round as does a potter's wheel": Ipuwer quoted in Barbara Bell, "The Dark Ages in Ancient History," *American Journal of Archaeology* 75, no. 1 (1971): 1–26

121 "a rapid, significant loss of an established level of sociopolitical complexity": Joseph Tainter, *The Collapse of Complex Societies* (Cambridge University Press, 1988), 4.

122 sharp decline in pollen: Christopher E. Bernhardt et al., "Nile Delta Vegetation Response to Holocene Climate Variability," *Geology* 40, no. 7 (2012): 615–18.

122 core taken from a desert lake: Mohamed A. Hamdan, "Climate and Collapse of Egyptian Old Kingdom: A Geoarchaeological Approach," *Proceedings of the Workshop "Italian Days in Aswan,"* edited by Giuseppina Capriotti (2013).

122 sediment fell into the already low Nile: Michael D. Krom et al., "Nile River Sediment Fluctuations over the Past 7000 Yr and Their Key Role in Sapropel Development," *Geology* 30, no. 1 (2002): 71–74.

122 the Palermo Stone: Bárta, *Analyzing Collapse*, 55.

122 archaeological evidence from Elephantine Island: Bárta, *Analyzing Collapse*, 58.

123 began to include desert animals: Bárta, "Long Term or Short Term? Climate Change and the Demise of the Old Kingdom," in *Climate and Ancient Societies*, edited by Susan Kerner et al. (Museum Tusculanum Press, 2015).

123 fossilized stumps and roots of long dead trees: Bell, "The Dark Ages."

123 "the desert is throughout the land": Bell, "The Dark Ages."

123 "the land was in the wind": Bell, "The Dark Ages."

123 the appearance of sandbanks and sandbars: Bell, "The Dark Ages."

123 thick layers of mud deposited by those floods: Bárta, *Analyzing Collapse.*

123 they considered rain to be a curse: Bárta, *Analyzing Collapse.*

124 the royal family was forced to loosen its grip: Bárta, *Analyzing Collapse.*

125 "kinglets": Ellen Morris, "'Lo, Nobles Lament, the Poor Rejoice': State Formation in the Wake of Social Flux," in *After Collapse: The Regeneration of Complex Societies,* edited by Glenn M. Schwartz and John J. Nichols (University of Arizona Press, 2006).

125 they failed in their divine duty: Morris, "Nobles Lament."

127 "I am the hero without equal": Ankhtifi's tomb text quoted from Stephan Seidlmayer, "The First Intermediate Period (c.2160–2055 BC)," in *The Oxford History of Ancient Egypt,* edited by Ian Shaw (Oxford University Press, 2000), 118.

127 "I gave bread to the hungry": Quoted in Seidlmayer, "The First Intermediate Period," 118.

128 increase in the number of graves: Morris, "Nobles Lament."

129 tombs able to survive for four thousand years: Seidlmayer, "The First Intermediate Period."

129 "files of soldiers and hunters": Seidlmayer, "The First Intermediate Period," 122.

129 "exhibit[ed] an astonishing degree of originality": Seidlmayer, "The First Intermediate Period," 114.

130 a woman centered her "resources and morality": Mariam Ayad, "Women's Self-Presentation in Pharaonic Egypt," in *Living Forever: Self-Presentation in Ancient Egypt,* edited by Hussein Bassir (American University in Cairo Press, 2019).

131 "Millions, billions" of them: Interview with Matthew Douglas Adams, July 28, 2021.

131 nothing about their lives seems to have changed: Adams, "Community and Society in Egypt in the First Intermediate Period: An Archaeological Investigation of the Abydos Settlement Site" (PhD diss., University of Pennsylvania, 2005).

132 "The picture of the state in ancient Egypt": Adams interview.

132 images of anarchy, starvation, murder, infanticide: Morris, "Writing Trauma: Ipuwer and the Curation of Cultural Memory," in *"An Excellent Fortress for His Armies, a Refuge for the People": Egyptological, Archaeological, and Biblical Studies in Honor of James K. Hoffmeier* (Penn State University Press/Eisenbrauns, 2020).

133 "The highborn are full of lamentations": Ipuwer quoted in Bell, "The Dark Ages."

133 inversion of that social order: Morris, "Nobles Lament."

133 "careworn brows": Morris, "Nobles Lament," 67.

133 "good shepherds": Morris, "Nobles Lament," 71.

CHAPTER 6: HOW POSTAPOCALYPTIC SOCIETIES REINVENT THEMSELVES

136 "numerous and extensive cities, desolate and in ruins": John L. Stephens, *Incidents of Travel in Yucatan*, Volume 1 (Harper and Brothers, 1848), Chapter 1.

136 "the most extensive journey ever made by a stranger": Stephens, *Incidents of Travel in Yucatan*, Volume 1, Preface.

137 "lost, buried, and unknown": Stephens, *Incidents of Travel in Yucatan*, Volume 2, Chapter 24.

137 "It has been the fortune of the author": Stephens, *Incidents of Travel in Yucatan*, Volume 1, Preface.

137 Aké's ruins sat adjacent to a hacienda: Stephens, *Incidents of Travel in Yucatan*, Volume 2, Chapter 24.

137 built by giants: Augustus Le Plongeon, in Roberto Rosado-Ramirez, "Living with Ruins: Community Regeneration After Political Collapse at the Ancient Maya City of Ake, Yucatan, Mexico" (PhD diss., Northwestern University, 2021), 212.

138 "the existence of these ruins was entirely unknown": Stephens, *Incidents of Travel in Yucatan*, Volume 1, Preface.

138 "never bestowed upon them one passing thought": Stephens, *Incidents of Travel in Yucatan*, Volume 2, Chapter 1.

138 "Involuntarily we turn for a moment to the frightful scenes": Stephens, *Incidents of Travel in Yucatan*, Volume 2, Chapter 24.

143 merchants vied with the nobility: Scott R. Hutson and Bruce H. Dahlin, "The Long Road to Maya Markets," in *Ancient Maya Commerce: Multidisciplinary Research at Chunchucmil* (University Press of Colorado, 2017).

144 suddenly turned themselves into walled fortresses: Arthur A. Demarest et al., "Classic Maya Defensive Systems and Warfare in the Petexbatun Region: Archaeological Evidence and Interpretations," *Ancient Mesoamerica* 8, no. 2 (1997): 229–53.

144 drought likely hit these southern cities: Peter M. J. Douglas et al., "Drought, Agricultural Adaptation, and Sociopolitical Collapse in the Maya Lowlands," *Proceedings of the National Academy of Sciences* 112, no. 18 (2015): 5607–12.

145 archaeologists have found mass graves: Patricia A. McAnany and Tomás Gallareta Negrón, "Bellicose Rulers and Climatological Peril? Retrofitting Twenty-First-Century Woes on Eighth-Century Maya Society," in *Questioning Collapse: Human Resilience, Ecological Vulnerability, and the Aftermath of Empire*, edited by McAnany and Norman Yoffee (Cambridge University Press, 2010).

145 Aké built a wall: Rosado-Ramirez, "Living with Ruins."

146 An even more severe and prolonged drought: David A. Hodell et al., "Terminal Classic Drought in the Northern Maya Lowlands Inferred from Multiple Sediment Cores in Lake Chichancanab (Mexico)," *Quaternary Science Reviews* 24, nos. 12–13 (2005): 1413–27.

150 the forest gives way to the town of Aké: Visit to Aké with Rosado-Ramirez, July 12–13, 2022.

154 the remains of ninety-six small houses within the monumental core: Rosado-Ramirez, "Living with Ruins."

156 stripping bark from trees for food: Scott L. Fedick and Louis S. Santiago, "Large Variation in Availability of Maya Food Plant Sources During Ancient Droughts," *Proceedings of the National Academy of Sciences* 119, no. 1 (2021).

156 like they'd heard the Itzás had in their capital: Jason Yaeger and David A. Hodell, "The Collapse of Maya Civilization: Assessing the Interaction of Culture, Climate, and Environment," in *El Niño, Catastrophism, and Culture Change in Ancient America*, edited by Sandweiss and Jeffrey Quilter (Dumbarton Oaks, 2008).

160 rendering their decorations invisible and meaningless: Interview with Scott Hutson, January 31, 2023.

160 ancient ruins are not empty: Lizzie Wade, "Ancient People Lived Among Ruins Too. What Did They Make of Them?," *Science*, March 30, 2023.

162 Mayapán's monumental architecture looked messier: Visit to Mayapán with Rosado-Ramirez, July 14, 2022.

162 drought struck again: Douglas J. Kennett et al., "Drought-Induced Civil Conflict Among the Ancient Maya," *Nature Communications* 13, no. 1 (2022): 3911.

CHAPTER 7: HOW THE APOCALYPSE OF COLONIALISM HAS HIDDEN IN PLAIN SIGHT

172 set off an explosion: Bernal Díaz del Castillo, *The Conquest of New Spain*, translated by J. M. Cohen (Penguin Books, 1963), 91.

172 *I will possess them*: Matthew Restall, *When Montezuma Met Cortés: The True Story of the Meeting That Changed History* (Ecco, 2018), 130.

173 sending an eagle to land in front of them: Camilla Townsend, *Fifth Sun: A New History of the Aztecs* (Oxford University Press, 2019), Chapters 1 and 2.

175 "buildings rising from the water": Díaz del Castillo, *The Conquest of New Spain*, 214.

175 an unusually decentralized and equitable republic: Lizzie Wade, "It Wasn't Just Greece: Archaeologists Find Early Democratic Societies in the Americas," *Science*, March 15, 2017.

176 the climate-driven collapse of their capitals: David Graeber and David Wengrow, *The Dawn of Everything: A New History of Humanity* (Farrar, Straus and Giroux, 2021), Chapter 11.

176 performative generosity of the rich: Graeber and Wengrow, *The Dawn of Everything*, Chapter 5.

176 farmers harnessed technologies like irrigation canals: Pekka Hämäläinen, *Indigenous Continent: The Epic Contest for North America* (Liveright, 2022), Chapter 2.

176 intentionally remained egalitarian hunter-gatherers: Graeber and Wengrow, *The Dawn of Everything*, Chapter 5.

178 The trade embargoes were growing harsher: Keitlyn Alcantara-Russell, "The Diet of Sovereignty: Bioarchaeology in Tlaxcallan" (PhD diss., Vanderbilt University, 2020).

180 launched a surprise attack: Federico Navarrete Linares, *¿Quién Conquistó México?* (Penguin Random House Mexico, 2019), Chapter 4.

180 an attack on traitorous Cholula: Restall, *When Montezuma Met Cortés*, Chapter 6.

180 "conquest procedures": Restall, *Seven Myths of the Spanish Conquest*, Updated Edition (Oxford University Press, 2021), Chapter 1.

181 "subdue and exploit": Restall, *Seven Myths*, 24.

181 Preexisting Spanish law: Restall, *When Montezuma Met Cortés*, 78.

181 "the term they use to make free people into slaves": Quoted in Restall, *When Montezuma Met Cortés*, 78.

181 "horrible, abominable, and deserving punishment": *Five Letters of Relation from Fernando Cortes to the Emperor Charles V*, translated and edited by Francis Augustus MacNutt (G. P. Putnam's Sons, 1908), 78.

182 as a form of state violence: Restall, *When Montezuma Met Cortés*, Chapter 3.

183 the city's *tzompantli*: Wade, "Feeding the Gods: Hundreds of Skulls Reveal Massive Scale of Human Sacrifice in Aztec Capital," *Science*, June 21, 2018.

183 "That fatal Friday morning": Quoted in Hämäläinen, *Indigenous Continent*, 66.

184 eating their own dead: Joseph Stromberg, "Starving Settlers in Jamestown Colony Resorted to Cannibalism," *Smithsonian*, April 30, 2013.

187 Marina translated his words literally: Townsend, *Malintzin's Choices: An Indian Woman in the Conquest of Mexico* (University of New Mexico Press, 2006), 95.

188 the level of the local community: Townsend, *Fifth Sun*.

189 "awestruck or paralyzed with fear": Townsend, *Fifth Sun*, 125.

189 "more of a psychological than tactical advantage": David M. Carballo, *Collision of Worlds: A Deep History of the Fall of Aztec Mexico and the Forging of New Spain* (Oxford University Press, 2020), 121.

190 "The key aspect of Spanish power": Navarrete Linares, *¿Quién Conquistó México?*, Chapter 4, my translation from Spanish.

190 keeping the Spaniards prisoner: Restall, *When Montezuma Met Cortés*, Chapter 4.

192 provided the perfect cover: Restall, *When Montezuma Met Cortés*, Chapter 6.

193 the Mexica killed approximately six hundred Europeans: Townsend, *Fifth Sun*, 117.

195 "a scab in a blanket": Townsend, *Fifth Sun*, 118.

195 Some Europeans also fell dreadfully ill: Carballo, *Collison of Worlds*, 218.

195 "There was indeed perishing": *Florentine Codex, Book 12: The Conquest of Mexico*, translated by Arthur J. O. Anderson and Charles E. Dibble (The University of Utah Press, 1975), 82.

196 colonial contexts in Florida: Clark Spencer Larsen, "Colonialism and Decline in the American Southeast: The Remarkable Record of La Florida," in *Beyond Germs: Native Depopulation in North America*, edited by Catherine M. Cameron, Paul Kelton, and Alan C. Swedlund (University of Arizona Press, 2015).

196 before direct contact with European colonists: Matthew Liebmann, "Colonialism and Indigenous Population Decline in the Americas," in *The Routledge Handbook of the Archaeology of Indigenous-Colonial Interaction in the Americas*, edited by Lee M. Panich and Sara L. Gonzalez (Routledge, 2021).

196 Kathleen Hull excavated in the Yosemite Valley: Wade, "From Black Death to Fatal Flu, Past Pandemics Show Why People on the Margins Suffer Most," *Science*, May 14, 2020.

197 the Awahnichi left their traditional home: Kathleen L. Hull, "Quality of Life: Native Communities Within and Beyond the Bounds of Colonial Institutions in California," in *Beyond Germs*.

198 "the most explosive Indigenous expansion". Hämäläinen, *Indigenous Continent*, 101.

199 switched its allegiance: Townsend, *Fifth Sun*, 121.

199 "They will suffer worse from hunger": Díaz del Castillo, *The Conquest of New Spain*, 389–90.

200 a tour of postapocalyptic Tenochtitlan: Interview with Raúl Barrera Rodríguez, June 1, 2022.

200 "smallest, but most visited, archaeological site": INAH, "Pirámide de Ehécatl," April 23, 2009, my translation from Spanish, website now archived: https://web.archive.org/web/20210625030747/https://inah.gob.mx/boletines/2051-piramide-de-ehecatl.

202 hundreds of skull fragments: Wade, "Feeding the Gods."

203 "aren't eyewitness accounts": Interview with Restall, June 6, 2022.

203 "rich and evocative" language: Townsend, *Fifth Sun*, 224.

204 "desperately needed to come to terms": Townsend, *Fifth Sun*, 98.

206 "all houses should be pulled down": Díaz del Castillo, *The Conquest of New Spain*, 369.

CHAPTER 8: HOW SLAVERY CREATED THE MODERN WORLD

209 "illusion of health": Interview with Alicia Odewale, July 11, 2019.

210 "royal slaves": Alicia Odewale et al., "In Service to a Danish King: Comparing the Material Culture of Royal Enslaved Afro-Caribbeans and Danish Soldiers at the Christiansted National Historic Site," *Journal of African Diaspora Archaeology and Heritage* 6, no. 1 (2017): 19–54.

212 museums and collections of Moctezuma: Lawrence Weschler, *Mr. Wilson's Cabinet of Wonder: Pronged Ants, Horned Humans, Mice on Toast, and Other Marvels of Jurassic Technology* (Pantheon, 1995).

213 "local, serf-like labor": Carballo, *Collision of Worlds*, 90.

213 4.8 million enslaved Africans: Wade, "Caribbean Excavation Offers Intimate Look at the Lives of Enslaved Africans," *Science*, November 7, 2019.

214 "The rules of society get suspended": Interview with Douglas Armstrong, September 11, 2019.

214 "get sugar going within a year": Armstrong interview, December 4, 2018.

214 how lucrative, and transformative, the switch to sugar was: Armstrong, "Early Seventeenth Century Settlement in Barbados and the Shift to Sugar, Slavery, and Capitalism," in *Power, Political Economy, and Historical Landscapes of the Modern World*, edited by Christopher R. DeCorse (State University of New York Press, 2019).

215 "full-scale capitalism": Armstrong interview, 2018.

215 "turning individuals' lives into energy": Interview with William White, July 11, 2019.

216 Steam technology may have arrived: Charlotte Goudge, "Man vs. Machine: Betty's Hope and the Industrialisation of 19th-Century Caribbean Factories," *Industrial Archaeology Review* 41, no. 1 (2019): 45–51.

216 "terraforming": Interview with Justin Dunnavant, July 10, 2019.

216 the water table had plummeted: Interview with Mark Hauser, September 5, 2024.

217 lead, mercury, and arsenic: E. Christian Wells et al., "Social and Environmental Impacts of British Colonial Rum Production at Betty's Hope Plantation, Antigua," in *Archaeologies of the British in Latin America*, edited by C. E. Orser, Jr. (Springer, 2019).

217 terror of dying of disease: Odewale, "An Archaeology of Struggle: Material Remnants of a Double Consciousness in the American South and Danish Caribbean Communities," in *Transforming Anthropology* 27, no. 2 (2019): 114–32.

217 artifacts directly related to their skills: Odewale et al., "In Service to a Danish King."

218 The archaeologists I'd gone there to visit: Reporting trip to St. Croix, July 9–11, 2019.

219 "The most difficult part": Dunnavant interview, July 10, 2019.

220 "No one has touched": Field reporting, July 10, 2019.

220 database of material excavated from sites of slavery: Digital Archaeological Archive of Comparative Slavery, https://www.daacs.org.

222 "making no mention of any minimal standards": Odewale et al., "In Service to a Danish King."

223 plant remains from all over the world: Sarah E. Oas and Mark W. Hauser, "The Political Ecology of Plantations from the Ground Up," *Environmental Archaeology* 23, no. 1 (2017): 4–12.

223 "engineers solving problems": Hauser interview, 2024.

224 drifted with ocean currents: Dunnavant, "Have Confidence in the Sea: Maritime Maroons and Fugitive Geographies," *Antipode* 53, no. 3 (2021): 884–905.

225 a collection of iron blades: Armstrong, "Cave of Iron and Resistance: A Preliminary Examination," *Journal of the Barbados Museum & Historical Society* 61 (2015): 178–99.

225 "engage in the slave rebellion": Armstrong interview, 2018.

226 "ability to reintegrate after disorder": Quoted in Armstrong, "Cave of Iron," 184.

CHAPTER 9: WHY WE'VE STAYED TRAPPED IN THE APOCALYPSE—AND HOW WE CAN FIND OUR WAY OUT

228 the flood would begin: Louisa Hoberman, "Bureaucracy and Disaster: Mexico City and the Flood of 1629," *Journal of Latin American Studies* 6, no. 2 (1974): 211–30.

230 "The construction materials are the same stones": Barrera Rodríguez interview, 2022.

230 the remains of the new palace: "Descubren en Monte de Piedad restos del Palacio de Axayácatl y de una casa construida por orden de Cortés," Secretaría de Cultura, July 13, 2020, https://www.gob.mx/cultura/prensa/descubren-en-monte-de-piedad-restos-del-palacio-de-axayacatl-y-de-una-casa-construida-por-orden-de-cortes.

233 "it starts to test the limits of pre-Columbian engineering practices": Interview with John López, January 27, 2018.

233 "were stranded in the upper floors": Hoberman, "Bureaucracy and Disaster."

234 at least forty-seven hundred Indigenous workers: Hoberman, "Technological Change in a Traditional Society: The Case of the Desagüe in Colonial Mexico," *Technology and Culture* 21, no. 3 (1980): 386–407.

234 visiting naturalist Alexander von Humboldt: Hoberman, "Bureaucracy and Disaster."

234 finally announced in 1900: "El Desagüe del Valle de México," *Mirador*, Mexico's Secretary of Infrastructure, Communications and Transportation, https://elmirador.sct.gob.mx/manos-a-la-obra/el-desague-del-valle-de-mexico

234 porous volcanic rock and soil: Zoë Schlanger, "Solving Mexico City's Cataclysmic Cycle of Drowning, Drying, and Sinking," *Quartz*, May 18, 2018.

235 The latest was completed in 2019: "Inauguran Túnel Emisor Oriente que permitirá evitar inundaciones en la Ciudad de México y Edomex," Gobierno de la Ciudad de México, December 23, 2019, https://jefaturadegobierno.cdmx.gob.mx/comunicacion/nota/inauguran-tunel-emisor-oriente-que-permitira-evitar-inundaciones-en-la-ciudad-de-mexico-y-edomex.

235 incredible engineering marvel: Jonathan Watts, "Mexico City's Water Crisis—from Source to Sewer," *The Guardian*, November 12, 2015.

235 "more intense rains, which means more floods": Quoted in Michael Kimmelman, "Mexico City, Parched and Sinking, Faces a Water Crisis," *New York Times*, February 17, 2017.

236 "exceeded the capacity of municipal and state teams": "Mantiene Conagua las labores de desazolve y desalojo de agua anegada en el municipio de Chalco," Comisión Nacional de Agua, August 22, 2024, https://www.gob.mx/conagua/prensa/mantiene-conagua-las-labores-de-desazolve-y-desalojo-de-agua-anegada-en-el-municipio-de-chalco.

236 residents attended meetings: Mariana Martínez Barba, "Residents of Mexico City Suburb Are Anxious After Living over a Month in Black Sewage Water," Associated Press, September 14, 2024.

238 "like a grounded ship": Solnit, *A Paradise Built in Hell*, 136.

238 ricocheting around the basin: Maya Wei-Haas, "How Mexico City's Unique Geology Makes Deadly Earthquakes Even Worse," *Smithsonian*, September 20, 2017.

238 trembling bowl of Jell-O: Robert A. Jones, "Pattern of Destruction: New Lessons from Quake in Mexico," *Los Angeles Times*, September 26, 1986.

239 regular, controlled burning: Cassandra Rowe et al., "Indigenous Fire Management Began More Than 11,000 Years Ago: New Research," *The Conversation*, March 11, 2024.

239 "It was soul-destroying": Interview with Mark Koolmatrie, August 4, 2020.

239 half of Kangaroo Island: Jamie Tarabay, "There's No Place Like Kangaroo Island. Can It Survive Australia's Fires?," *New York Times*, February 4, 2020.

240 Indigenous fire control practices were denigrated: Livia Gershon, "The Global Suppression of Indigenous Fire Management," *JSTOR Daily*, October 12, 2020.

240 evolved to nurture bison: Christopher J. Preston, "Why Grazing Bison Could Be Good for the Planet," BBC, November 2, 2023.

240 "never came back": Hauser interview, 2024.

240 directly in the path of landslides: Hauser interview, September 13, 2019.

241 wetland and ecological park: Matthew Ponsford, "Restoring an Ancient Lake from the Rubble of an Unfinished Airport in Mexico City," *MIT Technology Review*, February 13, 2023.

241 cultivated along the side of a highway: Claire Potter, "The Search for Mexico City's Lost Water," *Nextblue*, November 28, 2023.

241 "You can't reverse five hundred years": López interview.

242 "I lost my only family": Quoted in Elena Poniatowska, *Nada, nadie: Las voces del temblor* (Ediciones Era, 1988), 66, my translation from Spanish.

243 the ruins of a clandestine factory: Patrick J. McDonnell, "Mexico Didn't Wait Long After the Earthquake to Raze a Building That Housed Low-Wage Textile Workers. Neighbors Want to Know Why," *Los Angeles Times*, September 26, 2017.

243 "the seamstresses pinpoint the day": Phoebe McKinney, "Fighting to Survive: Mexico's 19th of September Union," *Women and Labor* 10, no. 9 (1989). Also quoted in Solnit, *A Paradise Built in Hell*, 138.

243 the first representative local government: Alejandra Reyes, "The Evolution of Local Governance in Mexico City: Pursuing Autonomy in a Growing Region," *IMFG Perspectives* 25 (2019).

244 "This is a city that reinvents itself": Barrera Rodríguez interview.

246 Caramanica saw how well the system worked: Ari Caramanica et al., "El Niño Resilience Farming on the North Coast of Peru," *Proceedings of the National Academy of Sciences* 117, no. 39 (2020): 24127–24137.

247 "Today the only thing that grows": Interview with Ari Caramanica, December 8, 2020.

EPILOGUE: THE BEGINNING

251 first handmade and then government issued: Matthew Magnani et al., "A Contemporary Archaeology of Pandemic," *Journal of Social Archaeology* 22, no. 1 (2022): 48–81.

251 colorful messages of solidarity: Dante Angelo et al., "Private Struggles in Public Spaces: Documenting the COVID-19 Material Culture and Landscapes," *Journal of Contemporary Archaeology* 8, no. 1 (2021): 154–84.

251 wooden spoons: Science Museum Group, "COVID-19 Collecting Project Final Report," https://www.sciencemuseumgroup.org.uk/projects/collecting-covid-19.

251 trash bags worn by American nurses: Roger Catlin, "First Vial Used in U.S. Covid-19 Vaccinations Joins the Smithsonian Collections," *Smithsonian*, March 9, 2021.

SELECTED BIBLIOGRAPHY AND FURTHER READING

CHAPTER 1

Many of the primary sources about the discovery of the first Neanderthal are freely available online, including Hermann Schaaffhausen, "On the Crania of the Most Ancient Races of Man," translated by George Busk, *Natural History Review* (1861), and William King, "The Reputed Fossil Man of the Neanderthal," *Quarterly Journal of Science* (1864). I drew on those articles, as well as Charles Lyell, *Geological Evidences of the Antiquity of Man* (John Murray, 1863), Chapter 5, to reconstruct the scene of discovery. For a recent reexamination of what remains of the Neanderthal type site, see Schmitz et al., "The Neandertal Type Site Revisited: Interdisciplinary Investigations of Skeletal Remains from the Neander Valley, Germany," *Proceedings of the National Academy of Sciences* (2002).

Svante Pääbo's *Neanderthal Man: In Search of Lost Genomes* (Basic Books, 2014) is a behind-the-scenes look at the quest to sequence the first Neanderthal genome and all the work that led up to it. An interview with Johannes Krause also helped me reconstruct the ancient DNA lab and the discovery of both the Neanderthal and Denisovan genomes.

The book *Kindred: Neanderthal Life, Love, Death and Art* (Bloomsbury Sigma, 2020) by Rebecca Wragg Sykes is a vivid, up-to-date examination of Neanderthal history and culture, including where they lived, how they hunted, and how they handled their dead. Conversations with Paige Madison, as well as her article "Characterized by Darkness: Reconsidering the Origins of the Brutish Neanderthal," *Journal of the History of Biology* (2020) helped me understand how colonialism and scientific racism influenced beliefs about Neanderthals until well into the twentieth century. Madison has also written, delightfully, about the practice of dating fossil bones by licking them: "Anthropology Is Far from Licking the Problem of Fossil Ages," *Aeon*, July 12, 2016.

For a more detailed account of how scientific hypotheses regarding possible relationships between Neanderthals and *Homo sapiens* changed in the late twentieth century, see Chris Stringer, "The Development of Ideas About a Recent African Origin for *Homo sapiens*," *Journal of Anthropological Sciences* (2022).

It's possible a Denisovan skull has already been discovered in northern China. See Ann Gibbons, "Stunning 'Dragon Man' Skull May Be an Elusive Denisovan—or a New Species of Human," *Science*, June 25, 2021.

CHAPTER 2

My main source for the creation of the first map of Doggerland, as well as how its ecosystems changed over the course of the Great Drowning, was *Europe's Lost World: The Rediscovery of Doggerland* by Vincent Gaffney, Simon Fitch, and David Smith (Council for British Archaeology, 2008). Gaffney's team and many other archaeologists in countries around the North Sea have continued to seek out evidence of Doggerland since the first mapping project. For the most recent report from Gaffney's team, see *Europe's Lost Frontiers: Volume 1*, edited by Vince Gaffney and Simon Fitch (Archeopress, 2022). For a view of recent Doggerland archaeology from the Netherlands, see Andrew Curry, "Europe's Lost Frontier," *Science*, January 31, 2020.

I first wrote about Tel Hreiz's seawall for *Science:* Lizzie Wade, "This 7000-Year-Old Wall Was the Earliest Known Defense Against Rising Seas. It Failed," December 18, 2019. Ehud Galili described his technique for finding underwater sites in an interview for that story. The primary source of information about Tel Hreiz and its seawall is Ehud Galili et al., "A Submerged 7000-Year-Old Village and Seawall Demonstrate Earliest Known Coastal Defence Against Sea-Level Rise," *PLoS ONE* (2019). Information about Atlit-Yam and Neve-Yam is collected in Ehud Galili et al., "Israel: Submerged Prehistoric Sites and Settlements on the Mediterranean Coastline—the Current State of the Art" in *The Archaeology of Europe's Drowned Landscapes* (Springer Cham, 2020). *The Remembered Land: Surviving Sea-Level Rise After the Last Ice Age* by Jim Leary (Bloomsbury, 2015) is an imaginative study of the drowning of Doggerland and its people's possible emotional and spiritual responses to losing their home.

Versions of the Ngarrindjeri story about Ngurunderi and his wives were written down in the nineteenth and twentieth centuries by white missionaries and anthropologists, as well as the Ngarrindjeri author David Unaipon. I've drawn on a summary of those versions compiled by Patrick Nunn in *The Edge of Memory: Ancient Stories, Oral Tradition and the Post-Glacial World* (Bloomsbury Sigma, 2019) and supplemented it with information shared with me by Mark Koolmatrie, a Ngarrindjeri elder who gives tours based on Aboriginal knowledge through his company Kool Tours. The exact sources of the other myths are cited in the Notes, but for an overview, *The Edge of Memory* is a comprehensive collection of stories about ancient sea level rise from all over Australia.

Archaeologists are catching up to Aboriginal knowledge about Australia's deep past and beginning to search for—and find—sites in Sea Country. For a recent overview, see Clare Watson, "Stepping Off Shore and into Sea Country," *Hakai Magazine*, February 2, 2021.

CHAPTER 3

I reconstructed Dan Sandweiss's experience as a graduate student finding unexpected oyster shells in the Santa Valley from interviews with him, as well his article "Oscillations: What Effect Does the Weather Have on the Development of Human Culture?," *Phi Kappa Phi Forum*

(2015). For a recent encapsulation of Sandweiss's decades-long work on El Niño, its changing patterns, and its possible cultural impacts, see Sandweiss and Kirk A. Maasch, "El Nino as Catastrophe on the Peruvian Coast," in *Going Forward by Looking Back: Archaeological Perspectives on Socio-Ecological Crisis, Response, and Collapse* (Berghahn Books, 2020).

A Paradise Built in Hell: The Extraordinary Communities That Arise in Disaster by Rebecca Solnit (Penguin Books, 2009) is the definitive historical and journalistic account of twentieth-century "disaster utopias" and a powerful counterpoint to ingrained cultural assumptions that people will inevitably turn on each other during a crisis. Solnit's deep research and vivid reporting was invaluable to me as I tried to imagine how past people would have reacted during and after apocalypses.

The Dawn of Everything: A New History of Humanity by David Graeber and David Wengrow (Farrar, Straus and Giroux, 2021) is an invigorating new consideration of why and how complex societies formed all over the world—and why, in the authors' view, complexity's origins have been misunderstood.

For the discovery of the Los Morteros monument, see Sandweiss et al., "GPR Identification of an Early Monument at Los Morteros in the Peruvian Coastal Desert," *Quaternary Research* (2010). For information about its early use of adobe architecture, see Ana Cecilia Mauricio et al., "The Earliest Adobe Monumental Architecture in the Americas," *Proceedings of the National Academy of Sciences* (2021).

For details about the construction, rebuilding, and abandonment of Huaca Cortada, see Jason Nesbitt, "El Niño and Second-Millennium BC Monument Building at Huaca Cortada (Moche Valley, Peru)," *Antiquity* (2016).

CHAPTER 4

My reconstruction of the collapse of Harappa was primarily informed by the work of Gwen Robbins Schug and Cameron Petrie, as well as interviews with both of them. Petrie, "Diversity, Variability, Adaptation and 'Fragility' in the Indus Civilization," in *The Evolution of Fragility: Setting the Terms* (McDonald Institute for Archaeological Research, 2019) is a comprehensive overview of the Indus Civilization, including its collapse. Adam S. Green, "Killing the Priest-King: Addressing Egalitarianism in the Indus Civilization," *Journal of Archaeological Research* (2021) examines the long history of archaeological evidence for cooperative government and social equality in Harappa and the other Indus cities. For an explanation of how Harappa grew and developed, as well as a slightly different view of its possible hierarchies, see Jonathan Mark Kenoyer, "Changing Perspectives of the Indus Civilization: New Discoveries and Challenges," *Journal of the Indian Archaeological Society* (2011).

The extent, significance, and even existence of a worldwide 4.2-kiloyear drying event is still somewhat debated, especially among geologists and paleoclimatologists; see Paul Voosen, "Massive Drought or Myth? Scientists Spar over an Ancient Climate Event Behind Our New Geological Age," *Science*, August 8, 2018. Archaeologists must be careful to analyze *local* paleoclimate data for evidence of ancient droughts to be sure such an event affected the societies they study. For evidence of local climate change, including drought, in the Indus Valley beginning around forty-two hundred years ago, see Petrie et al., "Adaptation to Variable Environments, Resilience to Climate Change: Investigating Land, Water and Settlement in Indus Northwest India," *Current Anthropology* (2017).

Robbins Schug reports on evidence for violence in Harappa during different time periods in "A Peaceful Realm? Trauma and Social Differentiation at Harappa," *International Journal of Paleopathology* (2012). Her article "Infection, Disease, and Biosocial Processes at the End of the Indus Civilization," *PLoS ONE* (2013) addresses evidence for disease in the city's various cemeteries before, during, and after the collapse.

All the primary sources I quote about the Black Death come from *The Black Death*, translated and edited by Rosemary Horrox (Manchester University Press, 1994). It is a gift to have so many voices from all over Europe compiled in one place and translated into English, and Horrox's organization of the material, as well as her section introductions, are excellent. The account of Mongol soldiers using the plague-infected bodies of their dead comrades as weapons comes from the account of Gabriele de' Mussis, included in *The Black Death*. For an alternative perspective on how and why the plague entered Europe, see Hannah Barker, "Laying the Corpses to Rest: Grain, Embargoes, and *Yersinia pestis* in the Black Sea, 1346–48," *Speculum* (2021).

Information about the excavation of the Jewish mass graves in Tàrrega can be found in Anna Colet et al., "The Black Death and Its Consequences for the Jewish Community in Tàrrega: Lessons from History and Archaeology," in *Pandemic Disease in the Medieval World: Rethinking the Black Death* (Arc Medieval Press, 2015). The article also includes quotations from primary sources about the massacre.

I first wrote about Sharon DeWitte's work on inequality and the Black Death in a feature for *Science*: "From Black Death to Fatal Flu, Past Pandemics Show Why People on the Margins Suffer Most," May 14, 2020. A recent overview of her many years of research and results, combined with helpful historical context, can be found in DeWitte and Maryanne Kowaleski, "Black Death Bodies," *Fragments* (2017). For post–Black Death health improvements, see especially DeWitte, "Stress, Sex, and Plague: Patterns of Developmental Stress and Survival in Pre- and Post-Black Death London," *American Journal of Human Biology* (2018). For the economic context in England leading up to the Black Death, including the Great Famine, see *The Great Transition: Climate, Disease and Society in the Late-Medieval World* by Bruce M. S. Campbell (Cambridge University Press, 2016). Campbell also offers an analysis of how environmental factors led to the rapid spread of the plague in the mid-fourteenth century.

CHAPTER 5

My depiction of a worker's life in the Giza pyramid town is based on Mark Lehner's articles "The Pyramid Age Settlement of the Southern Mount at Giza," *Journal of the American Research Center in Egypt* (2002) and "Labor and the Pyramids: The Heit el-Ghurab 'Workers Town' at Giza," in *Labor in the Ancient World* (ISLET-Verlag, 2015). Richard Redding did fascinating work on resource distribution in Old Kingdom Egypt, including the labor and diets of people in Lower Egypt's herding towns: "A Tale of Two Sites: Old Kingdom Subsistence Economy and the Infrastructure of Pyramid Construction," in *Archaeozoology of the Near East X* (Peeters, 2013). For a more authoritarian interpretation of Old Kingdom government and conscripted pyramid labor, see *The Rise and Fall of Ancient Egypt* by Toby Wilkinson (Random House, 2010).

The astronomer Barbara Bell was among the first to attribute the Old Kingdom's collapse to a period of low Nile floods. Her article "The Dark Ages in Ancient History," *American Journal of Archaeology* (1971) remains influential in Egyptology and was an important precursor to studies of the 4.2-kiloyear event. It also includes translations of many key ancient Egyptian texts, including Ipuwer's *Admonitions*.

Two seminal works about what collapse is—and isn't—were published in 1988 and remain vital to understanding how archaeologists think about this important kind of apocalypse: *The Collapse of Complex Societies* by Joseph Tainter (Cambridge University Press) and *The Collapse of Ancient States and Civilizations*, edited by Norman Yoffee and George L. Cowgill (University of Arizona Press). An important recent addition to collapse studies is *Understanding Collapse: Ancient History and Modern Myths* by Guy D. Middleton (Cambridge University Press, 2017), which contains chapters on Old Kingdom Egypt, the Indus Civilization, and the Classic Maya.

For a comprehensive study of how environmental and political factors intertwined to push the Old Kingdom toward collapse, see *Analyzing Collapse: The Rise and Fall of the Old Kingdom* by Miroslav Bárta (The American University in Cairo Press, 2019). Stephan Seidlmayer, "The First Intermediate Period (c.2160–2055 BC)," in *The Oxford History of Ancient Egypt* (Oxford University Press, 2000) is a refreshing and counterintuitive look at the creativity and freedom made possible by collapse. It also contains extensive quotations from Ankhtifi's tomb texts.

New archaeological excavations of the Old Kingdom and the First Intermediate Period are rare because most of the sites are inaccessible. Matthew Douglas Adams's dissertation project in Abydos, "Community and Society in Egypt in the First Intermediate Period: An Archaeological

Investigation of the Abydos Settlement Site" (University of Pennsylvania, 2005) is a welcome and illuminating exception.

Ellen Morris offers a helpful analysis of how collapse made ancient Egypt's class system more flexible and changed how the country thought about kings in "'Lo, Nobles Lament, the Poor Rejoice': State Formation in the Wake of Social Flux," in *After Collapse: The Regeneration of Complex Societies* (University of Arizona Press, 2006). For a study of the Old Kingdom that focuses on its remarkable stability, rather than its collapse, see Morris, "Ancient Egyptian Exceptionalism: Fragility, Flexibility and the Art of Not Collapsing" in *The Evolution of Fragility.*

There is debate about whether Ipuwer really was an eyewitness to the Old Kingdom's collapse and its aftermath, because the oldest surviving copy of his *Admonitions* dates to centuries after the First Intermediate Period. Morris makes a strong and generous case for his apocalyptic experiences in "Writing Trauma: Ipuwer and the Curation of Cultural Memory" in *"An Excellent Fortress for His Armies, a Refuge for the People": Egyptological, Archaeological, and Biblical Studies in Honor of James K. Hoffmeier* (Penn State University Press/Eisenbrauns, 2020).

CHAPTER 6

John Lloyd Stephens's travelogues about visiting Maya ruins were bestsellers in their time and are now freely available online: *Incidents of Travel in Yucatan,* Volumes 1 and 2 (Harper and Brothers, 1848). Frederick Catherwood's engravings of Maya architecture and art are truly stunning and did as much as or more than Stephens's books to inspire future Maya archaeologists.

The most comprehensive source of information about Aké in the Classic and Postclassic periods is Roberto Rosado-Ramirez's PhD dissertation "Living with Ruins: Community Regeneration After Political Collapse at the Ancient Maya City of Ake, Yucatan, Mexico" (Northwestern University, 2021). I visited Aké and Mayapán with Rosado-Ramirez in July 2022. Vicente Cocon López and the community of Ruinas de Aké were tremendously generous with their time and knowledge.

My descriptions of Classic period culture, as well as the timeline of the collapse, draw on Rosado-Ramirez's "Living with Ruins," along with dozens of interviews I've conducted over many years of reporting on Maya archaeology. For accessible accounts of life and politics in the Classic period, centuries before the collapse, see Wade, "The Arrival of Strangers" *Science*, February 27, 2020, and Erik Vance, "In Search of the Lost Empire of the Maya," *National Geographic*, September 2016. For information about Maya markets and merchants, see Scott R. Hutson and Bruce H. Dahlin, "The Long Road to Maya Markets," in *Ancient Maya Commerce: Multidisciplinary Research at Chunchucmil* (University Press of Colorado, 2017).

A comprehensive compilation of studies about the Classic period collapse and how it spread throughout the Maya world is *The Terminal Classic in the Maya Lowlands: Collapse, Transition, and Transformation*, edited by Arthur A. Demarest, Prudence M. Rice, and Don S. Rice (University Press of Colorado, 2004). A helpful recent look at the collapse, including its political and economic transformations, is Jason Yaeger, "Collapse, Transformation, Reorganization," in *The Maya World* (Routledge, 2020).

The chronology, political organization, and collapse of Chichén Itzá are all surprisingly unclear for such a significant and well-known site. For two different views of the timing of its collapse, and the role played by drought, see Julie A. Hoggarth et al., "The Political Collapse of Chichén Itzá in Climatic and Cultural Context," *Global and Planetary Change* (2016) and Yaeger and David A. Hodell, "The Collapse of Maya Civilization: Assessing the Interaction of Culture, Climate, and Environment," in *El Niño, Catastrophism, and Culture Change in Ancient America* (Dumbarton Oaks, 2008). The Yaeger and Hodell article also includes summaries of paleoclimate data about drought in the Maya lowlands.

Marilyn Masson and Carlos Peraza Lope have done extensive work on Mayapán; see, for example, their book *Kukulcan's Realm: Urban Life at Ancient Mayapán* (University Press of Colorado, 2014). For a new study of the city's collapse, see Douglas J. Kennett et al., "Drought-Induced Civil Conflict Among the Ancient Maya," *Nature Communications* (2022).

For a broader examination of how communities in Mesoamerica, and especially the Maya area, think about and interact with ruins, see Wade, "Ancient People Lived Among Ruins Too. What Did They Make of Them?," *Science*, March 30, 2023.

CHAPTER 7

The most widely read conquistador account of the Spanish-Aztec war is *The Conquest of New Spain* by Bernal Díaz del Castillo. I've quoted a lively, streamlined English translation by J. M. Cohen (Penguin Books, 1963).

The idea of Moctezuma as a voracious collector comes from *When Montezuma Met Cortés: The True Story of the Meeting That Changed History* by Matthew Restall (Ecco, 2018). It was one of my main sources for reconstructing the conquest of Mexico from an Indigenous perspective, along with *Fifth Sun: A New History of the Aztecs* by Camilla Townsend (Oxford University Press, 2019) and *Collision of Worlds: A Deep History of the Fall of Aztec Mexico and the Forging of New Spain* by David Carballo (Oxford University Press, 2020). Restall provides astute analysis of the conquistadors' propaganda, and his *Seven Myths of the Spanish Conquest* (Oxford University Press, updated edition, 2021) remains vital reading. Carballo focuses on the deep history of central Mexico and the Iberian Peninsula, as well as the archaeology of both. Townsend reconstructs her history of the Aztecs from the historical annals written in Nahuatl by Indigenous scholars after the conquest. These texts are a rich and, until recently, underappreciated source of knowledge.

For more information about Spanish violence as well as the decisive, strategic role played by Indigenous allies during the conquest, see *¿Quién Conquistó México?* by Federico Navarrete Linares (Penguin Random House Grupo Editorial, 2019). For more about the translator Marina, also known as La Malinche, see *Fifth Sun* and Townsend's earlier *Malintzin's Choices: An Indian Woman in the Conquest of Mexico* (University of New Mexico Press, 2006).

I wrote about the archaeology of Tlaxcallan and its differences from Tenochtitlan for *Science* in "It Wasn't Just Greece: Archaeologists Find Early Democratic Societies in the Americas," March 15, 2017. My feature on the *tzompantli* is "Feeding the Gods: Hundreds of Skulls Reveal Massive Scale of Human Sacrifice in Aztec Capital," *Science*, June 21, 2018.

The online graphic novel series *Aztec Empire* by Paul Guinan and illustrated by David Hahn is an exciting new account of the Spanish-Aztec war. Their illustrations of Tenochtitlan are particularly stunning, and Guinan's historical and archaeological research, explained in comprehensive notes, is top-notch. As of this writing, the series is still in progress, with all completed episodes freely available here: https://www.bigredhair.com/books/aztec-empire/about/.

I first wrote about Kathleen Hull's work on Awahnichi survival after a colonial epidemic in my 2020 *Science* feature "From Black Death to Fatal Flu, Past Pandemics Show Why People on the Margins Suffer Most." For more evidence against epidemics indiscriminately wiping out Native Americans, see *Beyond Germs: Native Depopulation in North America*, edited by Catherine M. Cameron, Paul Kelton, and Alan C. Swedlund (University of Arizona Press, 2015). Pekka Hämäläinen also complicates assumptions about how disease affected Native American communities in *Indigenous Continent: The Epic Contest for North America* (Liveright, 2022).

CHAPTER 8

I first wrote about Estate Little Princess and the archaeology of slavery in the Caribbean in "Caribbean Excavation Offers Intimate Look at the Lives of Enslaved Africans," *Science*, November 7, 2019. The Estate Little Princess field school is led by members of the Society of Black Archaeologists, and the students from St. Croix were supervised by Alexandra Jones, the founder of Archaeology in the Community. I did field reporting there on July 9–11, 2019, as well as extensive interviews, in 2018 and 2019, with archaeologists working on other islands.

For an examination of the lives of the "royal slaves" in Christiansted, see Alicia Odewale et al., "In Service to a Danish King: Comparing the Material Culture of Royal Enslaved Afro-Caribbeans and Danish Soldiers at the Christiansted National Historic Site," *Journal of African Diaspora Archaeology and Heritage* (2017). For information from Barbados about slavery and sugar plantations' role in the creation of capitalism, see Douglas Armstrong, "Early Seventeenth Century Settlement in Barbados and the Shift to Sugar, Slavery, and Capitalism," in *Power, Political Economy, and Historical Landscapes of the Modern World* (State University of New York Press, 2019). Details about the hidden cave and iron offerings found in Barbados can be found in Armstrong, "Cave of Iron and Resistance: A Preliminary Examination," *Journal of the Barbados Museum & Historical Society* (2015).

CHAPTER 9

I first learned about flooding in colonial Mexico City and the *desagüe* from John López, when we both had Fulbright grants in Mexico City in 2009. His work on the history of water management in Tenochtitlan and Mexico City is fascinating and helped me unlock my thinking about the modern world as a postapocalyptic landscape. For information about how colonial flood control might have proceeded without the disastrous *desagüe*, see López, "'In the Art of My Profession': Adrian Boot and Dutch Water Management in Colonial Mexico City," *Journal of Latin American Geography* (2012).

I reconstructed the flood scene based on information in Louisa Hoberman, "Bureaucracy and Disaster: Mexico City and the Flood of 1629," *Journal of Latin American Studies* (1974), as well as more than a decade of personal experience with Mexico City's rainy season storms. Hoberman's "Technological Change in a Traditional Society: The Case of the Desagüe in Colonial Mexico," *Technology and Culture* (1980) provides historical information about the *desagüe*. Historical photographs of the Grand Drainage Canal, showing its scale, are available here: https://elmirador.sct.gob.mx/manos-a-la-obra/el-desague-del-valle-de-mexico.

Jonathan Watts, "Mexico City's Water Crisis—from Source to Sewer," *The Guardian*, November 12, 2015, is a fascinating investigation of the incredible everyday workings of Mexico City's present-day water system. Michael Kimmelman, “Mexico City, Parched and Sinking, Faces a Water Crisis,” *New York Times*, February 17, 2017, offers a terrifying look at what may be in store for the city as climate change intensifies.

Nada, nadie: Las voces del temblor by Elena Poniatowska (Ediciones Era, 1988) is the definitive chronicle of Mexico City’s 1985 earthquake. Solnit also writes about the earthquake and its positive effects on Mexican civil society in *A Paradise Built in Hell*.

For details about the ancient canals in the Pampa de Mocan built to catch El Niño floodwaters, see Ari Caramanica et al., “El Niño Resilience Farming on the North Coast of Peru,” *Proceedings of the National Academy of Sciences* (2020).

EPILOGUE

For archaeological studies of the material culture of the COVID-19 pandemic, see Matthew Magnani et al., “A Contemporary Archaeology of Pandemic,” *Journal of Social Archaeology* (2022) and Dante Angelo et al., “Private Struggles in Public Spaces: Documenting the COVID-19 Material Culture and Landscapes,” *Journal of Contemporary Archaeology* (2021). For COVID-19 artifacts collected by museums, see Roger Catlin, “First Vial Used in U.S. Covid-19 Vaccinations Joins the Smithsonian Collections,” *Smithsonian*, March 9, 2021, and Science Museum Group, “COVID-19 Collecting Project Final Report,” https://www.sciencemuseumgroup.org.uk/projects/collecting-covid-19.

For additional information about how museum curators collect objects to document present-day crises, see Ryan P. Smith, “How Smithsonian Curators Are Rising to the Challenge of COVID-19,” *Smithsonian*, April 15, 2020.

INDEX

Note: Page numbers in *italics* indicate maps.